A HISTORY OF RED TAPE

Great Seal of Edward II

A HISTORY OF RED TAPE

An Account of the Origin and Development of the Civil Service

BY

SIR JOHN CRAIG

K.C.V.O., C.B., LL.D.

*Late Deputy Master and Comptroller
of the Royal Mint. Author of* The
Mint *and* Newton at the Mint

London
MACDONALD & EVANS, LTD.
8 JOHN STREET, BEDFORD ROW, W.C.1
1955

First published 1955

PRINTED IN GREAT BRITAIN BY RICHARD CLAY AND COMPANY, LTD.,
BUNGAY, SUFFOLK

PREFACE

THE author remained for forty years in the Civil Service in complete ignorance of his predecessors, apart from a few uncomplimentary legends. Precedent-ridden though it is, no profession is more careless of its past. Yet that history is not without interest or repute.

Trevelyan's attack on the calibre and recruitment of the service, of which the centenary was celebrated with laudations in 1954, appears to have been a biased abuse of his position. The notorious sinecures which were abolished a generation earlier were automatic growths from the way the service was financed, and were used, on the whole reasonably, for what appeared to be national interests. Earlier than that, the higher Civil Service had been subsidised for half a millennium, up to the breach with Rome, by a share of the plums of the Church; in the circumstances of the time, it was a rational use of public moneys to maintain a national service.

This sketch attempts an outline of the constitution, rewards and outlook of the Civil Service from its origin among the domestics of ancient kings to its proliferation into a hundred separate departments. It stops short of recent developments, which would require statistical treatment and which will doubtless be adequately expounded by the current Royal Commission.

Oblivion has naturally overtaken all but the greatest of the older personnel. It would have been misleading to dilate on the most famous of all, Sir Isaac Newton, who was granted a sinecure and proved a useful official for thirty years. Pride of place was rather due to Roger le Poer and his family in the twelfth century, Thomas Cromwell in the sixteenth, Pepys in the seventeenth, Chadwick in the nineteenth and Morant in the twentieth, as great reorganising administrators, but an effort has been made to include a sufficiency of commoner types and lesser men.

The author records with pleasure his immense debt to the authorities listed in the bibliography, and to many another; in particular he is indebted to the works of Mr. Edward Johnson on the Royal Household and the Exchequer, of Mr. G. R. Elton on Thomas Cromwell, and of Mrs. Higson (Miss Evans) on the earlier Secretaries of State. His gratitude is equally due to the learned institutions, of which the names are set against the several illustrations, for their permission to reproduce this copyright material.

J. C.

CONTENTS

		Page
Preface	. . . .	v
List of Illustrations	. . . .	ix

Chapter

1	WHO ARE CIVIL SERVANTS?	1
2	THE KING'S HOUSEHOLD	6
3	THE THREE SEALS	13
4	THE EXCHEQUER	24
5	THE MINT AND OFFICE OF WORKS	42
6	WOLSEY AND CROMWELL	49
7	SECRETARIES OF STATE	59
8	THE TREASURY	78
9	THE TAX OFFICES	91
10	THE ADMIRALTY	108
11	THE WAR OFFICE	123
12	THE POST OFFICE	130
13	PRIVY COUNCIL DEPARTMENTS	142
14	WELFARE DEPARTMENTS	159
15	THE PRE-VICTORIANS	169
16	THE GIANT STRIDE	182
17	LITERARY LIGHTS	197

Bibliography	. . . .	201
Index of Subjects	. . . .	205
Index of Persons	. . . .	209

LIST OF ILLUSTRATIONS

Great Seal of Edward II . . . . . *Frontispiece*
By permission of the Public Record Office

Facing page

Counterseal of Edward II 22
By permission of the Public Record Office

Privy Seal and Signet of Elizabeth I 23
By permission of the Public Record Office

Entry in Exchequer Accounts, 1831. From " Compotus Receptoris Revencionum Com'. Surr." for 1831 38
By permission of the Public Record Office

Exchequer Tallies 39
By permission of the Public Record Office

Thomas Cromwell, Earl of Essex. After Holbein . . . 86
By permission of the National Portrait Gallery

Whitehall Palace. After Knyff, about 1695 87
By permission of the British Museum

Receipt of Custom. The Long Room, London, 1841 . . . 102
By permission of the British Museum

Robert Burns, Excise Officer. By Peter Taylor 103
By permission of the National Galleries of Scotland

John Palmer 150
By permission of the University Museum, Philadelphia, U.S.A.

Sir Edwin Chadwick. Bust by A. Solomon 151
By permission of the National Portrait Gallery

Sir George Rose. By W. Beechy 166
By permission of the National Portrait Gallery

1

WHO ARE CIVIL SERVANTS?

HEROD was eaten alive by worms; the Roman Empire was bled to death, so some say, by an excess of bureaucrats; the wane of Great Britain's power coincides with a tropical growth of officials. The likeness of the two Empires can only be skin-deep, for officials in this country do not make major history; they are not self-created, and their array, with the counter-army of accountants, auditors and form-fillers which it has evoked in private business, is entailed by actions and equities in tune with the temper of the realm. That these numbers could not have existed or been borne in earlier times is obvious. It is not the purpose of this book to delve into the deeper reasons for the change, but to present some of the personnel and structure of the past. There will perhaps be observed throughout the story a tendency to stand on ancient ways, to prize the avoidance of wrong more than the pursuit of right, and to prefer promotions in turn to the advancement of the fittest.

One difficulty obtrudes at the outset. Civil Servants are understood to be precise, even meticulous to the edge of unintelligibility; yet the name and scope of their calling are, on the contrary, vague, ambiguous and uncertain. Where does the servant cease and the politician begin?

Two recent writers have asserted that of all mediæval institutions, the fourteenth-century Civil Service is most parallel to that of today. But in dealing with the past, modern historians do not restrict the term "Civil Servant" to the almost anonymous rank and file of quill-drivers and accountants. So great a figure as Hubert Walter, Archbishop of Canterbury, Chief Justiciar and Chancellor under Richard I and John—being thus head of both Church and secular administrations—has been praised as "a great Civil Servant." The most recent historian of Henry VIII's administration even discriminates between two Treasurers of the Household, heads of the then main financial department, classing the earlier, Sir John Heron, as a minister,

in contrast to his successor, the " cautious careful Civil Servant,"
Sir Henry Tuke; though Heron in turn drops to a senior Civil Servant when compared with the great Thomas Cromwell, the Principal
Secretary.   Yet he places Cromwell's successor as Principal Secretary,
Sir Thomas Wriothesley, who later became Lord Chancellor and
Earl of Southampton, in the cadet group, as " the most successful
Civil Servant of his age."   " Father of the Civil Service " is the
sobriquet constantly bestowed by his latest biographer on Samuel
Pepys, supreme head of the Admiralty 150 years later.   After the
Revolution, Lord Godolphin, Queen Anne's head of Government,
has been credited with " a Civil Service mind," though he was definitely a politician.   Now there was no constitutional or legal
difference between any of these men.

Popular ideas about who exactly is and who is not a Civil Servant
are liable to vary.   Some omit the hewers of wood and the drawers
of water, the charwomen, porters and labourers, while others exclude
only the most eminent, such as ambassadors and heads of great departments.   A worthy admiral once claimed that Civil Service vacancies
should be filled entirely from the lower deck and Army uncommissioned ranks, and was taken aback at the idea that the proposal
would affect the recruitment of his equals.   Civil Servants, he said
firmly, are messengers or men on that level.

Some laxity of interpretation is understandable.   The phrases
" Civil Servant " and " Civil Service " are of comparatively recent
origin.   They came into use some 200 years ago to describe the men
whom the East India Company engaged under covenants for work
in the sub-continent.   Such convenient terms seeped over a good deal
later into the home service without any exact limits.   Their first
official interpretation was quite wide.   When the Civil Service Commission was set up in 1855 to manage recruitment, its empowering
Order in Council was headed " Admission of persons to the Civil
Service of the Crown."   The Commissioners none the less immediately began to handle the granting of commissions in the Army,
overseas appointments as writers for Ceylon, and the recruitment of
staffs for public but certainly not governmental bodies, such as Chelsea
Hospital, the Ecclesiastical Commission, Police Offices and the Commission of Northern Lights.   None of these staffs would now be
regarded as Civil Servants.

Sixty years later, the Royal Commission appointed in 1912 to review

the public service was given a new definition in its terms of reference
—and such terms are usually drafted with care—" the Civil Service,
including the Diplomatic and Consular Service and the Legal Departments." The Commission took the Judiciary to be included, but was
shy of touching His Majesty's Judges, as personages too high for its
attention. It also assumed that " the Civil Service " included miscellaneous bodies of a public type, notably the Ecclesiastical Commission,
India Office, Crown Agents, Trinity House and the English College
of Heralds, though, as none of these was paid for by the Home Government, it did not feel called upon to deal with them.

While somewhat vaguely admitting that unpensionable, unestablished or temporary employees were also Civil Servants, the Commission concentrated on the permanent, which to it meant the pensionable or established, staff. This " permanent Civil Service " it
declared to be an entity clearly defined by statute. Lord Halsbury in
his *Laws of England* states the exact contrary : that " established Civil
Servant is not a statutory term." He defines this name cautiously as
meaning, for the purposes of the Superannuation Acts 1834–1935, " a
person who has been appointed directly by the Crown or who has
been admitted into the Civil Service with a certificate from the Civil
Service Commissioners and who has served in an established capacity
in the permanent Civil Service of the State and whose salary has been
provided out of the Consolidated Fund or out of moneys provided by
Parliament." This does not make much clear, except that the 1912
Commission was mistaken.

The next Royal Commission, the Tomlin Commission of 1929–31
—the last before that now sitting—fell back on a " working definition "; in its view, Civil Servants were roughly " servants of the
Crown, other than the holders of political or judicial office, who are
employed in a civil capacity and whose remuneration is paid wholly
and directly out of moneys voted by Parliament." Distinction between permanent and temporary employment had vanished; and
miscellaneous clients of the Civil Service Commission were excluded
from the definition. The word " directly " explicitly cut out staffs
of many bodies which get their money in the lump from Parliament;
it also excluded a type of employee which had been common but was
already almost extinct, i.e., personnel engaged for public work by
Government servants from allowances made to them for the purpose.

The personal retinues, officers or servants, of the Sovereign are most certainly not Civil Servants, although they might seem to be in the most obvious and direct sense servants of the Crown. Their stipends are paid from Her Majesty's Civil List, whereas the term " Civil Servant " now implies payment from money voted by Parliament annually, or in a few cases from the Consolidated Fund.

Members of the Government are not Civil Servants, though they are likewise paid from the Votes, and are still, by ancient usage, dubbed servants of the Crown. All who worked directly or indirectly under the monarch were once servants or ministers, and ministers were the lesser of the two. A series of statutes has since picked out specific posts which alone shall not disqualify the holder for the Commons, and these political offices, whether held by members of the Lords or of the Commons, constitute the Government. Nor is a member of the House of Commons, though paid from the Votes, a Civil Servant; by those statutes he can hold no post that is not political. And the officers and servants of both Houses, though accredited to them by the Crown, are nevertheless not in its service, but in that of Parliament. Judges are not Civil Servants; their independence has been a constitutional shibboleth these 300 years.

The three fighting forces are naturally not civil, not even the medical, spiritual and accountant branches, which are sometimes termed civilian, nor their ancillaries in the field. But in Whitehall and Kingsway, and in dockyard and arsenal, similar work is divided between members of the fighting forces and immense masses of Civil Servants; workmen, clerks, accountants or administrators may be in either category.

A prison warder is a Civil Servant, but a policeman is not. When the decayed local watch was superseded, it was arranged that the new police should also be servants of local authorities, as the watch had been. Even though the authority responsible for the largest force of all—the London Metropolitan Police Force—is the Home Secretary, the metropolitan policeman remains outside the Civil Service.

A postman or telephonist is a Civil Servant; a miner, a railway porter, a worker in gas or electricity is not, nor is a Bank of England clerk. When these undertakings were acquired by the Government, it was careful to erect a screen of intermediate employers, and so escape responsibility for the employees.

The distinction between one branch of nationalised work and another has been criticised by theorists. Ambassadors and diplomats have sought exclusion from the Civil Service classification as lesser men have pressed for inclusion, for advantages in finance or prestige. The work is too heterogeneous for a common factor to be found, except that one or another member of the Government can, in general, order how a Civil Servant's job shall be done. But many Civil Servants are bound to act judicially, and staffs of some independent Boards, such as the National Galleries and Museums, are nevertheless Civil Servants.

As to other bodies mentioned above as being grouped by the 1912 Commission with the Civil Service, the India Office, when it existed, was paid for by India; Trinity House supports itself from dues; the Crown Agents for Overseas Governments and Administrations and the Church or Ecclesiastical Commissioners are paid for by their principals.

The exact limits of a title that could vary so much in a generation or two are irrelevant for the public service of the past. The cleavage between political and non-political posts did not appear till the Stuarts quarrelled with their Houses of Commons, and it did not begin to be defined till the eighteenth century. So long as kings were supreme, all their servants were subordinates, and the highest had to the monarch somewhat of the relationship that the Civil Servant has to the political head of his department. A man of any grade might then, and all who could contrive it did, sit in one or other House. Nor could the soldier be distinct from the civilian until there was a standing army, while judges and administrators were originally one and the same. The judges, indeed, " the lions beneath the throne," were largely exempted from the supreme executive's control by their professional tradition until James II wrecked their immunity and made them rather the hounds of justice. Once upon a time the head of the Treasury might lead an army, and he was bound in peace to sit on the bench in one of the Courts of Law.

The scale of things has, of course, altered radically. Taking a large, even an impressionist, view of the figures, the change from the time of Elizabeth I to that of Elizabeth II may be put in round numbers as follows :

The home population has increased 10 times;
The Civil Service has increased 1,000 times;
Government expenditure has increased 20,000 times.

2

THE KING'S HOUSEHOLD

OUR early kings, Anglo-Saxon and Norman alike, kept about them a galaxy of magnates and their sons, with knights and priests, to manage the business of the country and the chores as well as the ceremonial of the Court. These men lived in and about the palace and accompanied the King on his endless peregrinations; the Court was mobile and restless. The principal of them attended the Great Council of the Realm, the forerunner of the House of Lords, whenever it was called together under the presidency of the King, and they constituted the majority of that smaller and more frequent committee out of which grew the Courts of King's Bench and Common Pleas and the Privy Council.

This personnel, the King's Household, in the words of Prof. Poole, was " the centre of administration and the source from which all Government departments developed. Out of the Household was slowly born the Civil Service." Slow indeed, and indirect, was its growth. The Court of Chancery and the Lord Chancellor's department, the Exchequer (now represented by the Exchequer and Audit Department), and the first Secretaries of State, the originals of Home, Foreign, Colonial and other offices, derive directly, and the Treasury indirectly, from Palace staffs; but some of the greatest departments crystallised at two or three removes from it, while others derive from the Privy Council, and of some the sole parent is an Act of Parliament.

The titles of its dignitaries betray the domestic origin of the Palace staff. The Lord Great Chamberlain in his first incarnation looked after the Royal bedroom in default of chambermaids. The King kept his cash and bullion by his couch, as the redoubtable Bess of Hardwick still did in Tudor days; so the Chamberlain became the financial officer, as he still is in some municipalities, though in the Royal service he was superseded by his assistant under the title of Treasurer. The steward may once have been the pig-keeper, the sty-ward; the same officer in Norman times had become the Dapifer, the carrier of a nap-

6

kin. When the Chamberlain, or rather his deputy, in much later times concentrated on the ceremonial of the Court, the Steward—or his deputy's deputy—still overlooked its provisioning and physical comfort, as the Butler saw to its wines. Constable is a corruption of *comes stabuli*, Comrade of the Stables, and his one-time subordinate, the Earl Marshal, was the man who tended the horses and mares.

The posts, wages and perquisites of the Palace establishment about the year 1136 are set out in a schedule, the *Constitutio Regis Domus*, which was probably drawn up on the accession of Stephen for his information or for the guidance of a paymaster. The staff, nine-tenths of whom naturally had to do with eating or hunting, was organised in five divisions, with some subdivisions, respectively headed by the Chancellor, Steward, Butler, Chamberlain with Treasurer, and Constable.

The subordinate establishment is not without its interest. The bottom grade of the hunt staff under the Constable and his assist-ant, the Marshal, each got 1*d*. a day; this also was the pay of the twenty " servientes," usually translated sergeants, and of the five men in charge of dogs of three out of the six breeds. The dogs themselves were assigned money allowances: 1*d*. daily was allowed for four of one kind and six of another, but greyhounds or lime-hounds received ½*d*. a day each. Fixing an allowance for which a job should be done, whether at a loss or a profit, became a standard Government device for many more important functions; it is at the root of all the farming-out and deputy arrangements. In this organisation it was carried further for the wolf-hunters, who were given as a group 20*d*. a day for both wages and the keep of their horses and thirty-two hounds, with another £6 a year for the purchase of new horses; they were at that time claiming an increase of this last figure to £8. Incidentally, the keep of baggage-horses in other divisions was fixed at 1*d*. each.

3*d*. a day each was allowed to the next grade in the hunt: the men taking charge of the three more important breeds of dog, the horn-blower, and some others. Still higher came the huntsmen and the archers, with 5*d*. a day each, unless they were knights. Knights here, as in the other divisions, received the daily 8*d*. that was the customary salary of that rank when called out for war.

Common rates of pay, rank for rank, ran through the other divisions. A great many of the buttery, kitchen and pantry staff—cooks, scullions, cellarmen, fruiterers, wafer-makers, linen-men, cup-bearers, watch-

B

men and the like—received nothing but the run of their teeth and $1\frac{1}{2}d$. a day for the hire of a subordinate. A few were allowed two employees and $3d$. a day; some—for example, servants and watchmen in the chapel—were allowed double board. The only wench was a laundress, whose pay was controversial.

We are more concerned with the upper ranks. The five divisions, one having two heads, were presided over by six officers, each of whom drew $3s$. $6d$. a day with full board, or $5s$. a day without board, but with certain perquisites in kind. Five of them remain among the traditional great Officers of State. To give them their later magnificent titles, they were:

Lord Chancellor, in charge of chapel, chaplains and writers.
Lord Great Chamberlain, in charge of finance and, apparently, the private apartments and the section that became the Wardrobe.
Lord High Treasurer, in charge of finance with the Chamberlain, but not in constant attendance.
Lord High Constable, in charge of outdoor activities and the prison.
Chief Butler, in charge of the provision and service of wine.

The other four great Officers of State are later creations—the Lord High Admiral, the Lord Privy Seal, the Lord President of the Council and the Earl Marshal. The Earl Marshal was then a subordinate of the Constable, but he had also taken on certain duties of witnessing documents and safeguarding records, for which reason he is now titular head of the College of Arms and is vested with a particular authority at Coronations. The Chief Butler, still an important personage in the eighteenth century, could not be identified at the 1901 Coronation, and the Treasury and Admiralty posts have long been dispersed among Commissioners.

The Steward had two seconds-in-command, one for the pantry and the other for the kitchen and larder together, at a little over half these rates—$2s$. $10d$. without and $2s$. with board—and the Butler had a single lieutenant at the same pay. A third rank in these sections worked in rotating spells, a month or a quarter at a time, for $1s$. $7d$. or $10d$., according to whether they were boarded or not. The second line or heads of sections in other divisions got $2s$. with or $1s$. $2d$. without board; they included all the Under-Chamberlains, the Treasurer of the Chamber (who afterwards became a hereditary Under-Chamberlain of the Exchequer), the Under-Constables, the Head Marshal, the

Clerk of the Spence and the Head of the Writers. The remuneration for this last post had quite recently been increased from 10*d.* to 2*s.* for the benefit of Robert de Sigillo, Keeper of the Great Seal from 1131 to 1135, who was promoted in 1141 to be Bishop of London.

The ancient posts of Chamberlain, Steward and Constable, like many lesser offices of this period, were hereditary, the duties being in practice passed to deputies. The Great Chamberlainship was eventually divided into a number of shares, which were inherited by different families, but the High Stewardship was absorbed in the Crown by the accession of Henry IV, its owner. The three offices are now revived only for the period of a Coronation or a State Trial. The Lord Chamberlain and the Lord Steward of the Household in the modern Court descend from their deputies.

It will be seen that the deductions for board and lodging varied with standing: 5*d.* was retained from a wage of 8*d.*, 9*d.* from one of 1*s.* 7*d.*, 10*d.* from 2*s.* or 2*s.* 10*d.* and 1*s.* 6*d.* from 5*s.* Evidently all were not entertained in the Palace in equal luxury. Even when boarded, the superior officials received in addition enviable allowances in kind. The Chancellor and other top rankers each had a daily issue of four gallons of wine and enough bread for four men; the three next ranks, the Knights and equal ranks and, appropriately, the cooper, had each two gallons of wine, but were not deemed to need bread. For those not boarded these allowances were doubled, making a daily eight gallons of wine and bread for eight men at the top, while bread for two to four men each was issued to the lower officials. The forebears of Her Majesty's Civil Service need not be presumed to have dealt unaided with all that liquor; each had a staff of assistants to support.

Each higher official who was lodged out was also given, according to grade, one large or small unused candle and from twenty-four to forty of the stubs left from lighting the Palace.★ Those who lodged in received what candles they needed. Probably all, as in later times, also received annual issues of clothing or of cloth for its making.

★ In the same way, the stumps of office candles were a perquisite till the nineteenth century of the deputy " necessary woman " at the Home Office and with old pens and waste paper brought her in some £20 a year, whilst the Foreign Office housekeeper sold her official candle ends to the gentlemen clerks to light their homes.

The cash allowances cannot be translated into modern terms. What we can now buy did not exist; what they could buy, we do not want. It would be otiose now, as it was then vain, to ask either of the Archbishops to keep his train of caparisoned horsemen down to fifty. For what the comparison is worth, a workman now earns some 30s. a day, against the 1d. usual in Stephen's reign. Possibly the wages of the lowest ranks of Stephen's establishment might be multiplied by 200 or 300. The Chancellor and his peers might be equated with the head of a first-rank modern department, drawing £5,000. The latter has much more comfort, less glamour, more work, less wine. The multiplicator should accordingly diminish up the scale, say to fifty at the top, whereas the nominal money value of sterling silver has risen only threefold, and of gold bullion nineteen times. The value of "diet" in the Palace for a Secretary of State, an office in Stephen's age still far in the future, was reckoned at £406 a year under Henry VIII, had risen to £586 under Elizabeth I and was commuted after the Revolution of 1688 for £730 p.a. for the senior Secretary and £292 for his junior.

But faithful work won other rewards over and above the prescribed perquisites. Domesday Book is full of the names of cooks, huntsmen, foresters and so on who held manors or farms in recognition of their service at Court, and such grants continued to be available for Civil Servants till the end of the Stuart period. Zealous clerks or clerics—for literacy implied minor orders—could also expect ecclesiastical endowments; from the Conquest a large proportion of vacant canonries was distributed among clerks of the Household, and Bishops through the twelfth and thirteenth centuries were commonly men in the King's service who continued their old duties with this added emolument. The nominal rights of the Church to elect its chiefs were no hindrance. Thus there came about 1173 a letter from Henry II, "King of the English . . . to his faithful monks of the church of Winchester greeting. I order you to hold a free election, but nevertheless I forbid you to elect any but Richard, my clerk, Archdeacon of Poitiers, to be Bishop of Winchester." This Richard, the new Bishop, was a sub-Treasurer in the Exchequer. Similarly, when the monks of Worcester elected a priest of their own choice to be Bishop, their thoughtless act had to be set aside in favour of John de Gray, Henry's Chancellor. There were limits; the wiliness of the monks of Christchurch prevented the advancement under King John of this

John de Gray to be Archbishop of Canterbury and led to the great interdict.

In one way and another, posts in the service were very attractive, and considerable sums were paid to the King, or in later times to the holder, as entrance fees. Thus in the twelfth century £3,000 and again £3,334 were paid to become Chancellor; appointment as Treasurer was bought in 1158 for £400, and a simple clerkship in 1196 for £334.

Stephen's establishment list has gaps. It does not mention the Justiciar, who until 1232 was viceregent of the King when he was abroad and his right-hand man at home, holding that priority under the Crown which fell, till the death of Wolsey, to the Lord Chancellor, then passed for a time to the principal Secretary and was finally vested in the Treasurer or the First Lord of the Treasury. The Sheriffs, the administrators of the shires and chief collectors of revenue, are naturally omitted. But within the Palace, the Wardrobe, a century later the principal organ of government, is not mentioned, and, in addition, the Treasurer and the Treasurer of the Chamber must have employed clerks and tally-cutters. The head of the writing-room is duly recorded without indication of the numerous staff, doubtless regarded as outside the Household, who served under him.

Household officialdom was the main vehicle of central government, despite the creation of separate clerical and finance departments, till the middle of the reign of Henry VIII, when tighter organisation of the Privy Council and the focusing of general administration in the King's secretary threw it largely into the shade. But not entirely; it was the Comptroller of her Household who communicated the wishes of Elizabeth I to her earlier Parliaments; and "Groom of the Stole" was the office which William III chose for his chief assistant in foreign affairs, the Dutch Duke of Portland. As Groom of the Stole, also, Lord Bute grew to power under George III, and the person holding that title was included in eighteenth-century Cabinets.

Palace and public officials were alike supported from the King's income; there was at bottom no distinction between this and Parliamentary moneys until George III surrendered the Crown lands on his accession in 1760 and received a Civil List. But the Civil List continued to pay salaries to many officials outside the Household, until it was greatly reduced on Queen Victoria's accession and relieved of such public charges. The Household, on the other hand, has not escaped encroachments. Three of its offices—those of the Treasurer, Comptroller and Vice-Chamberlain—are now filled by the Government of the day from their adherents in Parliament.

3

THE THREE SEALS

F ROM the time when seals were first used—and that was far back in the heptarchy—clerks must have been employed to concoct and write documents; laymen generally could only make their mark by the sign of the Cross and attest it with their seal.

The Royal writers appear to have been individual workers until the reign of Alfred; a very few decades later—by, say, A.D. 925—they had evolved an artificial officialese of rare words and impressive phrases. Departmental jargon is as old as the Saxons. The maintenance of this special style through generation after generation is witness to a permanent cadre of professionals whose old hands infused the new with their peculiar technique.

The principal task of these clerks was to draw up charters, of which many survive, to confer or confirm holdings of land; later came grants of every kind, pardons, summoning of Lords and of Commons, proceedings and judgments of the Court of Chancery, writs and royal appointments. Apart from minters whose names are inscribed on the coins that they made, the first English Civil Servant known to us by name is Ælfwine, the faithful scribe of Æthelred the Unready, whom he rewarded in 993 by a gift of broad acres at Bampton Aston, Lew and Brighthampton in Oxfordshire.

Existing Saxon scriveners were kept on by William the Conqueror. Anglo-Saxon and Latin were superseded by Latin and French, and Latin formulas modified by French models, but the change was so gradual that it must have depended on wastage and replacements of clerks rather than on some brisk pronouncement of policy.

Perhaps shortly before, but probably a year or two after, the Conquest the new office of Chancellor, to which the Conqueror's chaplain Herfast was appointed, was created. His duties were to supervise these writers and the Chapel and Great Seal staff. As Chief Clerk under him, the Head of the Writing-Room became or remained responsible for recruiting clerks, allotting them to individual tasks and checking the accuracy of their work. Ælfwine had presumably held this post. Towards 1135, it will be remembered, its pay was raised from 10*d.* to 2*s.* a day, whereas other superior clerks received only 5*d.*, and the rank and file only 2*d.* or 3*d.* a day.

By this time fifty clerks were employed in the writing-rooms or Chancery. Their chief, the Chancellor, was already beginning to deal with petitions for equitable remedies and with suitors wishing to approach the men by whom the verdicts would have to be put into writing, although the conversion of this side of the Chancery into a court of equity for hard cases was not completed till some time in the fourteenth century. The remuneration of the various ranks was helped out by fees levied on the beneficiary of each service; these exactions were raised to such harsh levels that in 1199 the Chancellor laid down a schedule of fixed charges to prevent further extortion.

Hubert de Burgh, the last of the great Justiciars, was retired by Henry III in 1232 and replaced by an obscure lawyer. In 1238 the King abolished the Chancellorship also, for a period, in an attempt at more personal government; when it was reinstituted, the King kept the fees, and out of them granted the new head an allowance for staff; but fresh fees were invented, and continued to provide the bulk of the remuneration. No more Justiciars were appointed, and the Chancellor became the head and front of the King's administration. He directed his ecclesiastical patronage, managed elections to abbeys and Bishops' sees, ran the wardships and vacant baronies that fell to the Crown, and controlled resort to the Great Seal, so that all important business had to pass through his hands. He sat in all Councils and ruled the Exchequer as well as the Chancery. The latter had also much judicial business; Lydgate's " London Lackpenny " lamented in the early 1400s the financial obstacles to justice in this court of equity :

> " Unto the Rolls I got me from there,
> Before the clerks of the Chancery;
> Where many I found earning of pence
> But none all at once regarded me,
>
> . . . . .
>
> For lack of money I could not speed."

Chancellors were churchmen, with occasional lawyers interpolated; most of their subordinate staffs were also in Orders. On the expanding judicial side of this ecclesiastical structure, the former Master of the Writing-Rooms, always appointed by the King, became a judge;

he was, first, Curator or Clerk, then Master of the Rolls—the title used in statutes of Henry VIII. It is tempting to turn the superior Writers under him into the eleven other " honest clerks " or " masters " (in Chancery) who assisted him in the Middle Ages. Unlike their chief's, their appointment was vested in the Chancellor, but they lived in the Palace. Their payment was partly from fees and partly in kind; successive Chancellors acquired the gift of all livings worth less than twenty marks (£13 6s. 8d.) a year, expressly for bestowal on these lesser masters and other Chancery officials.

A step further down, the " six clerks " served under the Curator or Master of the Rolls; the patronage of the office as well as its discipline was his affair, and from him appointment was bought at a great price. After the transfer of their original work of drawing and examining writs to other officers of the Court, the six made their livings by supplying suitors, for very heavy fees, with badly executed copies— which the suitors did not need but dared not refuse—of documents for their cases. To prevent competition or ill feeling, they apportioned the victims alphabetically, and to avoid taking time wastefully from their private practices when later they became solicitors, they attended one at a time for a spell of two months to supervise the copying and to collect the cash. In the eighteenth century they made £1,000 a head in some years and £2,000 a head in others by this blackmail. By Tudor times the actual work had been devolved by them on their personal employees, the " sixty clerks," who were rewarded with a percentage of the takings, but in 1596 these underlings were established as officers of the Court of Chancery. Both the six and the sixty clerks were abolished in 1834.

A non-judicial officer of some importance was the finance officer, the Clerk of the Hamper, or Hanaper. He was closely attached to the Chancellor, and received 1s. 6d. for each day that he rode in the Chancellor's suite, besides a wage of 6d. In due time the Clerk naturally came to draw the 18d. for 365 days in the year. The pay was enough of a prize to be sought by officials who had nothing to do with the Chancery. By 1800 the Clerk's wage was less than £100 a year, but he took £1,700 as his share of the fees and got his work done by a deputy for £112.

The Chancery administered Parliament. It called peers and prelates to the House of Lords, over which the Chancellor presided; initiated elections to the Commons under the Great Seal, scrutinised the election returns, and decided disputed elections till the House took over that privilege. It helped members to recover their fees from reluctant constituencies. The Clerkship of Parliament, the holder of which looked after the Lords, commonly fell to one of its members, either a Master of the Rolls or one in the running for that office, or a plain clerk, until the emoluments became too tempting; and clerks in Chancery sometimes secured also the under-clerkship, whose holder looked after the Commons.

The Chancellor's clerks were the main administrative machine till about the reign of Edward III, and remained the largest clerical unit till the sixteenth century, although all initiative and decision had gradually passed elsewhere, and they had been relegated to the engrossment of the words of others on documents of dignity and to the preparation of routine and formal parchments. They gave this final touch to all summonses, pardons, licences and other Royal demands and concessions of any importance.

The goal and crown of all their labours was the imposition of the Great Seal. The seal with its counterseal was, and is, formed of two massive disks of silver, or sometimes (but rarely) gold, six inches across, and heavily rimmed to form a circular box when placed together. Each was engraved inside with a portrait of the ruler in traditional poses; on his throne on the one part, and on a horse on the other. A ribbon was threaded through a slit in the document to be sealed; both its ends were embedded in melted wax between seal and counterseal, and the wax was impressed with the two patterns by forcing these together. After wine, wax was the chief item in the English import trade. The emblem was hallowed with constitutional sanctity. King James II expected to plunge the affairs of the kingdom into chaos after his flight when he cast the seal into the Thames. A hundred years later the Opposition in the Commons, having the Government on the run, tried to prevent the dissolution of Parliament by theft of the seal. James, as usual, had chosen his spot ill, and the drowned seal was fished up; the politicians were frustrated by the miraculous production of a new seal in twenty-four hours.

In the Middle Ages, the Great Seal's usual place was under lock and key in the Exchequer strong-room, the Treasury of leagues or treaties. When it was to be used, the King sent a written warrant for its production to the three officers who held the keys. Three other men then came into play: the Spigurnel to provide and melt the wax—he was important enough to be given the seal's weight in silver when the design was changed—the Keeper of the Seal, and the Chancellor to apply it to the document. During the fourteenth century the last two became alternative titles; a man of low rank was designated Keeper, but if ennobled he became Chancellor. All this ceremony had been preceded by the delays of the careful clerks over composition and engrossment. Meantime the disappointed suitors had had ample time to canvass for reconsideration of their case. The Palace had other clerks and other seals for its domestic business. It was obviously much simpler for an eager King to bid a clerk write his decision and confirm it with the Wardrobe Seal. If an impression of the Great Seal was demanded by the dignity of the subject-matter, this Wardrobe warrant could be addressed to the Lord Chancellor as an order for a supplementary formal document.

This new practice, begun under John, was well established in the next reign, and by the end of the century a Keeper and two Clerks of the Privy Seal—as this Wardrobe Seal was called—had been set apart for its work. The King had, in effect, established a private Chancery for his public work. When the Lords Ordainers sought to correct the errors of Edward II in 1311, the Keeper of the Privy Seal was accordingly one of the officers whom they demanded the right to appoint. During that century and the next, the Privy Seal Office, enlarged to a Keeper, four clerks and some under-clerks, was the recognised public general office for administrative action.

The Keeper—the later Lord Privy Seal—was also for a time the King's secretary. Though the title was used earlier in a sporadic way, the continuous line of secretaries, who mostly started as chaplains, begins in Edward I's old age with " the royal clerk who stays continually by the King's side," John of Banstead, who was Controller of the Wardrobe from 1295 to 1305. He kept the Privy Seal and was assisted by two Wardrobe clerks to transcribe and enrol his letters. The title of Secretary generally went with the custody of the Privy Seal until 1367, when William of Wickham, founder of Winchester School and the then Keeper, was transferred to the Chancery. Thereafter the Keeper of a later seal, the Signet, was generally Secretary.

The Keeper of the Privy Seal was commonly a distinguished ecclesiastic on his way to a bishopric. William Lyndwood, however, the scholarly author of the monumental treatise on canon law, entered the office as secondary in 1430, was promoted to Keeper in 1433 and nine years later became in addition the Bishop of St. David's. His successor, Thomas Beckington, Fellow of New College, Oxford, had, after employment on an embassy, been acting Secretary for two and full Secretary for five years (1438–43) before he was promoted or transferred to be Keeper of the Privy Seal and at once made Bishop of Bath and Wells. Beckington is the best known of the early Secretaries, owing to the survival of his papers. He had two personal clerks: Thomas Chamberlain, a yeoman of the Chamber, who was twice elected to the House of Commons and was afterwards Governor of Carisbrooke Castle, and John Blakeney, who was found places in the Signet Office and in the Mint. The next two or three Keepers had previously been Clerks to the Council. Every Keeper from 1456 to 1530 either was or became a bishop, except for a stop-gap of three months in 1523 provided by Henry, Lord Marny, soldier and Court official. In 1530 the keepership was granted to Anne Boleyn's father. Two of these Keepers had previously been Secretary; two others advanced to be Lord Chancellor.

The lower ranks were usually in Orders, but not so the best known of them, Thomas Hoccleve, a friend of Chaucer's and a middling poet, described as garrulous, egotistic, not very strong-minded and slightly dissipated. He entered the Privy Council Office in 1387, when he was about nineteen, with the usual wage of 3*d.* a day, and so continued till his death nearly sixty years later. His clerk's wage was increased in 1399 by a personal addition of £10 a year, which was raised to £13 6*s.* 8*d.* (twenty marks) in 1409; and in 1424 he was further given a corrody, or annuity, charged on a monastery. A long-standing promise of a benefice did not persuade him to take Orders nor prevent his marriage. His manuscript book of office precedents is in the British Museum.

His colleagues seem to have been organised in two grades, with recruitment strictly confined to the lower. Even in the troublous reigns when the Crown thrice passed by violence, the staff stood on their rights under this rule. Edward IV appointed one Richard Bele direct to the upper grade; as soon as Richard III had seized the Crown, the under-clerks protested vigorously to him against the importation of Bele " contrary to the old rule and due order, by means of giving great gifts and other sinister and ungodly ways, in great discouraging of the under-clerks, which have long continued therein to have experience of the same "—that is, of the office, not the " ungodly ways "—and had thus " to see a stranger never brought up in the said office to put them by of their promotion."

John Gunthorpe, Dean of Wells, Clerk of the Parliaments throughout the twelve years of Edward IV's second reign, had just been promoted to be Keeper by Richard III. He was ordered to dismiss Bele, to whose place Robert Bolman, an under-clerk of long and diligent service, moved up. But the office, having thus attracted attention, was discovered to be over-staffed, and the same Royal warrant stopped all further recruitment till wastage brought the numbers back to what they had been under Edward III, 100 years earlier. The surplus clerks were allowed to work out their time.

The Privy Seal Office had followed the Chancery in becoming too bureaucratic to suit the monarch. About the time that Edward II's opponents sought to get control of the office, the King began to avoid resort to it by employing various other Palace clerks and seals. That called the Signet was definitely adopted for the King's more personal business, and as his secretary one of his chaplains was placed in charge of it, by at latest 1367, ten years before the death of Edward III. Under his successor, Richard II (1377–99), the Signet encroached rapidly on the Privy Seal, in spite of vain protests by the Commons against this unconstitutional action, and the new office became the principal vehicle of the King's will. Resort to the Signet naturally became suspect after his fall, and faded somewhat into the background until Henry VI fell back on it to escape baronial tutelage. Several ordinances between 1440 and 1444 so related the three offices as to secure the extreme of duplication. All action was to start in the Signet Office as a sealed warrant directing the Privy Council Office to send instructions under its seal to the Chancery to prepare a document in the same words under the Great Seal. The theory was that " such things as shall pass through many hands are less likely to pass to the prejudice of the King or other person." The Privy Seal Office continued, indeed, for nearly a century to be the starting-point for considerable business, and the Signet Office itself sealed many orders and much correspondence that did not need the senior seals. But the result was broadly that the Privy Seal Office was reduced partly, and the administrative side of Chancery wholly, to the automatic copying of words prescribed for them, and to collecting fees for so doing.

The Signet was held by the King's Secretary, who, besides its assistants, had a small personal staff. Under him the Signet Office was staffed at one time by five clerks, all of whom were important enough to be invited to Queen Margaret's wedding in 1445, but later by four, with some under-clerks who seem to have been their individual and personal employees. Each superior clerk was allowed accommodation at the Palace for three horses and two servants. They got their board there, later commuted for £30 a head, but no remuneration except fees. The clerk responsible for drawing up a warrant kept the fee paid for composing and writing it by the person interested; the fee for sealing it was divided among the head of the office and all four clerks. The latter fee ranged from 1s. to 6s. 8d. under Henry VIII to Mary; from 6s. 8d. to £3 under Elizabeth. The four clerkships were commonly filled by promotion from the Privy Seal Office and must have been reasonably attractive, for they were filled by distinguished men, some of whom were destined to go far. The clerks of 1535 were:

Thomas Wriothesley, afterwards Sir Thomas, then Baron Wriothesley, finally Earl of Southampton; previously, from 1522, in service under Cardinal Wolsey and Thomas Cromwell; Cofferer of the Household and King's Messenger; Clerk of the Signet 1530–40; Engraver to the Mint from 1536 onwards; afterwards Principal Secretary and finally Lord Chancellor.

Sir John Godsalve, whose portrait was painted by Holbein, a general utility man who was rewarded by the Comptrollership of the Mint, 1547–53, and who wrote Queen Mary's submission to the Pope.

Sir William Paget, first Lord Paget, said to be the son of a London mace-bearer, Clerk of the Signet from 1532 for life; afterwards, from 1540–3, Clerk of the Privy Council; 1543, Clerk of the Parliaments and Principal Secretary; 1547, Comptroller of the Household; Chancellor of the Duchy of Lancaster; and, after imprisonment and a fine of £6,000 for his defalcations in that office, back again as Keeper of the Privy Seal in 1555.

Thomas Derby, Clerk of the Council also from 1533.

There was also, at that time, a fifth clerk, Henry Conway, supernumerary and useless from age, but allowed to finish his life in the office.

These clerks originally attended in person to receive oral orders from the King, but for at least a century past they had found so many paid jobs and were employed so frequently on missions that their appearances at Court became very irregular. A fresh rule, made in

1536, that they should take duty in pairs in alternate months, must have been tacitly ignored, as twenty years later, on 16th March, 1557, four clerks of far less standing—William Honnyng, Nicholas Yetsweirt, a Fleming, John Cliff and Francis Yaxley—signed a formal agreement that they would attend the office one at a time in turn, each taking one month in the winter and two in the other seasons. The man on duty was to write the most important documents such as grants in perpetuity, supervise all four under-clerks, of whom each had provided one, and collect and divide the fees with his absent colleagues. Each agreed to pay one quarter of the cost of paper, parchment and wax and of a sum of £13 6s. 8d. a year, to be divided as wages among the under-clerks.

The Privy and Signet Seals had been devised to facilitate direct action by the King. His personal action was hampered, but co-ordination between the different branches of government was facilitated, by the growth of obscure machinery, which may be called the King in Council.

His chief officials and such of the territorial magnates and great prelates as seemed to him expedient were summoned by the King from time to time to a council in attendance, the " continuous " or Privy Council. Its name and nature fluctuated. These meetings, fabled to have been started by Alfred in 895, seem to have become constant during the reign of Henry III. The activities of the Council of the fourteenth century so dominated administration that endless protests were provoked against its encroachments and trespasses on the established and constitutional channels of Royal action. Informal, mutable, with no fixed terms of reference, and keeping no records, the Council brought together heads of Departments and such outsiders of influence as had or could command the King's confidence; and it evolved an inner ring to concert and direct decisions.

The Council was provided with at least two part-time clerks from other branches of the King's service, notably from the Privy Seal Office. A past Keeper of that Seal, Adam Moleyns, was its principal clerk in 1436–42, and was followed for twenty-three years by the second man in the Privy Seal Office, who retained his old duties as well, and was paid half as much again for them as for the Council work.

By the end of the fifteenth century the Council was made up almost wholly of Royal officials, under the very personal government, or, as some would call it, the despotism, of Richard II. A reaction then set in; outsiders, the magnates and nobles, pushed their way into the Council, seized control of it and presently appropriated the principal posts in the Household. This modified Council became the real government during the minority of Henry VI, who only recovered some measure of personal power, not without great friction and eventually civil war, by evading and by-passing it. The Council broke up during the Wars of the Roses; Henry VII restored it in a different form.

As the King's Secretaries' office developed, the work of both Privy Seal and Signet Offices was reduced to mere routine. A Secretary of State's letter sufficed for many purposes; for others, which called for the dignity of the Great Seal, a warrant to the Attorney- or Solicitor-General was written in the Secretary's office or in the Treasury, according to the subject-matter. This warrant, directing the Law Officer to draw up an instrument in such and such terms, was signed by the King and countersigned by the originating Secretary or Treasurer before it was sent to him. He wrote the requisite document, which had then to be submitted for the King's signature, countersigned by the Secretary, and delivered to the deputy-in-waiting of a Clerk of the Signet. The Signet Office made a copy, to which the Signet Seal was affixed, and this was despatched to the Privy Council Office. There a copy was made of the copy, and this second duplicate was forwarded to the Lord Chancellor's office, where letters patent in the prescribed terms were at last written and the Great Seal formally affixed to them. In matters for which a Signet or Privy Seal was good enough, the circulation stopped at the appropriate office, which issued a definitive document under its own seal. This circumlocution continued by sheer inertia till the middle of the nineteenth century; indeed, the procedure continued much the same, with the Signet stage cut out, till the Great Seal Act of 1884.

Four Signet clerks were appointed for life at the board wages of £30 a year each till 1831, when one vacancy was not filled for a time. Their shared fees rose to an annual average of £264 in 1810 and of £587 a year each in 1834. Each had long ceased to attend or to know or do anything but appoint a deputy, who had so little to do that three of the clerks appointed the same deputy; he drew thrice £111 a year, a single deputy's usual share.

The clerks of the Privy Seal had likewise ceased to labour before the

Counterseal of Edward II

Privy Seal and Signet of Elizabeth I

Restoration; such duties as remained were carried out by deputies, of whom Samuel Pepys was one for a short time. They too continued to be appointed by the Lord Privy Seal for life, until at the end of the eighteenth century one vacancy was left unfilled. The remaining three averaged £455 a year in fees in 1834, when the transfer of recognition to the deputies was recommended, not for the first time. The Signet clerks were abolished instead, with all their staff and works, in 1851, and of the Privy Seal department all has since been wiped out but the Lord Privy Seal, a minister without any departmental duties.

4

THE EXCHEQUER

THE Exchequer was the second department to be created. The Saxon kings had, of course, their treasuries, which from Alfred's time were in Winchester, the old capital, in charge of the Chamberlain; he in course of time was assisted by two deputy chamberlains, the later Chamberlains of the Exchequer, and by a Treasurer who eventually superseded him. The Chamberlains were laymen and, from the Conquest, their posts were hereditary; the Treasurer was an ecclesiastic and was not expected to have heirs.

This Treasury was expanded and remodelled under Henry I into the department known as the Exchequer by, at latest, 1110. There survives a writ of that year which was addressed to the Barons of the Exchequer about a levy of 3s. a hide on land to pay for the marriage of Henry's daughter, Matilda, to the Emperor. This was the first big financial effort of the new body.

The reorganisation was the work of Roger le Poer, a priest whom Henry I on his accession brought over from an incumbency in Caen and made Bishop of Salisbury, Chancellor and a little later Justiciar. He is said to have won the favour of Henry, ever a devotee of speed, by the pace at which he said masses. Family connections proved to be as potent inside as outside the Church. Roger le Poer, and his two nephews, Nigel, who got the bishopric of Ely, and Alexander, who got that of Lincoln, acquired immense wealth and influence and built themselves multitudinous castles as the reign of Henry I wore on. Some time before 1133 Nigel was made Treasurer of the Exchequer that his uncle had reformed. The next King, Stephen, reacted against this powerful combination; so powerful was it that his own misfortunes grew and he lost half his kingdom after seizing the strongholds and persons of the three Bishops in 1139. The Exchequer fell into confusion and decay without them. Henry II restored the trio, and Nigel, reappointed Treasurer, re-established the Exchequer. Nigel's illegitimate son Richard was given a high post in the Chancery, probably the Mastership of the Writing-Room; a little later, about 1158, his father bought for him from the King for £400 the succession to his own post of Treasurer. This Richard, besides being Treasurer, was advanced successively to be Archdeacon of Colchester, Dean of Lincoln and Bishop of London; he also became a Justice of Common Pleas and a travelling Justice in Eyre. About 1178 he wrote his famous account of his principal department, the *Dialogus de Scaccario*. He died in 1198, two or three years after passing the Treasurership to his brother or close relative, William of Ely, the third of the blood to hold the office in succession.

Crown revenue in the twelfth century was made up of fixed dues from each shire with occasional extra imposts, rents and yield of the King's lands, the produce of his forests, fees and fines from judicial proceedings, feudal levies on wardships, deaths, marriages and comings of age of important people, and taxes on certain imports and exports. Most of it was collected by sheriffs; a couple of towns had enough independence to account direct. Payments in kind had largely been converted into money payments so far as Crown receipts were concerned, though the right of purveyance—that is, of requisition at an arbitrary price of goods or animals required by the Crown—continued to be exercised and abused till the Civil War of Charles I.

The normal money revenue of the Crown from 1100 to 1500 varied up to some £100,000 a year; in bad years under John it fell as low as £20,000. This was collected in small sums, and entirely in silver pence, each about as large as a sixpence but only half as thick, until larger silver and gold coin was introduced from 1344 onwards. But by no means the whole revenue passed at all times through the Exchequer, as will be seen.

Winchester remained for a time the headquarters of the new department; some of its officials were domiciled in that city as late as 1178. But the centre of gravity shifted steadily to Westminster, whither the main mass of treasure was moved towards 1200, though subsidiary stocks of treasure were kept at Winchester and elsewhere till much later.

In Henry II's time the office was balanced between knights and clerics, since the former could neither write nor read, but the clerk's integrity was not trusted without close check by the laity. This was made possible for the most illiterate by two devices, the tally and the chequer-board or reckoning table.

The first of these financial tools, the tally, dated back to Saxon times. It was something like a thin cricket bat or sword. When an instalment was paid into the fisc, a cut, nick or scallop of varying width was made on one or other edge of the tally, in conventional positions, for each penny, shilling, pound, £20, £100 or £1,000 received; the amount could be read off from the shape, place and number of incisions. The completed tally was checked by various clerks against their records; identifying names and headings were written on the blade by the Writer of Tallies; the tally was cleft broadwise exactly in two, each part showing the serrated edges, for three-quarters of its length; the shorter slat was given to the payer-in, who produced it as a credit note in subsequent accountings, while that with the handle was hung up in the Exchequer to be then compared with it; if any of the notchings had been altered, the two pieces would not " tally."

The Exchequer later used tallies on a great scale as a means of payment instead of issuing cash. A tally or a number of tallies was cut for specific sums and inscribed as on account of a particular source of revenue, for example the customs taken at a named port; individual debtors were paid off by such tallies; and the paymasters of the Palace were commonly financed by their supply in bulk. If the tax collector on whom they were drawn could meet the payment, he took the tally and put it in as the equivalent of money with his next account; if he had not the necessary funds, the tally was returned like a refused cheque to the disappointed holder, and by him to the Exchequer for cancellation and issue of a new tally on a solvent source. Later still, the Exchequer issued tallies in quantity to the public in return for loans, usually at an enormous discount; the name Government " stock " comes from the stock or handle of the counterpart retained by the Exchequer.

The other device—the chequer cloth, which gave a name to the new department—reached England about 1100, being introduced either by Bishop Roger or an earlier King's clerk. This abacus was an enormous cloth, big enough to cover the Exchequer table, and ruled in columns and squares. Counters to depict the first item in a reckoning were set out upon it by the calculator, those for pennies in one square—six, if there were so many, being represented by a single counter at the top of the square; adjoining squares stood in succession for shillings, pounds, scores of pounds and so on. The next items having been similarly displayed, counters for twelve pence were removed when that figure was reached, and one counter added to the shilling square; counters for twenty shillings were removed and one counter added to the pound square; and so the game continued till the sum was complete. Subtraction was effected by the same process, done in the contrary order. Roman numerals, which remained in use in Government offices till the close of the sixteenth century, make the simplest sums so difficult and mistakes so numerous that the introduction of the chequer cloth led to a gain in speed and accuracy; XLI and LIX, for instance, add up to C or by subtraction give XVIII. None the less, the Exchequer still retained Roman characters till its extinction in the nineteenth century.

The new department had two divisions. The Upper Exchequer had all the pomp and power of a court of justice and high administrative tribunal. All questions of law or principle, all disputes and controversies, any matters that rose above settled routine, were decided there. It could issue orders, general or particular, summon witnesses and imprison offenders, and it had its own Exchequer seal to validate its instructions. It was in origin an embodiment of the King's Court sitting for a special field of affairs, till particular Barons and high officials were detailed to its service, though on occasion others might still attend. Besides exercising these functions of judgments and guidance, it was the receiver of the King's revenue, the accounts of which were critically examined, surcharged or passed. Unlike the modern Treasury, it did not control expenditure, except on its own service; the available funds were simply passed to the Treasurers in the Household.

The judicial functions of the Upper Exchequer gradually diverged from its finance business. Some professional lawyers were appointed to it under the second Edward, and by the beginning of the third Edward's reign the term " Barons of the Exchequer " no longer meant the Exchequer itself, but a distinct body with partly administrative but mainly legal functions. These it attempted to expand, presumably drawn by the magnetism of fees; by the end of that reign it had repeatedly been ordered not to trespass on the grounds of the Court of Common Pleas. This Exchequer court continued to flourish as the judicial tribunal for fiscal and revenue cases. Here, for instance, John Hampden was tried in the ship-money case. It retained one feature of its origin: its decisions were void unless delivered jointly by the Lord High Treasurer and the Lord Chancellor, until 1664, when

a statute permitted the Chancellor to act alone.   It was as Chancellor
of the Exchequer that Sir Robert Walpole, First Lord of the Treasury,
sat in 1735 with the Barons of the Exchequer to try the great case of
Nash v. *the East India Company.*

On the revenue side, sessions were held twice yearly, on the March
and September quarter days, for receipt of revenue, usually in the pre-
cincts of Westminster Abbey, but on occasions at Woodstock, Shrewsbury, York, Durham, Chester, even Carlisle or Berwick.   The principal tax-collectors, the sheriffs, came in person or by deputy to pay
their net takings across the Exchequer table and sit singly, with their
clerks, at its side for examination.   The great officers of the Exchequer, in scarlet-and-gold robes of the King's gift, were ranged round
the other three sides.   Other barons in attendance watched from the
background.   The Justiciar, or failing him the Chancellor, was titular
president; in the absence of both, the chair was taken by a clerk
appointed by the Chancellor.   But when Henry III suppressed the
Chancellor in 1238, the right to appoint this clerk passed to the King;
the clerk about that time usurped in part his master's title and was
christened Chancellor of the Exchequer.   Another nominee or scribe
of the Chancellor, who also wrote all writs and summonses, sat by his
clerk's side, and under his eye recorded on a roll all the figures as
they were called out.   A second record was taken by a clerk of the
Treasurer and a third by the King's Almoner at the time the *Dialogus*
was written.   For any subsequent action all three records had to be
consulted; a mistake was thus extremely unlikely and fraud impossible.   The same principle of independent and overlapping work
by different employees dominated Exchequer organisation.   As the
Treasurer said, " a triple cord cannot easily be broken."

The other officials entitled to seats round the table were the Treasurer,
the two Chamberlains of the Exchequer, the Constable, the Marshal,
each of the four accompanied by his clerk, the Master of the Writing
Office, the calculator who moved the counters on the board and the
cutter of tallies.   But of these the Treasurer, by now the equal of the
Chancellor and infinitely superior to the Chancellor of the Exchequer,
was much occupied with more difficult business and took little part
in Exchequer routine till the end of Elizabeth I's reign; the Constable,
who had to countersign in person or by deputy all Exchequer
writs, usually left these duties to his clerk; one at least of the
Chamberlains was always represented by a clerk; and the Clerk of the

Marshal, part of whose business was to detain unsatisfactory payers in custody, had taken both his master's place and name by about 1200.

The Upper Exchequer was also provided with an usher, or door-keeper and messenger, a hereditary appointment which carried no salary but only fees for conveying writs and summonses to every part of the country; and also with a watchman at 1*d.* a day, two hereditary officials—the melter or assayer and the weigher—and four tellers. The melter, weigher and tellers did their work in the Lower Exchequer. The melter was paid 2*d.* for each assay of silver by the sheriff concerned, but he also enjoyed Crown lands that have not been identified. The weigher got 5*d.* a day while actually employed, and had grants of Crown land at Broadwindsor in Dorset, Rhode Farm in Selborne and Soberton. Their appointments, and those of the ushers also, could descend to women. The four tellers were appointed by the Treasurer to count coin in and out in the Lower Exchequer for a wage of 2*d.* a day at Winchester, or 3*d.* a day when employed, as they usually were, elsewhere.

The Lower Exchequer, or Exchequer of Receipt, was the cashier's department and safe-deposit. Not only coin and bullion, but the Great Seal, Domesday Book and multitudes of charters and treaties, as well as the Exchequer's numerous accounts, were locked in its strong-holds. It had for separate staff two lay knights appointed by and representing the chamberlains, a clerk, who later was called under-treasurer, representing the Treasurer, further subordinate clerks—subordinate to all three jointly—and a doorkeeper, who was appointed by the chamberlains.

Money nowadays is valueless in itself. It was formerly worth almost its face value as bullion. As the silver pence, which con-stituted the whole currency before Edward I, were in the twelfth century worn, clipped and corrupt, the Crown had established its right to be paid many taxes at the full bullion value. The melter and weigher were accordingly required to establish in the Lower Exchequer the value in metal of each parcel of coin and the dis-count at which it should be accepted. Like other Exchequer officials, they were kept on long after work for them had ceased to exist.

Some clerks appear to have been supplied for service in the Ex-chequer from the staff maintained by the Master of the Writing Office.

Presently, the department relied on its own staff, and a formidable array of individual and separate offices was developed :

Four Tellers;
King's Chamberlain;
Exchequer Chamberlain;
Clerk of the Pipe or Great Roll, probably a development of the clerk of the Chancellor;
Clerk of the Pells—from the Latin *pelles*, English " skins," which, fastened end to end, composed the parchment rolls;
Clerk of the Pipe—from the tube down which records were dropped to him from an upper chamber;
Writer of the Tallies, who alone could get some general view of the financial position, and who had changed his name by the fifteenth century to Auditor of the Exchequer;
Cutter of the Tallies;
King's Remembrancer, to note and follow up outstanding debts in fluctuating revenues;
Treasurer's Remembrancer, to do the same for the revenues of constant amount;
Foreign Opposer, to examine accounts outside, that is foreign to, the Exchequer;
Clerk of the Estreats, to specialise in escheated estates;
Clerk of the Issues;
Nichill Clerk, to examine returns by sheriffs of debts irrecoverable —the short form " nil " was used by Treasury clerks till modern times in minuting that no further action was possible;
Marshal of the Exchequer;
Constable of the Exchequer;
Usher of the Exchequer.

These men were not linked in the modern hierarchical fashion, but each was independent in the execution of his particular duty; officers were not in the slightest degree interchangeable and vacancies were rarely filled by transfers from other sections. All these posts, with substantial blocks of clerks as substitutes for the more important, continued till the nineteenth century, together with additions made under Henry VIII; amongst others, the Remembrancer of First Fruits and Tenths and the three Auditors of Land Revenues, one for all England except four counties, a second for those counties and a third for Wales.

Money, or tallies in lieu of money, once in, could not be got out of the Exchequer without the use of elaborate machinery. Except for internal wages and small supplies, a writ from the King for the exact amount, properly countersigned, had to be produced and checked against documents; with the consent of the Knights Chamberlains of the Lower Exchequer and of the Writer of the Tallies, the doors could then be unlocked by their three keys and the money counted out by a teller.

The delays and difficulties in getting money to the spending departments were from century to century avoided in various ways; red tape was cut and the careful Exchequer short-circuited. If, indeed, this department had ever centralised all revenue, it lost the handling of large blocks of it, which in the reign of John were paid direct into the Wardrobe—the section of the Household which managed most spending. Under Henry III, Peter des Rivaulx, the protégé of Hubert de Burgh's rival, made the Wardrobe the King's principal financial department.

A reaction then set in. From the thirteenth century the Exchequer called before it not only sheriffs and wardens of towns, but also collectors of customs, escheators—Crown managers of escheated estates— Wardens of the Mint, forest wardens, and even the Keepers of the three Wardrobes; of whom the Keeper of the Great Wardrobe accounted, in arrear only, for £33,727 received and expended by him in 1244–51.

Walter de Stapeldon, the Lord Treasurer, reformed the Exchequer in 1323, late in Edward II's reign. It was not a particularly prosperous period, yet two years later the Exchequer clerks were snowed under with work, and vigorously demanded an increase of their numbers. The Great Roll was represented to be larger for a single year than for three or four under the King's ancestors; accounts were several years in arrear, and the volume of business was still growing. The work of the Treasurer's Remembrancer's office had so increased during this reign that one year necessitated as much writing of rolls and writs as once did five or six. Two extra clerks were conceded to the Comptroller of the Great Roll for outside accounts until things improved, and the Remembrancer also was granted the addition to his customary fee under previous kings of a " competent sum," which was fixed at twelve marks (£8) a year, for the hire of two more clerks. Before the fall in 1399 of Richard II, the Exchequer was again the sole financial department, and the Wardrobes were reduced to the role of account-ants for the Household expenditure.

The number of Government departments increased by one on the accession of Henry IV. His patrimony of the Duchy of Lancaster, with its vast wealth of farms and manors and feudal rights spilled beyond the original bounds over half England, was united for good and all to the Crown. Its administration remained autonomous, and almost as much divorced as before from Exchequer, Chancery and the Palace departments, save that its net yield was paid over to these last to spend. A separate Chancellor, with his Duchy seal, a remem-brancer, a solicitor and a staff of clerks at the Savoy and surveyors and agents in each shire, gathered in its wealth. Occasional transfers and promotions were arranged for the benefit of an individual. The Duchy Chancellorship in particular became a sort of Stellenbosch to crown a deserving but undistinguished career; quite a number of Speakers of the House of Commons found that haven. In general, the staffs of Duchy, Chancery and Exchequer were quite separate.

Office was usually permanent and commonly delegated. Henry IV undertook on his accession that no official of his in the Exchequer or elsewhere would be appointed for life, or even for a fixed term of years, and in 1406 that none should leave their work to deputies. Neither promise made any difference in practice. At this time—the early fifteenth century—the hereditary post of Marshal was held by the Dukes of Norfolk and that of Chamberlain by the Cromwells, who filled them as they pleased. The Usher's duties were distributed by him among under-ushers and a messenger. Perhaps half of the better-paid offices that were not hereditary were granted to and recruited from men who had already served the Crown in the House-hold or on the battlefield, but a number went to men who had entered the Exchequer as clerks in their early twenties and rose from the ranks. There were in all nine Chancellors of the Exchequer between 1410 and 1516 and eleven under-treasurers, an equivalent or superior office, between 1428 and 1505, a total of nineteen men in approximately a century, because one man—Richard Fowler—combined the two posts. Of these nineteen, three or perhaps four of the Chancellors and five of the under-treasurers had come into the Exchequer in low grades.

John Throgmorton, who became a clerk by twenty-five, was a man of some importance; he was elected to the Commons for Worcester-shire before he was thirty and sat thereafter in six Parliaments, and besides this and his clerking was an escheator for two years and sub-sheriff for four—not jobs of the highest class. It took him eighteen years from his entry to become under-treasurer and ten more to add to this a Chamberlainship of the Exchequer; he then held both posts till his death in 1443. A John Brown, also twice elected to the Commons, was successively Clerk of the Issues (1439), Chamberlain of the Ex-chequer (1447) and under-treasurer (1455). Hugh Fenn, born about 1420, entered the Exchequer before 1444; he was one of the auditors —there were two at this time—and in charge of a body of clerks before 1455, when he was paid £10 for compiling the first known budget statement. His task must have been arduous. Exchequer records aimed only at preventing mistake or fraud and enforcing payments, however slowly; comprehensive summaries of revenue and expendi-ture could not be extracted from their multiplicity of parchments with accuracy till the nineteenth century and were not often attempted in the fifteenth.

The Wars of the Roses, when, in King James I's vivid phrase, " one house was up to-day and another to-morrow and the Crown was tossed up and down like a tennis ball," wrought havoc among leading officials, and Edward IV, Richard III and Henry VII all made sweeping changes in the personnel that battle and the scaffold had not already cleared away. But the permanency of the bureaucracy lower down was not greatly infringed. After a few Exchequer officials had been dismissed in the first spasm of violence and sudden death, their col-leagues introduced a Bill in Parliament in 1456 to confirm " the laud-able and profitable custom " that men of the Exchequer must not be removed from office, even though held at pleasure, except for an offence proved at law, and to reinstate all those discharged since Easter 1454. Henry VII indeed adopted the doctrine of " the spoils to the victors," but he applied it wholesale only to the forestry and lands staff.

The scope of the Exchequer began again to be narrowed under Edward IV, and Henry VII, whose administrative ability is undoubted, pushed the department into the background. The only revenues allowed to reach it were the fixed dues collected by sheriffs or paid by some boroughs, the Customs and the rents of certain Crown lands. The Exchequer defrayed from these the wages and fixed charges of

Household and Wardrobe and handed the balance over to the Chamber, to which all other revenue was paid direct. Not only were the complexities of traditional accounting avoided, but all finance was brought under the eye of the careful King.

John Morton, Archbishop of Canterbury, Cardinal and Lord Chancellor also for most of Henry's reign, was presumably his financial adviser-in-chief. A famous dilemma for trapping money was known by his name to contemporaries. Under Morton's Fork, the man who lived sparsely was told that one who spent so little must have saved much with which to relieve his King's necessities; and the man who lived largely, that his obvious riches compelled a great contribution to the same end. But the King gave close personal attention to the details of finance. Three men, none of them connected with the Exchequer, did the detailed work which transformed their master from a semi-bankrupt into the wealthiest monarch in Europe.

Sir Reginald Bray, who had provided funds for the invasion of the kingdom in 1487, was forthwith appointed Chancellor of the Duchy of Lancaster, and soon doubled the yield from its lands. Richard Empson was made attorney of the Duchy in 1490. Edmund Dudley was probably engaged on financial work, for which he used the Privy Seal or the Signet, well before he was given official status as President of the Council. Each of these two was Speaker of the House of Commons while busy with the King's finance, Empson in 1491 and Dudley in 1504. Both worked in the closest touch with the King, who initialled, often daily, their diaries of what had been done and what was projected. These twin bloodsuckers of tradition seem to have been conscientious and diligent officials, who stirred no particularly deep and bitter feeling in their lifetimes. Their executions by Henry VIII after a delay of eighteen months were more a characteristic of that monarch than a criticism of their methods.

Henry VIII rioted away the savings of his predecessor, seized the income of the Church and the capital of the monasteries, taxed rigorously at home, and finally devalued the currency and borrowed extravagantly abroad. Prices soared and the Exchequer collapsed. It was all very modern. At the second stage, when the substantial fortune left by his father had been spent and fresh revenue had to be found, a number of new departments, modelled mainly on the Duchy of Lancaster and its methods, was set up. Nationalisation began with the first fruits (the first year's income of a new benefice) and the annual tenths of income hitherto paid to Rome by the regular clergy. A Court of First Fruits and Tenths was created in 1534 with its own chancellor, treasurer, attorney, two auditors, staff of clerks and seal, which by raising assessments and annulling compromises substantially increased the burden on the clergy and the benefit to the King. This body also dealt with lands seized on attainders, revenues accruing during vacancies in benefices, and ecclesiastical fines. Contrary to the first plan, tenths were left to be collected by the bishops and paid by them to the Exchequer. The Exchequer was ordered to hand over any relevant documents and specifically forbidden to interfere in any way with the new body.

The Court of the Augmentations of the Revenues of the King's Crown was created in 1537 to handle at a high level the confiscated property and revenues of monasteries; its operations were subsequently extended to chantries and to property dedicated to pious uses by lay bodies like the Livery Guilds of London. Besides a chancellor, treasurer, attorney, solicitor, ten auditors, a clerk, an usher, and a messenger in Whitehall, it had seventeen local representatives for groups of counties, and was given both a great and a privy seal of its own. Purchased as well as confiscated lands were put under its management, but properties either of monasteries in the Duchy or of monasteries founded by former Dukes of Lancaster, wherever situated, were excluded and left to the Duchy to handle. Forced sales of up to a third of the land in the country in the course of a few years entailed sacrificial prices. Fortunes were bound to be made by men with cash. The staff of this new department, the courtiers, the lawyers and not least the clerks who transferred from Thomas Cromwell's private office, were among them. As always in periods of stirring government, "jobs were found for the boys."

A Court of Wards, under a master with a separate seal, attorney, auditors and clerks, was expanded in 1540, again with an injunction to the Exchequer against interference, and the surveyors of liveries were incorporated in it in 1542. This Court managed all the Crown's rights of profiting from the lands of deceased tenants-in-chief during the minority of their heirs, selling the marriages of heirs or heiresses, and all like feudal dues. It also maintained representatives in the provinces.

The administration of Crown lands was reorganised in 1542 on a county basis, under a Court of two surveyors, an attorney, a master of woods, auditors, clerks and forty-one local receivers. No fewer than six distinct departments had thus been created outside the Exchequer, almost entirely under Thomas Cromwell's management, for the collection of revenue; the sum involved was of the order of £275,000 a year.

From 1544 onwards further funds were raised by depreciating the currency. The time-honoured administration of the Mint by Warden, Master and Comptroller was scrapped in order to entrust it to under-treasurers under the Cofferer or head accountant of the Household. No new finance body was created; the profits of debasement were paid to the Court of Surveyors.

Unification of his multiple and costly organisation began seven years after Cromwell's execution, possibly under the influence of Sir William Paulet, one of Wolsey's old officials who ran through the full gamut of financial posts to become the great reforming treasurer of 1550–72. The Court of Augmentations and the Court of Surveyors of Lands were amalgamated in Henry VIII's last month, on 1st January, 1547; the receipt of their pooled revenues was shortly afterwards transferred to the Exchequer. A simple consolidation of the remaining departments and the abolition of surplus posts were estimated to save £6,431 a year; their amalgamation and consolidation in the Exchequer were expected to raise the saving to £18,500.

On Mary's accession an Act was passed to permit the dissolution of all Henry's new departments, on condition that all existing officers should be secured in their salaries and fees and perquisites. Sir Edmund Peckham, to whom the reorganisation had been entrusted, visited the Exchequer in state the following Christmas day, 1553, to exhibit to it the Royal warrants and to complete formally the reabsorption in the Exchequer of the Courts of Augmentations and Land Revenues and of that of First Fruits and Tenths. Mary restored its ecclesiastical revenues to the Church in 1555. A few of the staff thus freed were taken over by the Exchequer, even if it meant duplication of posts. The remainder of the first-fruits staff received full pensions, or even more. Sir John Baker, their Chancellor, got £100 a year more than his salary of £133 6s. 8d., presumably in consideration of the fees that he lost; the Clerk exchanged a salary of £40 for a pension of £33 6s. 8d.; Sir Walter Mildmay, the general surveyor, received a pension of £200, which he still drew in 1568 in addition to twofold salaries as Chancellor of the Exchequer and as under-treasurer.

Elizabeth I at once resumed this ecclesiastical revenue, which was handled by her Exchequer. Anne returned the money to the Church as Queen Anne's Bounty, but its collection and accounting continued in a first-fruits section of the Exchequer until the reorganisation in 1833, when the work was handed over to the Ecclesiastical Commissioners.

After Elizabeth's accession, the Exchequer was charged in 1559 with the scrutiny and auditing of the receipts and outgoings of the Great Wardrobe, the Chief Butler and the Hanaper of Chancery; and of expenditure on buildings, the Navy, ordnance, war and Ireland. It also took over the auditors of prests.

All these transfers were made on one condition: that the Exchequer's complicated routine of record and account should not apply to the new work. The simpler methods evolved outside, and the use of English instead of Latin, were to be retained for the work taken over, while the antique " course of the Exchequer " continued undisturbed for work that it had never lost. Officials bred in the old tradition kept their faith. " So perfect it is in all parts," one of the clerks assured Lord Burleigh when he was Treasurer, " that the best wits cannot find out what to add or take away in any particular without injury to the whole." Such devotion won the day after forty years of conflicting methods; in 1597 the old ways were extended to all Exchequer work.

The Exchequer, inflated by these auditors, receivers and clerks, with economies effected as surplus hands and pensioners died off, was at last once more in appearance the sole financial department, covering everything but the feudal dues under the Master of Wards. This swollen Exchequer could even produce periodical financial statements. In fact, it had been reduced by other events to the status of a recorder and cashier. For after a line of nominal Treasurers, high finance— and finance received paramount care in Elizabeth's reign—had become the lively interest of three great Treasurers, Paulet and after him the two Cecils; and the Treasurer, who incidentally often secured the lucrative post of Master of Wards, had been sundered from the Exchequer by the move of the Palace from Westminster to Whitehall in 1530. The Chancellor of the Exchequer also had gone there; from being little more than the keeper of its Seal, he was put in immediate charge of some of the business, given the right of appointing some of the staff and accorded the post of under-treasurer in addition to his own, with the salaries and fees of both. Thenceforward fiscal decisions were taken by the Treasurer and his private office, and the way was open for him to deal with new taxes outside the Exchequer.

With the rise of the Treasury and the permanent creation of separate and independent paymasters to whom funds were issued in large sums for each of the forces, their pensioners, civil contingencies and so on, the Exchequer sank into the background as an old-fashioned book-keeper, and became " a museum of archæological antiquities " in the eighteenth century. The remuneration of the traditional officers was enormously enhanced by the operation of piece-work rates on the increased receipts and payments that nominally passed through the books. In 1730 the Writer of the Tallies was getting, as Auditor of the Exchequer, £7,000 instead of the £10 a year of 300 years before, when he actually did the work; and later he got twice as much, £14,000. The Clerk of the Pells took £7,600 a year during the war with the American Colonies. The four tellers advanced from 3*d.* a day to £500 a year under the Commonwealth, when the posts were already sinecures; in the eighteenth century each teller averaged £23,000 a year during the same period of war. Such handsome incomes were naturally appropriated to worthy claimants, the offices being in the gift of the First Lord of the Treasury; the Auditor's income, for instance, went to swell the remuneration of Walpole, himself First Lord. The work was done for workaday salaries on unchanging lines by the deputies whom the great men appointed. Envy, or a moderate desire for economy, struck at last. The offices of the two chamberlains, the usher and the tally-cutter were ordered in 1783 to be abolished and indented cheques to be substituted for tallies; but only on the deaths of the respective officers. The tally-cutter lived on till 1826 and the tallies continued to be cut and used for accounting during that time. The chamberlains were got rid of in 1783 for a pension of £2,000 a year each, such work as they did being transferred to the Auditor's staff.

The Auditors of Prests or Imprests, who had been created under Henry VIII for the scrutiny of the final expenditure of money advanced to other departments, were abolished with their staffs in 1785 and replaced by two Commissioners of Audit of Army expenditure at £500 a year each, and three for civil expenditure at £1,000 a year each; although they employed thirty clerks, the total salary bill was reduced eventually from £33,687 to £8,650. The duties were unaltered.

Entry in Exchequer Accounts, 1831

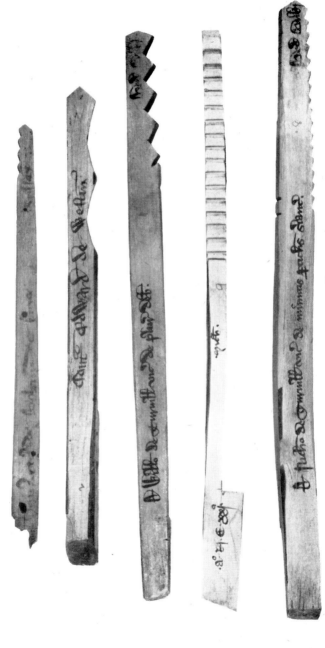

Exchequer Tallies

Procedure at the end of the eighteenth century remained much as before. An official who had money to pay into the Exchequer wrote his name, the amount and the account to which it should be credited in what was called, appropriately or not, the waste-book. The clerk in charge copied these particulars in Latin on a piece of parchment—the bill—which he shot down to the Tally Court through the pipe. There the deputy chamberlains and tally-cutter prepared the piece of wood, of which one piece—the foil—was retained and the other—the tally proper—was given to the payer. When his department sought to complete its accounts, the tally was presented, and one deputy chamberlain read out its amount, while the other held the foil and agreed it. No account could be passed without tallies. At the time the tally was prepared, the staffs of the Clerk of the Pells, the Clerk of the Pipe, and the Auditor recorded the particulars diversely arranged in their several ledgers. Similarly, when a payment out had to be made, the teller's clerk handed out the money on receipt of a " debenture " or order duly signed after all particulars had been recorded elsewhere. All money that reached the Exchequer passed in and out through the hands of that one of the four groups to which the account had been allocated. Such was the theory. In practice all moneys were received and issued by the Bank of England after the suspension of gold payments, and only nominal entries passed through the Exchequer.

Till its end in 1834, the Exchequer retained parchment on which it continued to record amounts in Roman numerals of the obsolete Tudor script; some of its accounts were kept in Latin throughout. The main account was a tub-like roll, difficult even to lift.

The Exchequer clerks boasted, with departmental pride, that the elaboration of their methods had prevented a single fraud in their whole history. Other officials enjoyed more latitude. Edmund Burke, in his eagerness to reform the Pay Office, reinstated in 1782 two clerks who had been discharged by his predecessor for embezzlement. So encouraged, they took a further £250,000 before being caught. A little later, Rose of the Treasury gave a chief clerk's job to one Chinnery, a friend of Lord Chancellor Thurlow; he embezzled £70,000.

The pay of each of the four tellers was marked in 1786 for reduction to £2,700 a year, as the holders died and new appointments were made. Two tellers of the old dispensation remained in 1810, when,

D

owing to heavy war expenditure, their gross fees were £23,000 odd each and their net incomes over £21,000 apiece. One of the old tellers, the Marquess Camden, granted the job in 1766 and succeeding to it in 1780, still survived in 1834. His gross fees had shrunk to the still respectable average of £12,857 p.a. (for the years 1829–33); the Marquess, however, kept only £2,700, like his colleagues, and, after paying his taxes and his staff, handed over more than half the fees to public funds. The other three drew £2,700 each. At both dates all the tellers were either peers or cadets of peers, except the son of the murdered Prime Minister, Spencer Perceval.

To do the actual work, each teller had a similar staff—a first clerk at £1,000 p.a. and four other clerks at £800, £600, £400 and £200, or figures close to those levels.

The salary of the Auditor of the Exchequer had been cut to £4,000 a year in 1794. All his work was done by a deputy, Robert Jennings, at £1,000, three superior clerks at £300, £500 and £550, and four assistants on salaries from £40 to £187.

The Clerk of the Pells had £3,000 a year about 1730, rose to £7,600 during the American war, and was immediately afterwards limited to £3,000. His deputy, E. W. Roberts, who had done all the work for forty-five years, averred in 1810 that the labour of recording every receipt and issue of public money had much increased since 1780 and needed his close attendance. He was well satisfied that thereby " the public have the most perfect security," but he felt that he would not have the weight to be the check " on the Lord Treasurer," without his background chief. The offices of Deputy and Chief were combined in 1823 at a salary of £1,400.

The Clerk of the Pipe drew just under £1,000 p.a. in fees (£968 in 1810, £996 in 1829–32), out of which he paid his deputy, who did all the work, £100 a year. The Clerk of 1797–1834 certainly could not meddle in the office; he became the Governor-General of India, Lord William Cavendish Bentinck.

The Comptroller of the Pipe drew a beggarly £205 a year, but the holder from 1801 till he died in 1847, John Tekell, was also Foreign Opposer in the Exchequer, with a salary of £40 and fees of £265; and Comptroller of the Mint for life with £298 10s. He had one deputy at the Mint, another for his two Exchequer posts; the latter deputy had in his own right a third Exchequer post, Clerk of Estreats, which he avowed to be underpaid at fees averaging £274 a year, and to entail great labours which he, with his own copying clerks, performed personally. A former salary of £96 13s. 4d. in addition to the fees had been stopped.

The King's Remembrancer averaged £1,633 in fees in 1810 and left all the work to his deputy till 1823, when his death enabled the two posts to be combined at a salary of £1,000, the fees being paid over to the Treasury. The Treasury Remembrancer, with a salary of £64, had fallen to average receipts of £196 in 1834, but professed to have too much work to do for that sum. The Surveyor of Green Wax, Lord Mahon, taking £260 a year, could leave all the work to a deputy. The Clerk of the Nichills actually performed in person, for £30 a year, duties which he considered laborious and responsible.

In the main, the Exchequer survived till 1834, when an Act of Parliament, in remodelling the Government system of dealing with money, virtually abolished the department in favour of a Comptroller-General of Receipt. The six ancient offices which still survived, with the fifty-three persons whom they employed, were replaced by a staff of thirteen, all, except the Comptroller-General, selected from the old staff. The annual bill fell from £40,500 to £6,800.

The lately discarded tallies, having been stored for fuel, caught fire, as it were in vengeance, and burnt down the Houses of Parliament in that year.

The extinction of the Exchequer was completed by another Act in 1866, which combined the new Comptroller-General with the Commissioners of Audit in the present Exchequer and Audit Department.

All that is left of the more ancient is a few ceremonies. The Queen's and Lord Treasurer's Remembrancer, uniting the two Remembrancers in the person of the senior Master of the Queen's Bench, presides over the trial of the Pyx by the Goldsmith's Company, collects from the City as annual rent for a forge a horseshoe and nails (which he always leaves behind, so that the same ones have served for centuries), and keeps the seal of the Chancellor of the Exchequer. The latter, or his other self, the under-treasurer (for he is still separately appointed to the two posts), formally attends the pricking of sheriffs.

5

THE MINT AND OFFICE OF WORKS

THE hoariest of all Government departments is the Mint. Ancient Britons and Romans coined money here, but the Mint's unbroken existence only begins a couple of years before A.D. 600, when St. Augustine founded one at Canterbury. A mint was started in London a few years later. Similar undertakings followed elsewhere, until they reached some fourscore in number at the end of four or five centuries. Some were owned and run by bishops or abbots; most, perhaps, were local enterprises; some were managed by the King. Egbert, for example, owned a mint in Winchester, from which he sent five men in 825 to Canterbury on its conquest, to coin for him, without dispossessing the Archbishop of his prior rights. London also was a King's mint.

The King assumed a general control of all mints during the ninth century by legislative orders and by restricting the legal making of dies to a single office, which William the Conqueror made hereditary; it continued to be a private possession for over 300 years. Tighter Royal control was applied in 1180, when the number of mints had greatly shrunk, by the appointment of an official, the warden, through whom all issues of coin had to be made.

A hundred years later, in 1279, the mints that still survived, with the exception of a few small properties of the Church, were brought under management of three officers based on London. The system then established remained in force till the nineteenth century. The three—a warden, a master worker and a comptroller—were independent of each other, and were intended to be mutual checks. The warden was the King's immediate representative. He collected the King's fees for the making of coin; from them he maintained the buildings, paid certain Royal officials, and handed the balance over to the Palace. He stopped coins that were below standard, and, as a judge, he tried all except the most serious law cases that were brought either against or by anyone in the mint. Like other groups of Royal servants, those of the mints were exempt from civil duties, were protected against ordinary legal processes and enjoyed the benefit of their own court. The first of those immunities survives in some departments whose officers may not be forced to serve as jurymen, sheriff or mayor. When more or less systematic steps against counterfeiters and clippers of coin came to be taken, they also fell within the warden's province.

The master was in effect a contractor for coinage, and was autonomous in his own sphere so long as his goods were up to standard. He paid all expenses, deducted from coins passed for issue a fee proportional to their weight, and made what profits he could. Save very occasionally he received no salary till 1626.

Comptroller had not its modern sense; it meant, as elsewhere, one who kept a counter-roll, an independent record of bullion received and coin issued, by which any cheating of King or merchant by warden or master could be exposed. Collusion between the three was necessary for the grosser frauds. A porter, a clerk of the papers to prevent tampering with the governing documents, and a teller and weigher of the coins were appointed by the King. They were paid by the warden, and were independent in the exercise of their particular duties. The Mint did not buy silver, nor later gold, for coinage; its duty was to coin bullion brought to it by King, merchant or offices of exchange. The Mint, indeed, was regarded even in James I's time as so separate from the public service that Bacon classed its officials with outside experts like lawyers and seamen who should appear before Council committees and not before the full Council. Until about 1400 the warden was usually chosen from the City of London, presumably to ensure the confidence of the commercial community. Exchequer officials, two of them Chancellors of the Exchequer, monopolised the post for another half-century. For yet another 300 years it was generally diverted to be an emolument of officials elsewhere; a Knight of the Body and King's Carver was followed in the office by the Master of the Ordnance, and he by a Lord High Treasurer; it was held under James II by the head official in the Treasury and by an Undersecretary of State. In the eighteenth century it oscillated between successful officials and undistinguished M.Ps.

The master was commonly a foreigner, mostly an Italian banker, as long as the wardens were City men; but from 1400 until the

Restoration the City shifted its grip to this post, which was filled as a rule by one of the Livery Company of Goldsmiths; or, if a greater man was master, a goldsmith was his deputy or was in charge of melting. Two Court appointments were followed by that of Isaac Newton, F.R.S.; the master's profits rising far above the salaries of warden or comptroller, the master from 1737 to 1850 was a minister, latterly one holding also another and more active ministerial post.

The comptroller was usually combined with the assayer, a professional technician, until 1438, when the posts became separate and the comptrollership was usually granted to an irrelevant official—someone in the Exchequer, or a Latin secretary or a clerk of the Signet; once it was assigned as security to a creditor of the King's. The City of London got its share in the seventeenth century; thereafter comptrollers were M.P.s or officials of other departments.

The clerks of these three officials were appointed by them severally during their pleasure, but were in practice permanent. The labourers and artificers required were impressed or hired, at first by the warden, later by the master. Numbers fluctuated greatly, and men came and went. The permanent element, however, formed a fraternity about the middle of the fifteenth century which contracted as a body with the master at piece rates for all coinage work except melting and casting of bullion into bars. The master, on his part, was bound to place the coinage work with them; his own task of melting and casting was presently arranged by him with separate and changing contractors at his discretion. The Company of the Moneyers altered its character when the adoption of primitive machinery in 1662 changed the kind of labour required. It became a small body of hardly more than half a dozen supervisors, who received piece rates, but hired the workpeople they needed at day rates. Moreover, they had the sole right of filling vacancies in their own ranks, and so nominated their successors; the company became hereditary in practice. A rise in the volume of work without reduction of piece rates made the company, like the master, very wealthy.

The warden left his duties to a substitute from 1600 onwards; the comptroller his from 1700; the master, who had been represented by a deputy as early as 1461, when the succession of goldsmiths was interrupted, also delegated his work from 1737 onwards. His post was acknowledged to be of " little or no attendance though one of occasional responsibility " in 1810, when it was held by the President of the Board of Trade. Consequently, the management of the Mint was transferred to a committee of the Privy Council from 1787 to 1816, when an energetic master, the brother of the Duke of Wellington, enabled the Committee to be dissolved; on his resignation, rule by deputies was resumed. Not only the principal officers, but also lesser lights like the clerk of the papers and the weigher and teller down even to the office-sweeper, were phantoms seldom seen, and were represented by deputies, of whom at least one was too aged to attend. The hierarchy remained intact; it had even been expanded, but it was manned by shadows. The physical labour in the melting-house was done by the workmen of the deputy master, whom the master had made his contractor, and in the other rooms by the work-men of the hereditary body who had a right to that contract. What remained unchanged was that three signatures were necessary on day-to-day documents, three keys to open a safe, and three consents at a board meeting to any business that did not lie within a single sphere.

The sinecure master's swollen fees were successively limited to £3,000, £2,500 and finally £2,000, in economy campaigns of the early nineteenth century. The sinecure warden was suppressed and his title attached to the master's. The sinecure comptroller was replaced by his deputy. At the same time quite considerable advances of pay were obtained by the deputies, lower officials and clerks.

The Mint continued to be run by the two head permanent officials till 1850 on personal lines. Refining of bullion, as well as melting and casting metal for coinage, were remitted by contracts at piece rates to the "master's second clerk," who combined in his mint-works an even more important business of refining at higher charges for the Bank and bullion brokers of the City. The other coinage operations were performed under contract by the Company of Moneyers. The moneyers' rates were not permanently reduced to take account of the economies of steam machinery, and both they and the master's second clerk did very well as the amount of gold coin increased. Big private incomes naturally irritated the Government; while the contract system was admitted to be the most efficient, it ought to be possible to seize the large margins for the Exchequer. Accordingly, these businesses within a business were abolished in 1850. The Government failed to find another suitable contractor for the coinage work; the refinery was sold; the melter and the Company of Moneyers were pensioned off, and their workmen became Government employees. The whole institution was placed under the direct orders of a whole-time and non-political master. The Treasury, moreover, withdrew, on grounds of principle, the liberty of private practice, exercised on a large scale, which was enjoyed by the assayer and the engraver. The former resigned; design in engraving gradually passed to outside artists.

Twenty years later, the master was replaced by an amalgamation of his two chief subordinates, the deputy master and comptroller, and the old titles of master worker and warden were transferred without pay to the Chancellor of the Exchequer.

Works

A second technical department was formed in the thirteenth century for the construction and maintenance of castles, palaces and manors; its organisation was probably completed in fairly final form about 1336. The technical services remained in the control of experts in each branch, who received standing retainers of 6*d*. or 7*d*. a day and hired the necessary hands, but were free to accept other contracts if their time permitted. There were King's master masons, King's carpenters, plumbers, glaziers, smiths and joiners, apparently one of each for an important building or group of buildings. Administration and financial control centred in a clerk or surveyor of works, who had deputies and clerks to keep the rolls and accounts, issue cash and materials, and check their use and the progress of the work. One clerk of works might cover London and its surroundings, or separate officers might be appointed for individual or isolated premises.

Professional knowledge was not looked for in a clerk of works. Thus, in 1389 Chaucer was appointed clerk for Westminster at 2*s*. a day and afterwards added Windsor. In 1443 John Somerset, the King's physician, was given, among other jobs, the surveyorship of Westminster, Sheen, the Tower and Eton; and a clerk of the Signet, Edmund Blake, became clerk in 1451 at 4*s*. a day of the King's works in Westminster, Sheen, the Tower, Eltham and at Clarendon. John Lematon, an Exchequer official and later Chancellor of the Exchequer, was clerk of works from 1442 for distant Berwick, Roxburgh and Carlisle, while in 1461 a fishmonger, Edward Gower, was appointed clerk of works of Clarendon for life.

Lay administrators were superseded under the Tudors by practising architects, of whom the greatest was Inigo Jones, under James I and Charles I. His salary of £150 a year, with £46 for a clerk and office, did not give the King the monopoly of his services. At the Restoration Sir John Denham, the poet, was appointed—not without protest—because the post was promised to him by Charles I, and Sir Christopher Wren could only be made deputy surveyor; Denham's death in 1669 freed for Wren the office of surveyor-general. Wren was in charge of Royal buildings for the substantial term of fifty-seven years, though they were far from monopolising his time. He fell into disfavour on the Hanoverian accession, and was replaced in 1718, after four years of continual friction, by William Benson, M.P., who made the immediate mistake of condemning the House of Lords as a dangerous structure and was discharged for this criticism of its stability when the House refused to fall.

The department was reorganised in the administrative turmoil of 1782 under a surveyor of works who, it was stipulated, must be an architect. Enlarged to surveyor-general, his sphere was extended to all Government as well as Royal buildings in 1814, and the Treasury set about the abolition of the jobbing contractors whom various departments independently employed on their own affairs, and the concentration under him of all civil buildings, maintenance and furnishings. Clerks of works were appointed for detailed supervision of groups of buildings, and appear to have enjoyed considerable discretion up to moderate financial limits.

Another wave of economy in 1832 absorbed the surveyor-general and his staff in the Board of Woods, Forests and Land Revenues. Some advocated the more intelligible course of transfer to the Ordnance, who were experts in buildings and from whom the surveyor-general drew much of his material, but this would not have served the economists' main purpose, which was to get rid, on suitable compensation, of a large number of officers maintained by the Woods and Forests. This, however, was a rich body, and independent of parliamentary votes and grants. Their land revenues were imperceptibly drawn upon for the needs of public buildings when the House of Commons was disinclined to grant funds; with the natural consequence after twenty years that the Works was again divorced from the Woods and Forests. Public buildings were brought under direct parliamentary control by the creation of a mock commission on the lines of Privy

Council committees. A First Commissioner, with a seat in Parliament, was created with a salary of £2,000, afterwards £5,000, a year; all the Secretaries of State and the President of the Board of Trade were appended to him. This Board of Works was given the right to appoint its architects, surveyors and technical staff; the Treasury reserved to itself the choice and appointment of a secretary, clerks and messengers. The Board never met or did anything else; in 1940 it was replaced by a Minister of Works and Public Buildings.

The Woods and Forests, with which public buildings had been brigaded, was itself, as the Department of Crown Lands, confined in 1923–4 to its investments and its finances were brought under the control of annual votes of Parliament.

6

WOLSEY AND CROMWELL

One of the secular revolutions coincided with the establishment of the Tudors. Education had for a century spread outside the fold of the Church. Literate laymen appeared by 1400; in 1500 they were in ample supply for the Royal service and other needs. Men's minds were altered by the rediscovery of the cultures and history of Greece and Rome. The printing-press was a new force in communications. The great breach with Rome was imminent. On the physical side, cannon had made private strongholds untenable and strengthened the control of the central Government. Ocean communication had been opened with the Far East; America had been discovered. Above all, money became much more plentiful. New mines in Bohemia and Germany swelled the supply of silver before the accession of Henry VII, and the flow of both silver and gold from the Eldorado across the Atlantic had grown to a deluge by his death. Crown revenue nearly trebled in that reign. It was the age of an expanding universe, and the power and comprehensiveness of government swelled continually.

The comparable revolution in the State service was delayed till the death of Cardinal Wolsey, its last great mediæval figure. Son of an Ipswich butcher and grazier, Thomas Wolsey, after a dazzling career at Magdalen, Oxford, obtained in addition to his inevitable fellowship a distant benefice by the kindness of a marquess whose son was one of his pupils. It was the first of several, for already the young man was a pertinacious pluralist. His next clear step up the ladder was a chaplaincy to the archbishop of Canterbury, on whose death he transferred to service in Calais under Sir Richard Nanfan, the deputy lieutenant. His master's age and feeble health caused the running of the colony to be left to this capable assistant, who showed his mettle so admirably that when at last Sir Richard retired he recommended Wolsey to Henry VII for his personal employment.

Wolsey, now a man of thirty-five, was accordingly made one of the

Household Chaplains in 1507. Henry VIII promoted him to be a councillor and his almoner on his accession two years later, and rewarded his services further with many Church livings in the next four years. Excellent organisation of men and materials for the French war of 1512–14—such work was still devolved on whoever, however unlikely, struck the King as most competent—and worthy conduct in the field brought Wolsey in 1513 the deanery of York, and in 1514 first the bishoprics of both Lincoln and Tournai, and then in July of that year the archbishopric of York. In 1515 he became lord chancellor; in the same year the Pope made him a cardinal and in 1518 legate.

Though an archbishop, Wolsey increased both his revenues and his field for patronage by holding also one bishop's see in his own name; he took Bath and Wells at first in 1518; that was exchanged in due time for the richer Durham; later, the still richer Winchester was substituted for Durham. He acquired the equity of three other sees— Salisbury, Worcester and Llandaff—by their conferment on Italian bishops on condition that they accepted fixed salaries, stayed in Italy and left Wolsey the profits and patronage. The richest of the abbeys —St. Albans—he reserved for himself; other abbacies, deaneries and vicarages he distributed for money or favours, sometimes to scandalous persons, including his bastard son. And he started the confiscation of the monasteries by seizing some twenty.

On the lay side, he grossed up his fees as Chancellor by sweeping all manner of cases out of the other law courts into that of Chancery, whether from greed or intolerance of their inefficiency. In one way and another, his income was said to reach a third of the King's, and he overspent it as prodigally. As the man with the ear of Henry VIII, Chancellor, Archbishop of York and Cardinal-legate, feared and courted by all and opposed by none, Wolsey ruled all domestic and foreign business, subject only to his alert and selfish master, and concentrated the Church and State machine in a single management. With his demoniac energy and insufferable ability, he in effect created the Tudor centralised government.

All this could not be done without more help than he could get from Palace and Government officials. Wolsey recruited what was in effect a Civil Service of his own within the immense personal staff or "household" which, like other successful men, he maintained on similar lines to the King's. His young men, passing on to Crown service, were the mainspring of the administration for a generation after his death, and their personal employees in turn continued the tradition.

Not very important among them, perhaps, was Pietro Vannes, an Italian whom Wolsey engaged in 1514 as his secretary for correspondence in Latin; about 1517 Vannes passed into the King's direct service as assistant to the Latin secretary, another Italian, whose death that year gave the assistant the succession. Vannes remained Latin secretary till he died in 1562; he was thrice sent on missions to the Pope and to Venice and was made Dean of Salisbury in 1540.

John Gostwick, another minor figure who entered Wolsey's service in 1517, was later one of Thomas Cromwell's right-hand men and was advanced by him to Treasurer of First Fruits in 1535.

A scholar, Richard Pace, after many visits and missions abroad, was taken by Wolsey as his chief secretary; he was advanced to be the King's for the decade 1516–26, but then went mad and had to be confined in the Tower. It was Pace who heard and recorded the King's summary of an ecclesiastical debate on the litany: " some be too styff in their old mumpsimus, others be too busy and curious in their newe sumpsimus."

Pace was succeeded as Wolsey's principal secretary by Dr. Stephen Gardiner, who also went on, in 1528, to be the King's; he surrendered this specific post when he was made Bishop of Winchester in 1531, but remained in the Royal service as councillor, leader of the Council, ambassador to France and to Germany, and odd-job man. The good Bishop's versatility was such that he earned the nickname of " Stockfish Stephen " by his briskness in provisioning the 1543 invasion of France, soon after his return from a year's embassy in Germany. The accelerated drive towards Protestantism under Edward VI cost him several years in the Tower; the accession of Catholic Mary not only released him but made him Lord Chancellor for the rest of his life.

Private employment under Wolsey started also on his career Sir William Paulet, finally Marquess of Winchester—" wily Winchester "—master of the Court of Wards, Lord Chamberlain and Lord Steward.

Thomas Wriothesley entered Wolsey's employment in 1522 when he was only seventeen; about 1529 he became Cofferer of the King's Household, the head accountant under the treasurer of that department, and a little later secured a clerkship of the Signet. When Thomas

Cromwell succeeded Wolsey in the Royal favour, Wriothesley combined service under him with employment under the King, added other jobs in the King's Bench and the Mint, and was enriched by numerous grants of manors and cheap purchases of monastery sites. He was made one of the two principal secretaries and knighted in 1540, shortly before Cromwell's fall. In 1544 he was promoted to Lord Chancellor; three years later he was removed from the Council and the Woolsack for delegating his duties to Masters in Chancery, but was comforted with the Earldom of Southampton and after a year restored to the Council.

Thomas Cromwell, Wriothesley's one-time chief, was the most variously dexterous of all Wolsey's minions; all agree on his capacity, drive and humour and his ease as a good mixer. Of lowly birth, for his father was an innkeeper and trader of Putney, he made that village too hot to hold him in early youth, and left it for the Continent. After spells as a private soldier in Italy, a banker in Florence and a business man in the Netherlands, he returned about 1512 to the City of London and set up in law and finance. In 1514 he was the collector of Wolsey's revenues; in 1523 he got a seat in the Commons; in 1525 Wolsey employed him in suppressing a number of small monasteries and in 1528 made him his secretary in succession to Gardiner, and so brought Cromwell into personal contact with the King.

For all his magnificence and authority, Wolsey remained a mere employee of that King's Majesty; " Had I but served God as diligently as I have served the King " were his dying words. In himself he was impotent. When failure to solve Henry's marital difficulty required a change, a mere word on 18th October, 1529, deprived him of the Great Seal; he was reft of all his offices and possessions except the archbishopric of York, to which he was banished, and which after many reluctant delays he saw for the first time. A craving to return from eclipse was immediately met by arrest; further proceedings were stayed by his death.

The King's service underwent three notable changes after this dismissal. His Majesty appropriated the ecclesiastical palace, York Place, though it had not been the property of Wolsey but of the see of York since 1245; renamed it Whitehall, enlarged it, and moved thither from his own decayed palace of Westminster with the Court and Household officers, secretaries, chancellor, treasurer and the rest. The Chancery and Exchequer were left in their quarters in Westminster; though the gap was but a quarter of a mile, it impeded continuous contact of subordinates and chiefs.

Secondly, at the very moment that the King was about to unite Church and State as Supreme Head of both, the age-old interlocking of the two hierarchies was ended. The lower ranks of the Wardrobe, the Privy Seal, Signet and Exchequer Offices had indeed long ceased to be monopolised by men in orders. When the " six clerks " of Chancery were permitted to marry by an Act of 1523 they observed that they were the very last Government clerks to be subject to vows of celibacy. But it was only now that high officials ceased to be recruited from churchmen. The Lord Chancellor had always been an ecclesiastic since the creation of the office some five centuries before, save for the occasional interpolation of a lawyer. No ecclesiastic was appointed to this high office after Wolsey, except during the reaction under Mary, when the Great Seal was entrusted to Bishop Gardiner and after him to Archbishop Heath, and brief appointments under the first two Stuarts—1621-5, John Williams, afterwards Bishop of London; 1635, William Laud, Archbishop of Canterbury. For the future the Lord Chancellor was to be a lawyer, with the occasional intrusion of a layman from outside both professions. Ecclesiastics did not at once entirely vanish from Government service; Elizabeth I found a use for bishops in the Council of the North and on diplomatic missions; James I put Archbishop Abbott into the Treasury; and Charles I made Bishop Juxon First Lord of the Treasury and Admiralty and Archbishop Laud First Lord of the Treasury, with unhappy results. The last clergyman to be appointed to high civil office was John Robinson, who, for his diplomatic work in Scandinavia, was advanced by good Queen Anne to be Bishop of Bristol in 1710 and Lord Privy Seal the following year. This archaism, and the inclusion of this Bishop in the delegation that signed the Peace of Utrecht in 1713, were received with hostile surprise.

The general anti-clerical bias which supported Henry's measures against the Church tended to exclude professional clerics from office once the Universities poured out educated laymen; most of the heads of the Civil Service from Tudor times onwards were Oxford or Cambridge graduates. Civil Servants, for their part, being no longer divines, lost their eligibility for the revenues of abbacies, bishoprics, canonries and deaneries. It was from this time that the practice became rife of accompanying a major promotion by a knighthood or, for the extremely successful, a peerage.

Thirdly, the Lord Chancellor lost the primacy in administration which he had enjoyed since the extinction of the Justiciar 300 years before. Exceptional Chancellors there were, like Lord Clarendon in the turmoil of the Restoration, but though not invariably a lawyer—the last non-lawyer appointed to the Woolsack was Lord Shaftesbury in 1672—Chancellors were for the most part limited to the administration of the judiciary. Wolsey was the last of his line, and leadership passed first to the King's principal secretary and later to the head of the Treasury.

Secretaries up to this time had ranked and messed with the chaplains. They were, of course, invariably ecclesiastics; it was expressive of the new outlook that Thomas Cromwell, whose assumption of the title was delayed a few years, was the first layman to be secretary. Though the secretaries conducted the King's own correspondence, which was thus withdrawn from the bureaucracy, as so much other business had been from time to time, they must long have become more of the official than the personal private secretary. Of the fifteen who enjoyed the status between the appointment of Beckington in 1438 and that of Cromwell in 1534, a number had only served a year or two before passing to more profitable posts, and only three tenures had been long—those of William Hatcliff, significantly enough also the Royal physician, for fifteen years under Edward IV; Dr. Thomas Ruthall, who had already attained his bishopric, for sixteen under Henry VII and Henry VIII; and his immediate successor, Dr. Thomas Pace, who held it for ten before he went mad.

The intrinsic importance of the post was clearly increasing with the growth of the King's business and with more involved foreign affairs. No regular diplomatic or consular service was created for centuries to come, but a resident consul was employed at Pisa from 1486. In Henry VIII's reign, Cardinal Christopher Bainbridge was resident ambassador to the Vatican for five years before his death in 1514, and Richard Sampson, afterwards Bishop of Chichester, was maintained as ambassador in Spain for the three years 1522-5. These were but a sample of the missions sent abroad almost yearly for shorter or longer periods. Correspondence so multiplied that additional secretaries, from whom the older post was distinguished as principal, though its holder had no authority over the rest, had to be created. Such an independent secretary for letters in French was employed from about 1450 and another for those in Latin from 1515. Secretaries were chosen largely for their foreign experience. Principal secretary Pace, and Knight and Gardiner, who came between him and Cromwell, spent much of their time abroad, so that the secretary was liable to become an itinerant envoy.

Cromwell, Wolsey's own secretary, did not automatically succeed to his power; it took him two years from his master's disgrace to win the full confidence of the King. By the end of 1531 he was acting as Henry's treasurer and was his leading councillor. He picked up the Court office of Master of the King's Jewels and the sinecure post of Clerk of the Hanaper during 1532, and the Surveyorship of Woods in 1533. In April of that year he became Chancellor of the Exchequer, and in April 1534 he ejected Gardiner and became principal secretary to the King. In this capacity he gathered into his hands all the domestic and Church affairs as well as the foreign work of the kingdom. The second phase of Henry VIII's reign proceeded; the breach with Rome was completed, and the property and revenues of the Church were nationalised. Cromwell was on top of the world, and as ruthless and grasping in his private as in his public character. When he wished to extend his City mansion, he was not content to remove his neighbour's landmark: he had rollers placed beneath the adjoining house—the home of the antiquarian Stowe—and the whole structure pushed to a suitable distance.

He held on to his secretaryship and some of his earlier offices while he enlarged his emoluments rather than his authority with others: Master of the Rolls forthwith, in October 1534; Vicar-General to the Head of the Church immediately afterwards, in January 1535, on the passage of the Act of Supremacy; Lord Privy Seal in April 1536. The secretaryship made him the vehicle of Royal authority and gave him control of the Signet seal. This was sufficient warrant for the use of the other seals, but though it carried with it board and lodging at the Palace and the right to fees, still small, for its use the post was still unpaid. Others of the cumulative offices were needed more for their revenues than for their dignity.

These were years of great activity. Apart from the heavy business of current affairs and a fermenting and unsuccessful foreign policy on a distraught continent, Cromwell personally managed the huge acquisitions of Church property at the highest level and created five new

E

departments, outside the Exchequer in his time, for its exploitation in detail. He reconstructed the internal organisation and discipline of the Household, when he put the Board of Green Cloth, the central control of Household finance, on a firm footing and introduced—a startling innovation—day attendance books. It was probably in the year that Cromwell became Lord Privy Seal, though the change had been in hand for some time, that he put the finishing touches to his reorganisation of the Privy Council.

In place of the old Council which the Wars of the Roses had broken up, Henry VII had created a panel of selected officials and statesmen who were individually sworn in as councillors and awarded the fee of £100 a year for life. Appointment as councillor might be an honour and an emolument for a successful permanent official in the Household or elsewhere, or it might give the King a lien on the loyalty and services of some useful man without a defined post. At any rate, no fewer than 170 appointments of councillor were made during his reign. So large a body would have been useless for committee work, and the panel never met in its entirety. The King called varying members together from time to time as his occasions required, but his normal operative council consisted of a much neater inner ring, which was composed mainly of the heads of the Palace departments. Though the Great Council of the Realm was still summoned occasionally, it had practically been replaced by meetings of the Lords and the Commons, equally too numerous and too temporary for detailed decisions. The inner Council, in close touch with the King and usually meeting under his chairmanship, settled every aspect of domestic government and foreign affairs, arranged all important appointments, and supervised and directed the sheriffs of counties, the justices of the peace who took over most of their civil functions, and the lords lieutenant to whom their military responsibilities were passed under Edward VI.

Besides its administrative business, the Council handled a great mass of judicial or semi-judicial work, either in the Star Chamber or in the committee which was set up in 1487 to deal with livery and maintenance, dangerous riots and the over-mighty subject generally. Its Court of Requests, which had been set up a little earlier by Richard III, furnished a poor man's court of equity.

A branch Council, reviving a body created by Edward IV, was set up soon after Henry VII's accession to manage Wales, and another, under the nominal presidency of little Prince Arthur, to run the north of England; they were kept in line with the main body by overlapping memberships.

The operative Council became more and more a body of officials, about a dozen in all; it died out under Wolsey; revived, it steadily increased its sphere of action. The appointment in 1529 of a lord president to take the King's place when he could not attend seems to have been of small importance; the president's existence is barely known. The Council appears to have been without a clerk from 1512; a new clerk, Thomas Derby, lately made a Clerk of the Signet, was again assigned to it in 1533, for his lifetime; about 1536 his functions were extended, and he was required then or in 1540 to keep regular minutes, a record of decisions and a register, while a second clerk looked after the Star Chamber. In 1540 its proclamations were given the force of law. Thus was forged the chief instrument for coordinating Government action for the next couple of centuries. Not the clerk, however, but the principal secretary remained its dominant figure; he devised the agenda and he in the main carried out decisions.

Cromwell, though he made some attempt to organise a faction of personal supporters in the House of Commons, can be regarded, like Wolsey, as an exaggerated head of the Civil Service, completely responsible to a superior, the King, who would neither be bored with detail nor forgive even those errors that he had approved. He had the Clerks of the Signet, the Privy Seal and the Council for routine work, but (again like Wolsey) depended largely on his private office, many members of which were rewarded sooner or later with posts in the Royal service. He took over from Wolsey at least John Gostwick and Thomas Wriothesley, both of whom concurrently held Royal posts. His secretary, Thomas Soulemont, was also, from 1536, the King's French secretary; he became Clerk of the Parliaments in 1539. Ralph Sadleir, future principal secretary, Master of the Wardrobe and Chancellor of the Duchy, began his career in the service of Cromwell, who conceded him a share in the fees of Clerk of the Hanaper; as did William Petre, who was principal secretary for thirteen years after Sadleir. Richard Taverner and Huttolph, employed in the private office from 1533, were four years later provided with clerkships of the Signet. Richard Pollard, also from the private office, became King's Remembrancer in the Exchequer. But William Body, whom Cromwell employed to take charge of the King's money, seems to have remained a private employee; as did Henry Potshead, who was employed on first-fruits and tenths. There were as many others.

How wholly Cromwell's power was delegated from the King was made manifest when he slipped up on the King's domestic life and, besides recommending the wrong party in Germany, foisted an unappetising wife on the uxorious Henry. Anne of Cleves was married on 6th January, 1540. All seemed well for a few months. Henry, as he poised to strike, was gracious to his victims till the last moment. Cromwell, a baron since 1536, was advanced to be Earl of Essex in April and received next day the antique if empty dignity of Lord Great Chamberlain. His secretaryship, however, was taken from him and given, with knighthoods, to two of his personal staff, Wriothesley and Sadleir.

Two months later, on 10th June, 1540, Cromwell was summarily arrested. The Cleves marriage was declared void on 9th July, and Cromwell, whose evidence had been needed for the nullity proceedings, was beheaded on 28th July. Sir Thomas Wriothesley and Sir Ralph Sadleir, as his fosterlings, were clapped in the Tower for some months before their release to resume, jointly, the status and duty of King's secretary.

7

SECRETARIES OF STATE

THE new importance of the office of principal secretary—the title was not enlarged to Principal Secretary of State till about 1603—was marked by the joint appointment of Sir Thomas Wriothesley and Sir Ralph Sadleir. The appointment, hitherto made orally, with transfer of a seal, was for the first time invested with the formality of a written ordinance under the Royal sign manual. The paper explicitly conferred on the two a single post, giving them " the name and office of the King's Majesty's Principal Secretary during His Highness' pleasure." Each was to hold an identical signet seal, maintain a register and have unfettered access to the other's register. One was to sit in the Lords and the other in the Commons, and they were to change places weekly unless some special matter required the attendance of both in a single House. Each was granted as councillor a salary of £100 a year for life, and as secretary half of the fees taken in the joint office, and board and lodging in the Palace.

The grounds for a twin appointment cannot have been the volume of work, as has been inferred. Great as that growth was, a single secretary was to suffice in the not less busy times of Elizabeth I. Possibly one of the colleagues was to attend regularly on the King and the other on the not yet dispossessed Cromwell, since Henry was often at a distant palace, while Cromwell stayed in Whitehall. More probably, the King wished to avoid dependence on a single expert, as had already befallen twice, by dividing to rule.

The holder of the Signet was the conduit between King and Council and between individual subject and King. All domestic and foreign business passed in and out through him, with all applications for passports, patents, grants and licences of every sort. Fortified by his private secretariat, he settled with the King the exact phrasing of every decision. His Signet Office had only to add formulæ according to precedent and was reduced to the quintessence of routine. The four clerks had long left most of the work to substitutes, and their posts had gone at least three-quarters of the way to becoming sinecures for rewarding services elsewhere.

When Sadleir retired in 1543 and Wriothesley was promoted Lord Chancellor in 1544, existing officials stepped into their shoes. Sadleir was replaced by William Paget, afterwards Lord Paget, the son of a London mace-bearer, who had entered Gardiner's personal employment in the 1520s and secured in 1532 a clerkship of the Signet, which was turned into a life tenure in 1540, when Paget was also made clerk of the Council. He now, April 1543, became simultaneously clerk of the Parliaments and one of the principal secretaries. The post vacated by Wriothesley went to Dr., afterwards Sir, William Petre, a tanner's son, who had entered the Chancery as a clerk about 1530 and advanced in 1536 to be Cromwell's deputy and his vicar-general for all ecclesiastical and monastic business, out of which he made the usual fortune. Two of his brothers also made successes of official careers, one in the Customs, the other as Auditor of the Exchequer. Cromwell had been secretary for seven years; Petre was retained for thirteen, till his health failed in 1557; while there were six changes in the person who held the other half of the post from 1540 to 1558.

On the accession of Elizabeth I, and for most of her reign, the dual secretaries were reduced to a single officer, provided by the Cecils, father and son. The family had already been in Court employment for two generations. David Cecil had emerged from Wales to be a yeoman, then sergeant-at-arms to Henry VII, with sundry other perquisites in the way of bailiffdoms; his son Richard, beginning as a page in the Wardrobe, reached the same posts under Henry VIII. His grandson William, Lord Burleigh to be, was taken by Somerset the Protector for his secretary, and advanced almost at once in 1550 to be one of the King's two secretaries, which he remained till the accession of Mary. Having been careful to court the rising sun, he was re-appointed, without a colleague, three days after the accession of Elizabeth in 1558. In 1572 Burleigh was promoted to be treasurer, and twin secretaries again replaced him. One was a protégé of his, just back from service as envoy in Paris, Sir Francis Walsingham, who remained in office till he died eighteen years later; the other, Sir Thomas Smith, died after four years in office, and his successor, Thomas Wilson, after five. Walsingham was, like Burleigh, sole secretary for his remaining nine years, except for the five months' company of poor William Davidson, he who was discharged, imprisoned and fined for sending on the Queen's order to execute Mary, Queen of Scots. Burleigh was not able to get the vacancy conferred forthwith in full form on his son, Robert Cecil, the future Marquess or Salisbury, and father and son discharged the duties together until Robert's official appointment in 1596. The second Cecil would not quit the secretaryship when he was appointed treasurer in 1608, but kept both posts till his death in 1612. He was indeed given Mr. John Herbert, a master of requests, explicitly as second secretary in 1600, but " Mr. Secondary Herbert," as he was dubbed, took a very subordinate and obscure part.

Thus, three men monopolised for most of half a century an office which had previously been divided, and was about to be divided once more. Burleigh's skill and the protracted experience of all three maintained it as the driving-wheel in the State machine. But all three remained subordinates. Everything was for the Queen's decision, and however she plagued them with procrastinations, action must be delayed till it was given.

Burleigh, whom the Queen named " Sir Spirit," remained, subject to her, the presiding genius of the reign, overshadowing the lesser lights, irrespective of title, till his death in 1598. Walsingham— " Moon " to Queen Elizabeth because he threw light on dark places— during his long term specialised on the secret service at home and abroad. Robert Cecil, Lord Salisbury, was summed up to James I by Bacon as the essential bureaucrat : " he was no fit counsellor to make your affairs better but yet he was fit to have kept them from getting worse."

Obviously the whole collecting and digestion of facts and correspondence on domestic arrangements, diplomacy, defence organisation and policing of a kingdom could not be handled by one man without staff. That it could be done with so few was due partly to the intrinsic advantages of a small organisation, partly to selectivity in enforcement of general policy. " Neither should all have the whip," wrote Elizabeth to James of Scotland, " though some were scourged." And if an advance in industry or trade or territory seemed desirable in the national interest, the monopoly of its exploitation was conferred on an individual or a group ; the vastest private profits that could be made were then believed to lead to the general benefit.

Apart from assistance by Clerks of the Signet and of the Council, the secretary engaged and paid a staff of his own. Personal clerks of this sort were employed by Petre, secretary from 1543 to 1548, as by Cromwell; they were no longer part of a mediæval household, as under Wolsey, but a separate office staff. These men classified and presented incoming correspondence to their chief, translated, drafted, fair-copied, kept registers and records, prepared diaries. Walsingham employed at least twelve; possibly a set-up of six or seven at one time. His chief clerk was Lawrence Tomson, a Fellow of Magdalen and master of twelve languages. Thomas Edmondes and Lisle Cave specialised in French, Thomas Phillips in breaking and decoding ciphers. But division of duties was very fluid. When Walsingham was away, the clerk of the Council acted for him; in later regimes one of the private office staff took his chief's place.

Several of these personal clerks were promoted to State posts and taken on the strength. Nicholas Faunt, who wrote an account of the office, was engaged by Walsingham as his private secretary about 1580, in his teens; he was employed on diplomatic missions abroad for most of the years 1581–8, during which time he managed, in 1585, to secure a seat in the House of Commons; before the end of the reign he was given one of the Signet sinecures. Thomas Edmonds became not only Queen's French secretary but also a clerk of the Council; he also was often sent to France on diplomatic business. Thomas Lake went further still. He entered Walsingham's service in his early twenties, about 1590, as a stenographer, whose skill won him from Queen Elizabeth the nickname of Swiftsure. After his master's death he continued into the service of his successor, Lord Salisbury—one of the two Cecils probably paid the personal staffs during the official vacancy in the secretaryship. In 1600, being about thirty-three, he was made a Clerk of the Signet, and in 1603 King's Latin secretary and Keeper of the Records; he entered the House of Commons and was the head of the secretary's clerks when he was further promoted and knighted.

These were for work in Whitehall. Abroad, a miscellany of envoys was paid from the privy purse. Some of them were sent to reside for several years in a given capital, while others only crossed for some particular business. The secretary employed in addition, as did other ambitious privy councillors, agents of his own for the collection of information on the forces, intentions and moves of foreign Powers, as well as a secret force of informers at home. England was menaced by a creed which it feared, which a foreign Power might back by force and which was supported by a fifth column of unknown strength within the island. Burleigh's intelligence organisation was reputed the best in Europe. Walsingham's spies pervaded England, while he employed close on fifty in various Continental cities, reaching even as far as Turkey; he was represented in thirteen towns of France, ten in the Netherlands and nine in Germany. All this cost more money than the secretary could get out of Queen Elizabeth for the specific purpose; the rest he paid out of his own pocket, or rather out of the fees and perquisites which would otherwise have remained in that pocket.

Burleigh complained that he died poorer than on his entry into the Queen's service; Robert Cecil, on the contrary, greatly swelled his fortune, although his allowance for secret service abroad was fixed at only £1,400 a year on James's accession. The secretaryship was reckoned worth £2,000 a year in 1603, but what paid, with a margin, the costs of office and spies was the grant to both father and son of the additional and immensely profitable office of Master of the Court of Wards.

Of Salisbury's private staff, Lake has been mentioned. Simon Willis, the chief clerk and thrice Member of Parliament, was dismissed, nominally for insolence, but actually, it is believed, because his secrecy was doubted. Levinius Munck was advanced to chief clerk and in due course made a Clerk of the Signet, as was Thomas Windebank, while Sir Thomas Smith was advanced to be King's Latin secretary. Robert Naunton, engaged in 1603, and George Calvert, taken on as a man of thirty-odd in or before 1605, both rose in time to be Secretaries of State.

With the union of the office with the treasurership by Lord Salisbury (Robert Cecil), it reached its zenith for the time being. When Salisbury died, the King appointed a new treasurer, but tried to run the secretariat direct with the aid of his favourite courtier, Carr, Lord Rochester, Earl of Somerset. The work of the department had, however, grown in the last century far beyond the possibility of detailed supervision by a King with many other interests and duties, even if he had been wedded to his desk, and the system of dual secretaries was resumed in 1614. Theoretically, they still shared an undivided post; their spheres abroad drew apart in practice, uncertainly and with much overlapping, till just before the Civil War, when a territorial division had grown up.

In spite of the amount of common work, the two clerical sections were separately staffed. Each secretary appointed his own staffs;

he might even take them with him if he shifted from the junior to the senior post; but succeeding secretaries generally reappointed the employees of their predecessor, and these enjoyed a practical permanence.

A good many of the Stuart secretaries were promoted officials already trained in the office. Salisbury's post, indeed, was filled by a diplomat, Sir Ralph Winwood, who had been since 1599 acting ambassador in Paris and agent in Holland, Düsseldorf, etc. When Mr. Secondary Herbert died in 1616, Winwood was given for colleague that Sir Thomas Lake who had risen in a quarter of a century from Walsingham's amanuensis to head of the office staff. Lake was driven to retire in 1619 by startling family scandals, but with ample compensation.

Meantime Winwood had died in 1618 and had been replaced by Sir Robert Naunton, a Fellow of Trinity, Cambridge, who, after some years abroad as a gatherer of news for Essex, had been taken on Salisbury's staff about 1603; employed mainly on diplomatic missions, during which he was elected to the House of Commons in 1606, he had been rewarded in 1616 with the posts of Master of Requests and of Surveyor to the Court of Wards. So little discretion was now permitted the secretary that when Naunton sounded a foreign ambassador on his own initiative, he was well scolded and retired in 1623 with a pension of £1,000 a year and the gift of the post of Master of the Court of Wards, which he kept till his death at seventy-two in 1635.

The dismissed Lake was followed by George Calvert, who had been engaged about 1605 by Salisbury and next year provided with a clerkship of the Crown in distant Connaught, of which the duties, if any, must have been done by a deputy. He entered the Commons in 1609, but continued a clerk in the secretary's office till he was made secretary himself in 1619. The ordinary and by now handsome emoluments of the post were increased in the following year by the grant to him of an annuity of £1,000 a year. A favourite of the Duke of Buckingham, he exercised no influence whatever in his office, though he is thought to have improved its organisation; in 1623 he sold it for £6,000 to Sir Albert Morton, the clerk of the Council. A peerage, as Lord Baltimore, and the retention of substantial estates in Ireland further eased his retirement. He prospered personally, though the schemes of colonial settlement, of which he was an enthusiast, all went agley. It was his son, the second Lord Baltimore, who was enabled by his father's spoils of office to settle Maryland. Sir

Albert Morton had little joy of his bargain, for he died at once, to be succeeded by Sir John Coke. Coke's introduction to official life was in Burleigh's office in 1591; since then he had done good service in reforming naval and Admiralty administrations as deputy treasurer and as one of the Commissioners when there was no Lord High Admiral, and enjoyed one of the customary supplements as a Master of Requests. He held his side of the secretaryship for a period that had become uncommon of late—fifteen years, from 1625 to 1640, when he was discharged as a scapegoat for Charles I's fiasco in Scotland. That term was covered on the other side by three colleagues: Lord Conway, a soldier, Lord Dorchester, and Sir Francis Windebank.

Windebank's father had been clerk of the Signet, clerk of the Council and a friend of the Cecils. The son was promised an eventual Signet clerkship when prior pledges had been met; he worked in that office from 1608, being then twenty-six, and got his clerkship in 1624. Then in 1632, " a new secretary brought out of the dark," he was advanced to Principal Secretary of State. By all accounts he effectively shouldered Coke out of sight, but as a Roman Catholic he himself thought it prudent to flee the country in 1640.

After an interval, yet another official was promoted in his place, Sir Edward Nicholas, who, after experience in the offices of the Chancellor of the Duchy of Lancaster and of the Warden of the Cinque Ports and as a Member of Parliament, was made Secretary to the Admiralty in 1625 and clerk of the Council in 1635. Various ephemeral appointments—Sir Henry Vane, Comptroller and Treasurer of the Household for two years, Viscount Falkland for one year, Lord Digby for another —to Coke's side still left Nicholas as the main channel of communication between Charles I and Parliament during the Civil War. He was reappointed as Secretary of State on the Restoration, but had soon to be retired at sixty-nine owing to failing health.

During the first two Stuart reigns up to the outbreak of the Civil War, the bureaux of the central administration were thus staffed by seven or eight men, commonly with good University careers and some personal knowledge of the Continent, who were picked by a Secretary of State at his discretion, were his servants, not the Crown's, but were kept on by his successor. The secretaries were to some extent selected by themselves, for each bought his appointment, subject to the King's approval, from his predecessor for £6,000, £7,000 or £8,000; they generally only left of their own volition, and in extreme cases were rather bought out than discharged. A fair number of them rose out of the office staff. Some of this staff, as well as most of the secretaries, were Members of the Commons, where the latter replaced officers of the Household as the representatives of the Crown. Blustering, tactless or merely tongue-tied, their general incompetence for that task doubtless contributed to the final rupture between Crown and Commons.

The Commonwealth commonsense gathered all the work of the Home, Foreign and Colonial Offices, together with intelligence work, the nascent Post Office and newspaper work into the single hand of John Thurloe, whose fingers reached into every recess of Government activity. He was provided with a staff of more than twenty for the secretarial work: two assistant secretaries at the unheard-of salaries of £500 each, a finance clerk at £400, and seven ordinary clerks at £120, while two of the Clerks of the Signet were given an extra £150 each to assist him. Besides these, there was a Walloon—John Rudolph Weckerlin—who had been working in the office since the last years of James I, and no fewer than ten sergeants or messengers. By his side, but independent of him, the Commonwealth employed the great John Milton and afterwards another poet, Andrew Marvell, for drafting correspondence in Latin and incidental propaganda articles at home. Thurloe, though Cromwell's right-hand man, was essentially an executant; he had no share in shaping policy, and was not even aware of it till it was shaped.

At the Restoration in 1660, Thurloe was imprisoned for a short time. The secretaries were again duplicated. Foreign States were apportioned between them on fluctuating and imperfectly observed territorial and religious lines. Of foreign parts, Spain, Flanders and Italy were generally dealt with by one, France, Holland, the Baltic, Germany and Turkey by the other. Germany was divided at the Restoration, its Catholic parts being added to the first group and its Protestant states to the second. Portugal, independent of Spain once more, was at its own request assigned to the second, while Spain remained with the first. Two years later Germany was reunited in the second or northern group, as it came to be called, while France and Portugal joined Spain and Italy as the south. The southern division on the whole took Ireland, but could not monopolise it. Not even the protests and appeals of Stafford under Charles I could get his work handled consistently by the same secretary. Home affairs were divided at random as the correspondence came in; where this work carried fees for the clerks, each side competed for it, so that occasions had been known when both secretaries issued rival warrants for routine business at home or conflicting orders to envoys abroad. Colonies were assigned to the southern division, which disputed the work with a committee of the Privy Council. The division between the two sides became official in 1704, when Sir Charles Hedges was specifically appointed to the southern.

The large ideas of Charles II were manifested in a further increase of the salary of each office to £1,850, apart from the fees and per-quisites which made it worth much more. The promoted official type of the old days disappeared, with a solitary exception. This was Sir Joseph Williamson, F.R.S., son of a poor clergyman and a Fellow of Queen's, Oxford, who was engaged at the Restoration as a clerk on the southern side by Sir Edward Nicholas, who had been educated at the same college. He was then twenty-seven. The office cannot have been over-burdened, for after less than two years, at the end of 1661, Williamson was able to earn an extra £160 by becoming also Keeper of the King's Library and, by purchase of the post from the previous holder, of the State Paper Office. He secured a post in the Post Office as well, and got various commissionerships, as for seizing prohibited goods and for running a lottery.

When the Court fled to Oxford from the great plague of 1665, one Muddiman founded a newspaper there which shortly became, as it remains, the *London Gazette*. Williamson, who, for all his other activities, had become the head of the secretarial staff, took over its compilation, editing and profits, and continued to run it after the return to London, and to make some hundreds a year out of this journalism. Excerpts from despatches to the office provided a good news service. The northern section published a competitive sheet, the *Current Intelligencer*, for a year or two, but its despatches apparently drew a smaller public.

Williamson, himself chief of five or six employees of the Secretary of State, employed as many more of his own, for his office work as well as for the *Gazette*. There were similar personal additions in the other division, and this example was followed by later chief clerks. This lowest tier were employees at two removes, if at all, of the Crown. Williamson succeeded in getting elected to the Commons in 1669 after four defeats; three years later he was appointed a clerk of the Council;

the next year he was sent to Cologne for a twelve-month on a futile embassy, and on his return bought his appointment to be Secretary of State for £6,000 from Lord Arlington, who went on to be Lord Chamberlain.

Those were the parlous years in which Charles II was abrogating the legal disabilities of Roman Catholics by his prerogative. Many of the formal documents had to be drawn up in Williamson's office and be signed by him. The Commons clapped him in the Tower on 18th November, 1678, for this formal work of making out commissions as army officers to disqualified persons. The King took him out on the morrow, and maliciously told the Commons that he returned courtesy for discourtesy by informing them of his action, although they had not told him of theirs. However, Williamson was given back his £6,000 and £500 besides to resign his secretaryship; but he remained Keeper of State Papers till his death, and was employed as a veteran diplomat after the Revolution at the Peace of Ryswick in 1697.

Williamson seems to have almost caricatured the traditional handler of papers and files—a dry, repellent man, obsequious to superiors and a sergeant-major to subordinates, whom neither King nor colleagues could abide and who never opened his lips in the Commons. But he was a founder member of the Royal Society and brought decent order and routine into the growing chaos in the secretary's office. He was in his element in the State Paper Office. This was a sub-department set up in 1578 by the principal secretary of the day for the preservation of documents concerning State or Council action. Previous repositories had only preserved treaties, Exchequer and law-court documents. However, the correspondence and files of the head of an office continued to be regarded as his private property, and were removed on his departure to perish or be hidden in family archives. Williamson, indefatigable in recovering past losses, in insisting that for the future office papers were public property, and in indexing and arranging the collections, " made " the State Paper Office.

The modern title for the permanent head of the secretary's office, " Under-secretary of State," was introduced for his successor as chief clerk, William Bridgeman. He it was who held up Pepys' remodelled Navy Board for a month after the King's approval, till his fees were paid.

Two other secretaries on the southern side were men who enjoyed more independent authority than would have been tolerated by the

Tudors and who foreshadowed the self-moving statesmen of the new epoch. Lord Arlington of the Cabal was secretary before William- son for the twelve years from 1662 to 1674; after him Robert Spencer, Earl of Sunderland, held office for seven years in two spells, 1679–81 and 1683–8. Sunderland actually voted in Parliament, in defiance of the King's policy, for the exclusion of James from the Throne; hence his dismissal in 1681; but his dissension did not prevent his return to power. Each gave the secretaryship of State dominance in the Government machine, and each was charged with being " Premier Minister."

On the other, less reputed, side, secretaries were chosen some for previous loyalty, some for diplomatic, some for parliamentary, experience. Sir William Morrice (1660–8) was a local magnate, sheriff and J.P. who ran his office efficiently without ever seeing the King's face. Sir John Tressor (1668–72) had been a member of the Commonwealth Parliament. Sir Henry Coventry (1672–80), a brother of the Sir William Coventry who was Pepys' superior, had shared the exile of Charles II and been employed since his Restoration as ambassador in Sweden and envoy at the Peace of Breda. Sir Leoline Jenkins (1680–4), head of an Oxford College, judge in the Admiralty Court, had served in the King's army during the troubles and had since been ambassador in Holland, among other diplomatic employments. Sidney Godolphin, Queen Anne's great minister, filled a gap of four months, and was followed by Charles, Earl of Middleton (1684–8), who had fought in the Civil War and been am- bassador in Vienna; he followed James II to St. Germains. All the last three were in the Commons.

The half-dozen clerks of each of the two offices were appointed and paid by its ministerial head for the time being, except a few who were the personal employees of his chief subordinate. They enjoyed more permanence in practice than the secretaries and were well paid as clerical salaries went.

John Cooke was chief clerk of the northern division from 1660 to after 1684. He directed the office, wrote documents for the King's signature, corresponded with the embassies abroad and settled any difficulty of form or precedent. In 1673 he was awarded £2,500 for long and faithful service, an annuity of £400 a year being substituted in the following year. He was further given the office of Latin secretary, with £200 a year from public funds, in 1681. This post, once secured by the secretariat, was gripped tight; it continued to be separately shown, and paid, till 1832. Cooke also retained a portion of the secretary's fees—£1 out of £6 5*s.*, 10*s.* out of £2, and so on. In 1672 Coventry brought in his nephew and secretary, Henry Thynne, to be second man in the office, but Thynne accompanied him on his departure and made a vacancy for the succeeding secretary Jenkins also to employ a relative of his own, Dr. Owen Wynne. The doctor, a civilian, who translated from Latin, French, Spanish, Italian and Dutch, had for standard duty to keep and produce papers for his chief, no doubt as a private secretary, and make up the mail with the proper enclosures. He was paid by Jenkins £140 a year plus board and lodging, and by his successor £200 a year inclusive. He transferred after the change to Sunderland's office, and while there added to his emoluments the wardenship of the Mint at £300 a year. Three other clerks—de Paz, Carne and Chute—at £40, £50 and £60 worked under Cooke; the first translated from all modern languages, the other two only from Latin and French; the best paid was a relative of the Lord Keeper Guildford. Finally, Cooke had his own clerk, Widdows, whom he paid £50 a year, plus 2*s.* 6*d.* for each signature; he did copying and indexing. There was also a door-keeper, and messengers were provided by the Palace.

One of the northern division rose further out of the ruck. William Blaythwayte entered it after the usual training abroad; he started at nineteen as an assistant in Sir William Temple's mission to The Hague, and visited successively Rome, Stockholm and Copenhagen, obtained a clerkship to the Council, £150 a year as secretary to its committee on trade, and engagement as Secretary of State's clerk in 1681. After some two years' service, he bought the post of Secretary at War in 1683, and ran almost the whole domestic side of the Army; notwithstanding that he was also from 1685 clerk or secretary of the Committee of the Council for Trade. Although taken abroad by William III as a Secretary for Foreign Affairs for a time after the fall of James, he remained a Commissioner of Trade and Secretary at War till 1706. Revolutions touched him not.

The Revolution of 1688 transferred power increasingly from the Crown to ministers, who diverged further from their officials. No more subordinates were promoted to be Secretaries of State. The pay of staff was met from the profits of the *London Gazette* and the fees charged for documents and instruments, supplemented as need arose by the Civil List or a Treasury grant, until the *Gazette* was transferred to the Stationery Office and the fees were appropriated by the Exchequer. Their emoluments were only charged on Parliamentary votes in 1849.

Servants of his servants were replaced by direct employees of the Secretary of State. The Secretary for the time being filled the lowest clerkship when it fell vacant, but might appoint someone on occasion direct to be his private secretary or précis writer or even Under-secretary of State. The northern divisions in 1768 had nine clerks, who entered at £50 and rose step by step in strict seniority, as death or promotion made vacancies, to first clerk at £170. A chief clerk, who was the finance officer, drew slightly more. The southern division had a similar establishment. Each was headed by an Under-secretary of State at £500. But these figures were much less than the actual emoluments. The Post Office made at least half of the clerks allowances varying from £40 to £110, to which men succeeded as they went up the scale. Towards the end of the eighteenth century, one was agent for Grenada at £172, registrar for London of the house duty at £240 and registrar of seizures at £240. Others were agents for other colonies, yet others, or the same, held posts in other Government departments; a little later one was superintendent of St. James's and Hyde Parks at £200 a year. All participated in proportion to their seniority in the tips expected from foreign Powers on the conclusion of a treaty. The amounts were not enormous; an average of £737 a year was distributed for the forty years before 1831. These gratifications were then abolished, and the compensation of existing staff was fixed at £830 a year. The under-secretary of 1782-9, William Fraser, drew in all not £500, but £2,255 a year; he had £300 as the office's German translator, £270 as the writer of the *London Gazette*, £218 as a Clerk of the Signet, and £90 as a Customs waiter, the last two posts being sinecures.

In 1782 the Home Office was brought to birth by the disentanglement under one of the Secretaries of State of domestic business, including Ireland, the Isle of Man and the Channel Islands. The rest, under the other secretary, constituted the Foreign Office. The change was made without formality by an oral direction, and both Secretaries of State were still considered, as they are to this day, to occupy a single post. The two departments continued to share the same State Paper Office, an almost independent office whither their

F

files were relegated after a few years. The Lord Chamberlain continued to supply office furniture, and the treasurer of the Palace Chamber went on providing and paying their joint corps of thirty messengers, presently raised to forty for journeys at home or abroad. Home and foreign service messengers were not separated till 1824.

The Foreign Office kept as its organisation two territorial divisions, each under an under-secretary. Either under-secretary or both might be indifferently in or out of the Commons. A recommendation of a Parliamentary Committee of 1784 that one should be permanent and the other a politician changing with his chief was rejected, but in the end things took that form. Richard Stonehewer, who spent fifty-three years in the combined offices and was promoted to under-secretary in 1765, was certainly a permanent official. So was William Fraser, under-secretary to four successive chiefs. George Aust, who succeeded him, had started as a clerk in the 1760s, and his position as permanent under-secretary was not affected by his election to Parliament. A change then set in and men from missions abroad were usually chosen till the promotion in 1854 of Edmond, afterwards Lord, Hammond restored the prize to the office.

The Foreign Office staff still numbered only twenty in 1821. The Secretary of State had £6,000; both under-secretaries rose to £2,500; the chief clerk received from one source or another £2,243; the nine clerks had become three seniors on an average of £1,190 and thirteen juniors on an average of £425.

By 1841 the numbers had risen to forty. Most of the perquisites and outside employments had been abolished. The salary of the Secretary of State had been reduced to £5,000, that of the permanent under-secretary to £2,000 and that of the parliamentary under-secretary to £1,500. Palmerston laid down for the main cadre below them scales which gave the chief clerk a maximum of £1,250, and provided six senior clerks who rose to £1,000, ten clerks who rose to £545 and seven junior clerks who rose to £150. A librarian, a translator, a private secretary, eight clerks of lower status outside the established cadre and a few subordinates made up the balance. Advancement within the cadre proceeded almost absolutely by seniority: so ingrained was the ideal of a band of brothers that Edmond Hammond, afterwards permanent under-secretary, protested strongly against his own promotion out of turn. In 1880 a Secretary of State fluttered the dovecotes by a pronouncement that selection for senior clerk, the second promotion, would in future be by merit; but the change was not rigidly enforced in practice until the third step in rank. Numbers, pay and grades have since been several times increased.

One perquisite was spared by Palmerston. Diplomats paid clerks at home a small commission for services that ranged from banking their salaries and buying their stores to forwarding their letters. These agencies too were abolished for conscience' sake in 1870. They had come to be concentrated in two clerks who earned thereby £4,000 a year and were granted two-thirds of that amount from public funds as compensation.

Appointment by the Secretary of State was made subject to a qualifying examination from 1857 and a competitive one from 1883, without altering, as all agreed, the quality of the appointees.

This staff, zealous and able and already expensive, remained throughout the nineteenth century a mere combination of registry, copying and despatch rooms. Incoming communications went straight to the permanent under-secretary for submission, with any essential explanation, to the Secretary of State for instructions. A recommendation for action would have been to Lord Salisbury, Prime Minister and Secretary of State in 1884, as gross an impertinence as to Lord Palmerston. Hammond in 1870 held that even the veriest trifles must be decided by the Secretary of State; " the under-secretary of State is merely a channel . . . he has no independent action at all." Sir Thomas, afterwards Lord, Sanderson, permanent under-secretary from 1894 to 1906 after thirty-five years' service, declared that he had never ventured to advise on policy or go beyond explanations, and those only on routine. " Lamps," as he was called, guided his subordinates in the most modern way by a booklet of his own, *Uses and Abuses of Red Tape*. After the minister had decided, the permanent under-secretary, or at most a senior clerk, might draft a letter for consideration, or senior clerks on demand prepare recitals of the previous facts. The main duty of the office was to docket and put away papers and produce them, if possible, when wanted; decipher incoming and put into cipher outgoing despatches; fair-copy letters and make up mails. The first typist was daringly engaged in 1889; a second not till five more years had passed.

The staff revolted in the end against neglect of brain-power. In 1905 routine and copying were organised and delegated to subordinates; even a junior was presently allowed to try his hand on a positive solution of questions of which he had learnt something. But the late Lord Norwich affirmed that even up to 1914, his work as a junior could have been done by any half-educated man, young or old.

Four-fifths, perhaps nine-tenths of all papers stopped short of the under-secretary half a century later, and only a fine residue was sieved through him to the minister.

Abroad, a consular service had to be created in the Near East on the abolition of the Levant Company in 1825, and the Foreign Office was increased within by a consular department. A Far Eastern service was similarly enforced by the rescission of the East India Company's monopoly. The rest of the world was served for a time by individual appointments which local merchants commonly filled in return for the fees charged, but salaried officials had increasingly to be sent out. Subordinates were hired by them out of allowances made for their offices. Not that these were overworked. When Charles Lever, the novelist, was appointed consul at Trieste in 1873, he was told by Lord Derby, " Here is £600 a year for doing nothing, and you are just the man to do it."

Resident diplomatic missions at foreign capitals increased after the Restoration. They were not overdone; the total cost to the Civil List had risen from £30,000 under James II to £203,500 in 1830, when the charge was transferred to the Consolidated Fund with a promise of reduction to £180,000. An amateur of sufficient breeding to meet foreign statesmen was usually nominated for the particular post; he was not transferable. Public funds provided him with one assistant in the late eighteenth century and a second in the early nineteenth, but envoys took into their households both unpaid attachés and others whom they paid. On the change in 1830, it was agreed that all attachés should be paid after six years' service, this being reduced to four years in 1861, when a qualifying examination was imposed; the diplomatic service then became a profession and career with a graded personnel that moved from capital to capital. Men at the top of the Foreign Office were occasionally appointed to embassies; Commission after Commission vainly recommended the amalgamation of service abroad and at home until the recommendations of the MacDonnell Commission were accepted after the First World War.

The other secretary's department, the Home Office, took pride of place from the separation of 1782, mainly, it is believed, because its

Secretary of State, Lord Shelburne, was the social superior of Fox. Growth of numbers, and the substitution of much the same salaries for perquisites, followed the same course. But because action or inaction affected the subject, or even the peace of the realm, so much more immediately, devolution of authority proceeded faster. The work was also much more miscellaneous from the outset than that on foreign affairs. The Home Office passed its colonial and army responsibilities to newly created ministers within a generation, but against that relief it was, with the Board of Trade, the focus of the philanthropic movements of the next century. In 1823 it began to take over the prisons, which had hitherto been local, or rather private, concerns; these eventually constituted a separate but not independent department. In 1829, a Home Secretary, Sir Robert Peel, founded the London Metropolitan Police; borough and county forces followed, all to some extent under the guidance and surveillance of his officers. The various measures for the protection of children which began in 1802, and for the betterment of conditions in, and the inspection of factories, which began in 1833, all centred on the Home Office and required the creation of new types of expert staff and itinerant officials. The supervision of remodelled local authorities was its natural inheritance, until, in 1871, this was transferred to a new department, the Local Government Board, which in due course was transmuted into the Ministry of Health.

Agriculture, freshwater fisheries and mines all in some measure fell under its ægis until they were transferred to the Ministry of Agriculture, the Board of Trade and a new Ministry of Mines.

The fissions of the office of Secretary of State became almost mystical. On the union of England and Scotland, parallelism of administration being implicit in the Treaty of Union, a third partner was added to the dual secretaries to handle Scottish affairs. This third secretary only lasted till the rebellion of 1745, when he was dropped and Scottish business was taken in charge by a Scottish Minister, usually the Lord Advocate.

There came to a head twenty years after this a long-drawn constitutional and bureaucratic struggle between the Secretaries of State of the southern department and the presidents of the Committee of the Privy Council for Trade and Plantations. Originally advisory, the Committee acquired and lost and won again some executive powers in plantation problems. These were again whittled away. An Order in Council in 1766 tried to clarify unpractical confusion by ordering " every executive business that has by degrees crept into " the Committee to be resumed by its proper department; but the proper departments were unable to bear the load. The proprieties were met by creating in 1758 an office of Secretary of State for the Colonies and conferring it on the president of the Committee, whose secretary was appointed an under-secretary of State. This arrangement continued for eleven years, during which the mainland plantations were lost in the War of Independence. It was not this loss that brought it to an end, nor yet the criticism that a secretary with a limited function who was not interchangeable with his colleagues was unconstitutional. The separation from the secretaryship of the presidency, to provide a job for the discredited Earl of Carlisle, provoked a storm in which both Colonial Secretary and Committee for Trade were abolished in 1782. For a time the Home Office carried instead a Plantations Office in its bosom.

The two Secretaries of State were again raised to a trinity under the pressure of war in 1794. The third, an appointment additional to and quite distinct from that of the Secretary at War, took over the responsibility of the Home Office for movements of troops. As the acquisition of enemy territory overseas became inextricably blended with war strategy, the Colonies were transferred to him in 1801. The Colonial Office formed round him, and the third partner was generally known as the Secretary for the Colonies. His office staff developed on the same lines as that of the Foreign Office, but devolution was more rapid.; junior clerks were permitted to minute on papers as early as 1870. Before that, the Crimean War had enhanced military responsibilities; the Colonial secretaryship was split in two in 1854, and the creation of a new Secretary of State *for* War raised the number of secretaries to four. A fifth soon followed, in 1858, as the minister responsible for India; he amalgamated the staffs both of the directorate of the Company at East India House and of the previous government body, the Board of Control. So things stood till the First World War produced a new fighting arm, the Air Force; the precedents of Navy and Army governance were disregarded, and the minister given to it at the war's end was a sixth Secretary of State. A seventh ensued in 1924 on the severance of Dominion from Colonial business, though both posts continued to be held by the same person. The separate minister created for Scotland in 1885 was transmogrified in 1926 into an eighth Secretary of State, and a ninth completed the tale of muses in 1935, when a distinction between Burma and India was needed.   Seven of these posts had nothing in common, neither work nor men nor buildings; but, to confirm the alien's observation that the saint of British organisation was the Holy Trinity, the nine offices remained in law not nine offices, but one office.

8

THE TREASURY

THE modern Treasury has persistently been credited with being a survival from the ancient Treasury of Receipt of the Lower Exchequer. The genealogy is untenable. The only old offices in the Treasury are those of Lord High Treasurer, now represented by the Board, and of the combined Chancellor of the Exchequer and Under-Treasurer, an otherwise invisible office which is always conferred on that Chancellor. These three belonged to the upper Exchequer. All posts of the Exchequer of Receipt are accounted for elsewhere, and the Treasury, unlike it, has never been either a store for money or a maker of payments. It is, in fact, an expansion of the private office of the Lord High Treasurer into the secretariat of the substituted Board.

The present department may be considered to begin when Lord Burleigh, becoming treasurer in 1572, continued to be busied in the palace of Whitehall on the general domestic and foreign business of the kingdom. His instructions and authorisations to the Exchequer, a quarter of a mile away, were transmitted through a secretary. His son, Robert Cecil, Lord Salisbury, remained Secretary of State during his treasurership, and likewise could not attend at the Exchequer in person. A body of commissioners with a secretary was appointed instead of a treasurer on Salisbury's death in 1612, and the instructions of a board could obviously not be given orally. The first preoccupation of the early Treasury was to limit expenditure, if possible, to the money available; the head officer of the Exchequer, the auditor, was accordingly required to pass every order for a payment, whether Royal writ or other formal document, to the Treasurer or Board, and only on their warrant direct it to a named teller for issue of the money. After 1660 a second warrant from the Treasury was required before payment could be made, to specify the particular tax or fund from which the money should be drawn. Numbers of warrants of the first sort survive from Burleigh's later years.

Individual treasurers and boards alternated until the accession of George I. The last Lord High Treasurer, Lord Shrewsbury, appointed by Queen Anne on her death-bed, was replaced on 13th October, 1714, by a board of commissioners, and the Lords Commissioners of the Treasury have ever since remained as executors of the Office of Lord High Treasurer. The commissioners, usually five in number, divided equally among them his salary of £8,000 a year, but were equal in no other respect. The First Lord became not only the minister for finance but, with occasional interruptions by a Secretary of State, also Prime Minister. The Second Lord—the Chancellor of the Exchequer—played no great part till the 1820s; by Gladstone's time he had replaced his chief as the minister for finance. The three junior Lords became Government Whips for ensuring a majority in the Commons, and their numbers are increased by adding unpaid members to the Treasury Board.

The Board met four times weekly, morning and afternoon, from the Restoration. Each session was allocated in rotation to the affairs of one or more departments. To these were summoned personally, to explain and be cross-examined on their proposals or shortcomings, the commissioners for the various taxes, of the Navy, of victualling, of the wounded and of transport; the Ordnance Board, the Comptroller of Army Accounts, the Surveyors of Lands and Woods, the auditor of the plantations in America, the professional staffs of the Works; and many another, as occasion arose. The King might preside; William III, for whom an anteroom was set aside in the Cockpit building allotted to the Treasury after the Palace was burned down, attended frequently; and Royal attendances did not entirely cease till the Regency. The First Lord and the Chancellor of the Exchequer stopped appearing in 1827, though the Board continued to meet twice weekly for thirty years more. After the nineteenth century it met only to greet a new secretary. All official action, however, still purports to be directed by the elusive Board, and it remained incumbent on the signatory of a letter in full form to assert that he had been directed by the Lords Commissioners of Her Majesty's Treasury to convey their views. Documents still more ceremonious maintain a pretence of being a minute of an actual meeting at which My Lords read such and such a document and reached the decision communicated. Until the nineteenth century the meetings were attended by a secretary, in full Court dress, to read the previous record, report action taken on it and note new decisions.

The secretaryship was sometimes held by approximations to permanent officials; much more often, being highly paid, it fell to bagmen politicians. One of the earliest was Philip Warwick, afterwards Sir Philip, son of the organist of Westminster Abbey, who was appointed to it in 1636, at the age of twenty-seven, by Bishop Juxon. In 1640 he got a seat in the Long Parliament, was in time expelled by the revolting members, fought on the royalist side at Edgehill and served Charles I as an amanuensis. His loyalty was rewarded at the Restoration by reappointment as Secretary to the Treasury, where the Treasurer, Southampton, left all the business to him. A " very able, right honest man," according to Pepys; " during seven years' management of the Treasury, he made but a moderate fortune out of it."

The Treasury was put in commission again on 29th May, 1667, on Southampton's death; Warwick was dislodged, becoming collector of customs in London port, by that intriguing knave, Sir George Downing, who gave his name to Downing Street and invented the division bell to call Government members from Whitehall to vote. He had been in his previous forty-four years a colonial, a ship's chaplain, a scout-master in the Commonwealth forces and finally Cromwell's resident envoy at The Hague at £1,000 a year. This Commonwealth man was succeeded in 1671 by a Cavalier, Sir Robert Howard, who had been knighted at Newbury. He worked hard at verses and plays " of a most freezing mediocrity "; an insufferable boaster, pilloried as " Sir Positive At All In," for all his talent at collecting Government jobs he only held this post for two years (1671–3). Warwick had obtained, in addition to his Treasury appointment, a clerkship of the Signet, Downing a tellership in the Exchequer from 1657, supplemented after he left the Treasury by a commissionership of Customs; Howard in 1677 got the more valuable auditorship of the Exchequer. The Signet and Exchequer posts were in each case for life.

Charles Bertie followed Howard from 1673 to 1678, and was succeeded by the jovial Henry Guy, a groom of the Chamber, an excise officer in the north of England and M.P. for Heydon. He was secretary to the Treasury for sixteen years, except for an interval when he was Commissioner of Customs. In 1695 and 1696 the House of Commons launched attacks on a broad front on Government departments. The storm was started by an extortion of money from the neighbourhood by some infantry in Norfolk; on inquiry it was found that their colonel and his agent had pocketed their pay; the

Colonel was cashiered, but investigation spread. A former treasurer, the Earl of Danby, now Duke of Leeds, narrowly escaped impeachment; the Speaker was deposed for accepting excessive gratifications for assisting Bills through the Commons (it was believed that he had made £10,000 a year instead of an accepted £4,000); the commissioners of hackney-coaches, a licensing authority, were discharged; Pepys at the Admiralty and Newton at the Mint were put in peril, and an early victim was Guy, who was committed to the Tower in February 1695 for having accepted a bribe of 200 guineas. The admitted emoluments of the post at the time were £2,400 a year; Guy left a fortune of £100,000 when he died in the reign of Anne.

Guy was replaced by a permanent official, one of the greatest of the Treasury secretaries, William Lowndes, who had entered Treasury service as a clerk in 1679 and had already been advanced to chief clerk before his promotion on 24th April, 1695, to secretary. Six months later he became a member of Parliament, but neither the rise and fall of parties nor the occasional loss of his seat affected his tenure. He remained secretary till his death in 1724.

One action of his immediately after his promotion was no less contrary to modern convention. Silver coins were at that time the basic money of the Christian world; the course of foreign exchanges and settlement of the balances of trade were governed by the amount of silver contained in the cash concerned. English silver coins fell into two very different classes: those minted since the introduction of machinery thirty years earlier were in good shape and of full weight, and were commonly hoarded; the money that circulated was much older and very worn, and was being rapidly and seriously lightened further by criminal clipping. A current crisis was believed to be a crisis of currency. The new secretary published his proposals in a brief history of English coinage compiled from his own researches, and proved by the historical method that money ought to be devalued. The Chancellor of the Exchequer incited John Locke, who was appointed in the following year to the Board of Trade, to publish a counterblast in which the contrary was proved from first principles. Lowndes's fundamental conclusion was flatly rejected in the proposals which the Chancellor then carried through Parliament. It was as if, with the proposals reversed, the harbinger of Stafford Cripps' devaluation had been the publication of a book by the Secretary to the Treasury in favour of restoring the gold standard.

The permanency of staff in the historic offices was established by age-old tradition, but the tenures of clerks appointed during their pleasure by ministers in the new departments were less clear; being but servants of the individual, adherents introduced by him might well have left with him. In the readjustment of parties at the end of William's reign, the triumphant Whigs demanded also the chief posts held by clients of the losers in the Treasury and like offices; so did the Tories when their turn came in 1710. Lowndes, with the backing of the leader of the winners, successfully resisted on each occasion, on grounds of efficiency, the dispersal of trained staff; and secured in the central services the principle that subordinates did not change with their ministers. Outliers suffered occasionally after later elections up to 1762, when Henry Fox's discharges so affronted opinion that the permanency of the Civil Servant was in practice established. Lowndes has been dubbed, before Pepys and more aptly, " father of the British Civil Service." His passion for small economies is preserved in the phrase he bequeathed to his official posterity, " Take care of the pence and the pounds will take care of themselves." In the House of Commons he devised the financial procedure known as *Ways and Means*. He was so proud of the name that he chose it as motto for his coat-of-arms, on which it girdled a device of coins. Harley became head of the Government and Treasurer in May 1711. His subordinate's post was divided in June to allow his relative Thomas Harley to be added to Lowndes as joint secretary to the Treasury. Henceforward there were always two, but their functions differed.

The numerous small bodies of commissioners that were set up to levy new taxes after the Restoration in 1660, and especially after the Revolution in 1688, had been placed under the Treasury in the interests of revenue—the Commissioners of Excise in 1660; those of Customs when those taxes ceased to be farmed in 1671; of the land tax, on its invention in 1692; of stamp tax, similarly in 1694; of hackney-coaches in the same year; of hawkers in 1698; and of salt tax in 1705, while in 1710 the two Postmasters-General and the Post Office were also placed under Treasury tutelage. Not only so, but the Treasury was given the right of choosing and appointing individually all the numerous subordinate staff, except in the Post Office, as well as the commissioners themselves.

Moreover, Treasury ministers impressed on William III very soon after the Revolution the changed position of the Crown by wresting from it the bestowal of lucrative sinecures in the Exchequer and elsewhere. The posts of Clerk of the Pells and of Auditor of the Exchequer were both rendered vacant by death in 1698. The first had been granted by Charles II in full form by letters patent to a Colonel Strangeways, of Dorset, on the first vacancy; the second had been promised by him on the first vacancy to Lord Carmarthen. William III had overridden this pledge and promised the auditorship to Godolphin. Charles Montagu was at the height of his power; although Godolphin was his chief colleague, and was to be Prime Minister for the next decade, he asserted that the gift of both posts vested in the Treasury, and not in either the past or the present King. Charles's letters patent were also set aside, and after a vacancy of only three days Henry Pelham, a leading Tory, was made Clerk of the Pells. With equal speed, the auditorship was diverted from Godolphin to Montagu's brother in trust for Montagu himself when he should be free; the brother was looked after by being appointed in addition a Commissioner of Excise.

This immense patronage, rivalled only by the Admiralty (whose influence was concentrated in a few dockyard towns), was one of the factors which lifted the Treasurer or First Lord higher in political estimation than the Secretaries of State. The " Treasury borough " was an important political power. One of the Treasury secretaries administered for the benefit of his party the recruiting of many posts in the Treasury's gift and was appropriately called the patronage secretary, until a generation or so ago the now less invidious title of parliamentary secretary took its place. He is better known as the chief Government Whip, being the superior of the junior lords. The other secretary, in charge of the general business of the office, became the Financial Secretary to the Treasury.

The Treasury in the eighteenth century was supported by the fees which it charged for its warrants of authority for expenditure or appointments. Treasury, Exchequer and any other official charges were naturally included in the proposed expenditure, and persons appointed to important offices were commonly repaid by their department the fees involved. The other departments also sent gifts of money, which were accepted as official expenditure, to Treasury officials on New Year's day. So the cost of Treasury staff fell on the King's or public funds no less than if it had been paid straightforwardly. Nevertheless the system continued for more than a century, becoming even more absurd in 1782, when in the Treasury, as in other offices, the receipts were pooled and fixed salaries paid out of them or from supplements from the Civil List.

In Lowndes's time the receipts were divided into three equal shares; each secretary took one, and the third was divided between the Treasury clerks, at that time four. The salary of each secretary was fixed in 1782 at £3,000, in addition to which he got about £270 from New Year's boxes; in 1800 the salary reached a peak of £4,000, from which it was steadily cut down in economy drives: to £3,500 in 1821, £2,500 in 1831, and £2,000 in 1851.

Both posts having been captured by politicians, a Parliamentary committee of 1786 recommended that one should become " stationary " with a reduction in salary to £2,000. The Treasury board indignantly rejected the debarment of one of their top officials from Parliament. The provision of a permanent head for the now numerous staff was accordingly effected, after a delay of twenty years, by the appointment in 1805 of a law clerk and assistant secretary; the post was filled by a transfer from the new Inland Revenue. Sir Alexander Spearman rose from the ranks; Sir Charles Trevelyan was an Indian Civil Servant; after them came (Sir) George Alexander Hamilton, who, having been a member of Parliament for seventeen years, was appointed financial secretary in March 1858, preferred permanency to politics and transferred to assistant secretary the next January. The title of the post was changed to permanent secretary in 1867. Hamilton's successor, Sir Ralph Lingen, had been secretary to the new Board of Education, to which he had been appointed at the age of thirty, for twenty years (1849–69), before transfer to the Treasury to be its permanent secretary for sixteen more, 1869–85. Sir Reginald Welby, K.C.B., who followed him, was a clerk in the Treasury, which he had entered in 1856, at the age of twenty-four; he was permanent secretary for nine years (1885–94). Sir Francis Mowatt, the next permanent secretary, was also a promoted Treasury clerk, who had entered in the same year (1856) at the age of nineteen. After their retirement, Lord Lingen, Lord Welby (for both had been made peers on their retirement) and Sir Francis Mowatt all played distinguished roles in the London County Council. They were respectively alderman, chairman and alderman.

The number of subordinates swelled from the four clerks, sharing possibly £1,000 a year among them, of Anne's reign, to a substantial staff, well paid when old, in the latter part of the eighteenth century. They numbered thirty-seven in 1793, divided into a revenue branch and a number of divisions; the superior staff was graded in three tiers. Five chief or principal clerks received salaries of £800 a year each, eight senior clerks were on scales rising to £500 and eleven assistant clerks rose to £280. The rest were miscellaneous ancillaries. As the pooled fees were insufficient, the balance of each salary was paid from the Civil List. Each clerk received a share of the New Year's boxes in addition; the amounts were appreciable, a Lord of the Treasury receiving on average £33 a year, the Chancellor of the Exchequer £80, and a senior clerk £50. The work was not so heavy as to prevent other earnings. Five chief and at least three senior and four assistant clerks held other public offices, and some of them more than one. Thomas Pratt, a nonagenarian, had £340 as Keeper of the Papers in addition to his salary of £800 and his £79 from New Year gifts. One senior was also a clerk in the Foreign Office, and with minor offices and a pension for posts he had lost drew just under £1,700 a year, of which only £450 was his Treasury salary. Other clerks were a Customs searcher at Newcastle-on-Tyne, a sluice-master at Purfleet and a comptroller of the Mint, and a number were commissioners of lotteries or agents for Colonies. Indeed, in 1806 the Treasury claimed for their staff the monopoly of Colonial agencies—the predecessors of the Crown Agents for Overseas Governments and Administrations—but they were despoiled of the prize by the Colonial Office.

The clerks were nominated by a secretary and usually entered the bottom grade. They progressed upwards by seniority alone, as death made room. A recommendation in 1782 that promotions to chief clerk should depend on merit does not appear to have had any effect. A promotion beyond £280 might be expected in fourteen to twenty-eight years, for in 1797 the assistant clerks in the general divisions had from five to fourteen years' service and those in the revenue branch up to twenty-seven years' service. A second promotion could not be expected in less than thirty-five years from entry, for senior clerks ran from fourteen to thirty-four years in the general divisions and up to forty years in the revenue branch, while the chief clerk most recently promoted had served thirty-five years. This stagnation was a reflection of the privilege of dying in harness. The oldest of the chief clerks in 1797, Thomas Pratt, had already the remarkable record of seventy-three years in the Treasury, while the head of the revenue branch had put in fifty-three years. Pratt's feebleness was admitted to throw work on his colleagues, but the Board of Treasury on consideration recoiled from the hardship of retirement for a man with three-quarters of a century of service.

The numbers employed were bound to increase, but the growth was for long moderate. The administrative staff of 1890 numbered nineteen—hardly more than it had been a century before; the growth of work had been met by the creation of subordinate grades. Total staff reached 141 in 1914 and a temporary peak of 373 in 1921 after that war.

The work of the department had been transformed in this long period. It is probable that its supervision of expenditure, or at any rate of new expenditure, was more direct and minute from 1660 to 1700 than ever before or after. When the land revenues of the Crown were surrendered, the Civil List reduced and expenditure transferred to Parliamentary funds, the interest of the Treasury in interference declined. The disposal of moneys provided for a particular minister by the House of Commons might be considered only his and its interest, and the Treasury sank into a comfortable routine of book-keeping.

Even the supervision of the currency was dropped. The oversight of the coins was left to a committee of the Privy Council from 1787 to 1816, and the striking change at the end of this period, the degradation of silver to a token currency, was the work of the leading member of the committee. To strengthen the market in Government stocks by confirming its promise to reduce debt, the Government tried to limit its own powers by the creation in 1786 of the National Debt Commission, which was to be independent of it. The commissioners were the Chancellor of the Exchequer for the time being, which was considered a mistake; the Speaker, various legal officers, the Governor of the Bank of England and his deputy governor. If the Commission ever met, it soon ceased to do so. The office became an appanage of the Treasury for issues and redemptions and for juggling with Government paper. An offshoot of it was the Government Actuary, who was called into being to calculate the annuities sold there. Three generations of Finlaysons held this post and discovered by their calculations that Chelsea pensions had also become hereditary; the average life of a pensioner was 135 years.

No investigations into the cadres of other departments had been

Thomas Cromwell

Whitehall Palace about 1695

made since the miserly days of Elizabeth I.   The criticism of entirely useless and extravagantly paid parts of the Civil Service which began in 1782 was the work of committees of the House of Commons.   The Treasury, itself purged and reorganised in 1784, only slowly and modestly pursued lines of thought opened by the committees.   But the inflation at the end of the Napoleonic wars compelled all-round increases of pay in lower reaches, even while the larger emoluments were still being spasmodically cut, and the Treasury was forced after the war to issue general directions for the raising, or lowering, of salaries, the granting of increments triennially, the standardising of hours and leave, and the keeping and signing of attendance books.

By 1810, applications for retirement pensions, as alternatives to other ways of providing for aged employees, had become so usual that the Treasury set up a general pension system which was administered by itself.   It thus became the omnipotent arbiter of one important emolument, and was betrayed into a more general interest in the Crown service.   A little later it was issuing instructions on the qualifications and training of recruits, as for instance that all clerks must be skilled in double-entry book-keeping.   In the 1850s the Prime Minister had acquired some say in the major Civil Service appointments made by other ministers, and the energetic permanent head of the Treasury was undertaking personal inspections of duties and organisation in other departments; in 1853 he issued a report which eventually centralised recruitment.   Neutral grades that could be employed anywhere and orders to departments on the kinds to be employed followed.   The control worked diversely: the employment of typists was pressed on the reluctant, but the use of electricity by the eager was retarded.

Such dominance over the personnel of other departments was acquired in the course of half a century that in 1872 the Chancellor of the Exchequer explained that his permanent secretary was " not an under-secretary of state; he was at the head of the Civil Service." This concentration was restated as a Government ruling in the Treasury Minute of 15th September, 1919, which enacted that the Treasury secretary " will act as permanent head of the Civil Service," and the following year appointments of heads, deputy heads and principal financial and personnel officers in all departments were made subject to the Prime Minister.   In 1919 also a separate sub-department, which had long been advocated by theorists, was formed within the Treasury to deal with Civil Service staffing.

G

Not that even the dwarf Treasury of the late eighteenth century was entirely careless of the organisation of public business. Each department—and they were already numerous—naturally bought its own quills and paper and ordered its own printing. The Treasury set up the Stationery Office in 1786, as a measure of economy, to purchase all parchment, vellum, paper and the like, from manufacturers, as far as possible at wholesale prices, and to undertake or contract for all binding and printing; the consuming departments were asked to deal through it as their current contracts expired. The influence of the central department was so slight that eleven years later, in 1797, fifteen departments still kept to their old arrangements, and not all were brought in, even for stationery, till 1830.

It was the Stationery Office that eventually abolished the red tape with which Government servants bound their papers together. Word was sent round soon after 1914 that this essential would be supplied no more as all contracts for the dye had been placed in Germany.

Similarly, the Treasury during the first quarter of the nineteenth century pressed its colleagues possessing buildings to stop individual contracting for upkeep and place all repairs and maintenance with the Office of Works. More oddly, when general penny postage was introduced in 1843, Sir Rowland Hill was taken on the Treasury staff to organise the change-over.

The liberty in detail of other great departments was decreased and the stringency of the Treasury veto on new spending was restored in the nineteenth century. Under the inspiration of Treasury ministers, the complicated accounting system was replaced in 1834 by a single fund into which all revenue was paid and out of which all expenditure was met. An intelligible budget at last became possible. At the same time, a new Department of Audit replaced the old-world Exchequer. The Enabling Act specifically required the auditors to compel their victims to refer expenditure to the Treasury for sanction.

That department not only prepared the annual budget containing the proposals for taxation for the year, but it also placed before the House of Commons the detailed proposals for expenditure of all civilian departments, while those of the fighting departments had to be agreed by it before their submission. Its ministers were in charge of the two great revenue departments and answered to Parliament for a host of minor departments which had no separate minister. It was in sole control of Government borrowing and its experts managed the Government overdraft, the technique of Exchequer Bills and Treasury Bills, of which the latter were invented by Lord Welby while still a subordinate, and the intricacies of a national currency.

With the inception of the Welfare State in 1909–11, the Treasury turned to the promotion of expenditure. " The business of a civil servant," Sir Francis Mowatt had said, " is to do as he is told." The new Chancellor of the Exchequer had a leading part in schemes for distributing cash to the old, the sick or the idle; his officials as in duty bound put all their abilities behind him. Advertisement of the Government's insurance scheme as " ninepence for fourpence " illustrated the new tone. But ancient ways are strong, and parsimony had been ingrained under so many careful Chancellors that these Civil Servants continued to look after the pence long after the pounds had been left to look after themselves. As late as 1927 a permanent secretary—Sir Thomas Heath—believed that the Treasury's main function was to enable the Chancellor of the Exchequer to reject proposals for expenditure and by intransigence prevent a multitude of such proposals from ever being made. Sir Thomas is said to have saved labour by having an initial sentence printed on all memorandum paper : " This is an atrocious proposition which must be sternly resisted." A more realistic view is that the machine has been so perfected and has so disregarded the dictum of Nicholas Faunt that " what can be done by fewer is badly done by more," that projects of small momentum get lost in its cogs. Later still the Treasury grew to such relatively vast dimensions that only superhuman labour keeps the engine turning over.

The progenitors of the modern Treasury, from the time that it had any existence apart from the Exchequer, worked in the privy gallery of the Palace of Whitehall. Their home burst into flames on the afternoon of 4th January, 1698, and by the following morning all but the banqueting-hall had been destroyed. Lowndes, the still-new secretary, accommodated all the clerks in his private house until a building on the Cockpit site across the street could be made ready for them and some other departments. Although this building only dated from 1675–6, it was found so dangerous in 1732 that the board and staff quitted it instantly for, appropriately enough, the Lottery office; there they abode for four years till William Kent had completed the present Treasury office on the old site. It too was shared with other departments. The growing Treasury thrust them out one by one, not many years ago; then burst its bounds and moved in mass, save for a few fragments, to Great George Street.

9

THE TAX OFFICES

Customs

THE customs are by far the oldest of taxes still in force. William the Conqueror, and probably his predecessors, had the right to one cask of wine off every ship that came in with ten, and one from those before the mast and another from those stowed aft in a ship that carried twenty or more; for some centuries half the imports into England were wine, an essential of life which was poorly produced by native vineyards. Another warmth-producing material, wool, was the principal export; various coast authorities were entitled to proportions of this, as well as of other goods, that varied with the harbours.

John imposed a nation-wide tax in his financial stresses of 1203; Magna Carta admitted only the traditional rates to be ancient and proper usages, " customs," and liberated trade from the new maltolts or evil tolls.

Systematic taxation other than that of wine began anew in 1266 when Prince Edward, put in control of foreign trades, was allowed to impose a universal tariff on exports and imports. His " first general parliament " as King in 1275 agreed to an export duty of half a mark (6s. 8d.) on every twenty-six-stone sack of wool or on 300 wool fells, and a mark on every last of leather, but freed other goods; these grants constituted for the future the " great and ancient customs," and though suspended for much of Edward II's reign, they were enjoyed by later kings without question. Edward I could no more than his successors refrain from further taxation. He imposed in 1295 heavy additional maltolts on wool exported and seized the wool when the merchants would not pay. But he had to yield, and to promise in his confirmation of the Charters in 1297 to take nothing beyond " the ancient aids and prises due and accustomed " except by common consent. A prise was seizure of a proportion of goods when cash could not be obtained. None the less, Edward I levied extra customs from 1302 onwards—2s. on each tun of wine, 1s. or 2s. on each length of various cloths, an extra quarter of a mark on each wool sack and half a mark on each last of leather, 1s. a quintal on wax, and 3d. a pound avoirdupois on all other goods. It is said that the extra wine duties were justified by resort to larger ships and smaller tuns. Foreign merchants agreed to the levy, the " new or petty customs "; native traders spurned it, and their imports of wine continued subject to prise.

The Parliaments of Edward III granted him customs subsidies of, usually, an additional £2 a sack of wool or last of leather for exports by native merchants and half as much again when the trade was in foreign hands; extra duties on the tun of wine also and *ad valorem* duties on the pound of foreign goods. Tonnage, which rose to 3s. a tun, and poundage, which rose to 1s. in the pound, were thereafter usually voted by Parliament for the King's life at the beginning of each reign, until James I annoyed the Commons by anticipation; subsidies continued to be occasional and restricted to short terms of years. The latter were supposedly for the land defence of the realm; the former to enable the King to keep the seas.

Duty according to value implies a price list, but the first book of rates seems not to have been drawn up till 1509. The Government were not very adaptable; notwithstanding the inflation and rising prices under Henry VIII and Edward VI, this book was left in force till 1558. A third book, drawn up in 1586, governed the customs till 1608; and the 1608 book was not amended till 1635.

The various duties on a single article were kept separate. Part of the charge on wine was appropriately a matter for the Chief Butler, and Deputy Butlers were appointed for groups of ports. Other complications were that certain foreigners acquired at times the right to pay only native rates or an intermediate rate, or that rates were reduced for shipments at some one port. Further additional duties, termed imposts, were added by the Stuarts by prerogative without benefit of statute. James I, a contemner of nicotine, started the innovation at once, with an extortionate impost of 6s. 8d. a lb. on tobacco in addition to the poundage of 1d. on plantation and 1s. on Spanish tobacco. An impost on currants in the following year was resisted by a merchant called Bates; he was taken to the courts, which declared this use of the prerogative legal.

The collection of customs duty in London port was run by the chamberlains of the City, who accounted direct to the Exchequer, for a good many years before 1200; they still did so in 1297, except for

wine duty, which was handled and presumably farmed by traders, the
" buyers of the King's wines "; the Pepperers' or Grocers' Guild also
had special privileges in the weighing and classification of the goods of
their trade. London was a special case; throughout the Middle Ages
it handled as much trade as all the rest of the kingdom. Elsewhere the
collection of tax was farmed out to contractors in the early twelfth
century. William of Wrotham, Archdeacon of Taunton, manager
of the Navy, also farmed the provincial customs with William of
Furnell; they paid £4,959 in respect of thirty-four ports and market
fairs for the years 1202-4, when Hugh Oisel, a great London merchant,
offered cut-throat terms to outbid them. As late as 1299, when export
of English coin was forbidden, each port was ordered to elect two
officials to search the baggage and persons of travellers and con-
fiscate any English coin found on the outward-bound and any inferior
foreign coin found on incomers. But that was not then a duty of the
Customs.

Before this, in 1297, two collectors of the duty on wool had been
appointed by the Crown at each of nine official ports, and direct collection seems to have become the practice for a time. Geoffrey
Chaucer, the poet, was appointed controller in London of one of the
duties, that on wool, in 1374, and of another, the petty customs, in
addition in 1382. The original London Customs House was built in
his time.

The capture of Calais and the location there of the English wholesale
market in wool cut across island organisation. The wool ' subsidy,'
being meant for the support of the garrison, was administered in
Calais.

Calais apart, the Customs organisation, from this time or shortly
after, was based on the occupation of sixteen ports. Named in order
from north to south and round the south coast, they were Newcastle-
on-Tyne, Hull, Boston, King's Lynn, Yarmouth, Ipswich, London,
Sandwich, Dover, Chichester, Southampton; three linked pairs of
ports which were regarded as units, Poole and Weymouth, Exeter and
Dartmouth, Plymouth and Fowey; Bridgwater, and, lastly, Bristol.
Other Customs stations were sometimes set up: Berwick for a time,
or St. Ives and Padstow in 1509; but in general, for several centuries,
these sixteen or nineteen stations were supposed to look after the
stretches of coast of up to 100 miles which separated them; even the
linked ports were up to twenty or thirty miles apart. Smuggling was

naturally rampant. The reverend abbot of Furness was one of the unlucky to be caught in 1423 exporting his wool without paying duty; it was the fifth annual ship of 200 tons burden that he had packed with wool. In 1557 the Venetian ambassador observed that three-quarters of the English customs revenue was lost by evasion and by the costs of collection. There was corruption as well. 275 tuns of wine were landed at Exeter in 1575; the Customs officials only noticed 77.

The fundamental officers in a station were three. The customer or collector took the cash and accounted to the Exchequer at its six-monthly meetings; the comptroller—the contra-rotulator—recorded the sums that should be taken in his counter-roll; the searcher per-mitted import or export of a parcel of goods on receiving a warrant for landing or a coket for export which both had signed. "Coket" is a corruption of the concluding acquittance on the document: "Quo quietus est" becoming "coketus est" and then "coket." The fraudulent ways of searchers caused about 1430 the appointment of a surveyor to watch them. Tide-waiters and land-waiters were the private servants of the customer or the surveyor; King's and letters-patent waiters came later. The full set-up of a port in the fifteenth and sixteenth centuries was a surveyor, two customers or collectors—one for outward and one for inward work—a controller, a searcher, a weigher (or troneur and peseur), a clerk, a gauger and a cranekeeper. Wool was weighed on a special type of balance called a tron: hence the weigher's double name. London had in the reign of Elizabeth I fourteen surveyors and receivers, two customers for the petty customs and three collectors with a clerk each for the other customs, and eighteen tide-waiters.

The upper men were appointed by the Lord Treasurer from persons or merchants of standing in the locality or from Household or Ex-chequer officials. A law of 1442 which prohibited for obvious reasons the ownership by Customs officials of vessels of their own was not long observed. Appointment was sometimes for life; at other times for a term of years. Some were explicitly permitted to do the work by deputy; others were expressly required to do it in person, which made no difference. Some men were granted several posts at opposite ends of the kingdom. Thomas Stoughton, a leading fishmonger of London and purveyor to the Royal Households of Henry VI and Edward IV from 1444 to 1476, was customer at Chichester, Ipswich and Sandwich from 1451; he was comptroller at Ipswich by 1460 and in London and

Sandwich by 1475. His brother John, employed in one of the Palace food departments from 1436, was customer in Calais at the same time, comptroller at Boston from 1443 to 1463 and clerk of weighing at Sandwich from 1460. He was incidentally spigurnel, that is, melter of wax for the Great Seal, from 1461 to 1465.

The pay of the top grades in the fifteenth century was £10 or £12 a year, but this could be supplemented by such handsome rewards that only the soft of heart or head can have been bribeable; one half or even the whole of goods whose importers attempted to evade duty was awarded to the vigilant Customs official. Less honourable additions were obtained by sharp practice; the Customs were notorious extortioners.

The clumsiness of bureaucratic control led again to farming customs duties out to contractors who paid a fixed rent and collected more diligently than the State, and the success of this was followed by extensions. Thomas Smyth, nicknamed the Customer from the way he made a fortune, contracted for tonnage and poundage in the port of London in 1557. In 1570 he undertook to pay £5,000 down and £17,500 a year for all import duties in London and its subsidiary ports. He raised subordinate officials' wages, increased their number by hired men of his own, and collected such large sums for his own benefit that on each of the three renewals of the contract the rent was hugely increased. Smyth had to pay £30,000 a year for his final spell of 1584-8, and even so cleared £16,000 on the deal. The easier export duties, being excluded from Smyth's contract, were farmed out in the same way to a syndicate whose head was the Secretary of State, Sir Francis Walsingham.

The revenue having been worked up to double by the incentive of private profit, the Crown saw no reason to waste money in contractors' profits, strengthened its staff with inspectors and resumed direct administration of the London customs for ten years. Disillusioned ministers then returned to farming the customs throughout the country in sections. The great customs and silk were one contract; wine and currants composed the petty farm; the imposts on tobacco and on sugar were let separately. Contracts were usually for three years, after which fresh offers were invited. Dishonesty in the highest quarters had an opening at this stage. The sugar-impost contract was for £5,667 a year when it expired in 1620; the Household treasurer, the Earl of Middlesex, who had been trained in a merchant's office and as Surveyor-General of Customs had greatly increased their yield, took a lease of this tax at only £2,000 in the names of his servants, and promptly let it to others for £6,000.

The customs duties were summarised and confirmed to Charles II on his restoration by the " great statute " of 1660. He was given tonnage on wine at rates that varied with the types and even with the port of entry; London cargoes paid an extra £1, and the difference in duty was supposed to be payable on wine transported across country to London. The old butlerage of 2s. a cask was levied in addition on all imports by foreign merchants, while cargoes of British merchants remained liable instead to prise. British importers paid on cloth two farthings and a half farthing—⅝d.—on the pound weight; foreign merchants were charged double, plus the old duty of 1s. 2d. a length. A poundage of 1s. in the pound, as set out in a table of values, was charged on all other goods imported or exported, except native commodities exported by stranger merchants, which paid double. These were the receipts afterwards called the " old subsidy."

The management was entrusted to commissioners and the detailed collection was farmed out. But the farmers of the customs were entangled in financial difficulties by the stoppage of trade in the great plague of 1665. The Customs house, last rebuilt in 1559, was destroyed by the Great Fire the year after the plague. In 1621 farming was abandoned, compensation to the dispossessed farmers being continued for a century, and collection returned to a board of commissioners, semi-political persons who drifted round the upper layers of Government departments and developed below them the usual small hierarchy. The appointments both of commissioners and of their subordinates down to the lowest vested in the Treasury after the Revolution. But the commissioners required the port staff, from at latest, 1700, to pass in competency after a short training course, and medium posts were filled by them to some extent by promotion from lower. A Select Committee of 1797 recommended both the extension of the requirement of certificates of competence and organised promotion up to collector.

On these rates were superimposed, as the years went by, both heavier taxes on named goods and general increases. The poundage rates were doubled in 1689 and were raised to threefold in two steps in 1703 and 1704. The various accretions accumulated undigested in a perplexing mass of separate orders, so that a single commodity paid a number of separate levies at different rates. The secretary of the commissioners, C. Carkesse, compiled a list of these customs duties, which ran to 117 closely printed pages. Following this, a new " additional " table of rates was drawn up in 1724 by the commissioners, in consultation with the trade. Walpole moreover eased the work at the ports by the repeal in 1724 of most of the export taxes and of the import duties on a number of raw materials.

Further growth in Government expenditure continued to be met by undigested particular and general increases, without regard to the cost of collection. The statute of 1660 and additional table of 1724 were laden with a multitude of extra rates, while the poundage was raised by a subsidy of 1748 to 20 per cent and by a further subsidy of 1759 to 25 per cent. And as the increases were assigned to particular services, manifold charges had to be made against a single commodity. A consignment of linen in 1784, on which the total duty was £70, was assessed under ten different orders, and the tax was credited to as many different heads. Pitt simplified collection in 1787 by abolishing some charges, combining others and directing all receipts to be paid alike into his new consolidated fund; but even in 1801 there still survived 1,500 separate customs rates, and every article imported was subjected to four different duties.

About 1820, James Deacon Hume, son of a former secretary of the Customs, and himself a Customs clerk of thirty years' standing, was given three years' leave to consolidate the 1,500 Customs statutes which were still valid. He reduced them to ten acts, which were passed in 1825, and was rewarded with £6,000. At the same time, Huskisson's reform of the tariff eliminated a host of pettifogging details; Peel's reforms of 1842 and 1845 and Gladstone's of 1860 reduced the customs for a time to revenue duties only.

Changes in trade and in the department's organisation were met by creating new posts, while continuing to fill the old in accordance with precedents. A review by a Parliamentary committee in 1782 discovered some 200 Customs officials who had no work; for the most part customers, comptrollers, searchers and those waiters who were appointed by letters patent. The pay was occasionally trivial—as low as £2 2s. a year for the customer at Sutton, £2 9s. 6d. for the one at Holbeach and £11 4s. 8d. for him of Eastbourne. But there were plums, too; the usher of the Long Room in the London Custom House had only £6 for salary, but his fees averaged £619 a year. The customer at Chester had £1,675. The comptroller in London for inwards and outwards trade, whose work had passed entirely to others, averaged £1,724 a year, mostly from seizures with which he had now no concern; the collector outwards and the collector inwards in London, both complete sinecures, averaged £2,132 and £2,732 respectively. All these posts were marked down for abolition on vacancies. About a quarter of the 200 fell vacant during the next fifteen years, during which period 450 new posts were created, but meantime holders of sinecures had been further enriched by growth of of business that they did not do. The Earl of Liverpool, still London collector inwards, was averaging £3,457 in 1797; the pay of the Duke of Manchester, as collector outwards, had risen to £2,788 in 1797 and in 1834 he was still going strong with an official income enhanced to an average of £2,928. One other rich post in 1797 was Lord Stavell's; as surveyor for both outwards and inwards traffic, he received an average of £2,391. But a fall in seizures had reduced the perquisites of the comptroller, the Earl of Guildford, to £278.

Smuggling changed its technique in the eighteenth century. The mediæval ship could not slip into and out of a quiet haven in a single night; the handier vessels of the seventeenth century could, and were not stopped by dispersion of watchers about minor creeks. The Customs called in the Navy to intercept suspected ships at sea, and built or hired a fleet of their own; the Board had thirty-seven cutters in commission in 1797. But, stimulated by high taxes, the professional smuggler flourished; it was estimated in 1784 that 40,000 men and 300 ships were engaged in the trade, and, as everyone knows, they were strong enough on land to fight considerable forces. It was estimated that half the brandy and over half the tea consumed in England paid no duty.

The coastguard was instituted after the war against Napoleon to stop the growing traffic. Nominally under the Customs, it was run by the Admiralty and by them converted into a reserve of officers and men for the fleet in war or emergency. This was called up in the Crimean War, regardless of the revenue's interest. Thereupon the Customs transferred the whole force in 1857 to the senior body. The coastguard also played an important part in saving life from the angry sea in conjunction with private institutions. By 1919 this was found to be its most vital function, and it was transferred to the Board of Trade in 1925.

It appears to have been this watch in coastal waters, technical changes in shipping and the control of inland markets which resulted from the excise rather than any brilliance on the part of the Customs commissioners which drove smugglers to more subterranean ways.

More than revenue work fell on the Customs Board and its officers. The collection of light dues, for the maintenance of lighthouses, beacons and buoys by Trinity House and parallel fraternities, had indeed devolved upon them from very early times. So, naturally, had the measurement, registration and record of transfer of ships. Statistics both of trade and of navigation were prepared partly at the out-ports and partly at the head office in London from early in the eighteenth century, and supplied by the latter to the Board of Trade. Copies of Customs bills of entry were also prepared and supplied to merchants at a price. The conduct of this business was in practice sold periodically to private undertakers from what was described in 1834 as a " very ancient date "; the contractors of 1834 had held it for seventeen years. But they in turn had sold the undertaking for £2,000 a year to a coterie of Customs House officials; the profits which the latter wrested from extortionate charges were eventually devoted to the first of the Civil Service and departmental benevolent funds.

Excise

One of Dr. Johnson's famous definitions was of excise as " a hateful tax levied upon commodities and adjudged not by the common judges of property but wretches hired by those to whom excise is paid." Its difference from other taxes in these respects is not deep. Excise at its origin differed from customs in falling upon goods produced at home, though some foreign commodities that had already paid customs duty were long subject to excise as well. It was obnoxious partly because it was novel, partly because it fell on articles of necessity, mainly because peering Paul Prys levied it, not at the ports but almost under the eyes of the consumer. And there were fewer holes in the taxation net than obtained in the Customs. The tax was levied at different points for different commodities. In some cases, as with hops, the grower paid; in others it was the manufacturer weekly on his production, or the retailer monthly on his sales, or even the purchasing consumer. The sanctity of the home was invaded in one case: the private house that made its own candles had to pay a commuted rate according to the number of its inhabitants.

Excise, well known in Holland, was proposed on beer in the reign of Elizabeth I, but it was left to a rebellious Parliament to introduce it in 1643. Beer, ale, cider and perry, starch, salt, hats, silks and other articles were the victims. The duties were not at first excessive : 6*d.* or 2*s.* 6*d.* a barrel on beer according to its strength, and 2*s.* on foreign beer. Only beer that was bought was taxable; home-brewed was always free. A tax on malt, however, struck at it through its raw material and affected professional beer twice over.

The new tax was levied by commissioners in London and sub-commissioners in the provinces. Charles I followed suit and applied the law for his benefit in the counties that he controlled. By 1649 Parliament began to farm out collection. The excise had been declared to be a temporary measure, but on the Restoration Charles II was reft of all the out-of-date feudal dues which his father had abused. The exactions on a death were to be revived long after by Gladstone, and purveyance reappeared in our own time under the name of requisition. In lieu of the feudal duties the King was granted the Commonwealth excises on liquor, one half as part of the hereditary revenues of the Crown and the other half for life. Tea, coffee and chocolate and British spirits, under the name of low wines, were added. The non-alcoholic articles that were at first excused were soon excised again. The King had the further advantage of fobbing off hundreds of loyalists' claims by Excise appointments.

Because of the difficulties of so dispersed a tax, the excise was generally farmed out, and longer than the customs. Direct collection was resumed in England in 1683, though farming continued for the remoter counties and remained usual in Scotland till the union of the kingdoms in 1707. It was placed under a board of commissioners, the Treasury enjoying all the patronage, as with the Customs.

Walpole's notorious attempt to widen the excise in 1733 was rather a customs measure. Bonded warehouses had been introduced in 1700 for the temporary reception of prohibited silks, to avoid stopping the re-export trade. One of the administrative slips on that occasion was both to prohibit the import of silk and to raise the duty on it; the ban had then to be waived or the revenue sacrificed. Bonded warehouses for pepper followed in 1709, and for tea, coffee and cocoa in 1724, when use of the facilities was made compulsory. The principle was that the importer paid a fraction of the customs duty when his goods were landed and taken into the warehouse; he could re-export them free or pay the rest of the duty if he removed them for sale at home. The Excise had powers of search and of checking goods in transit; no more than three gallons of wine could be moved without an excise permit, and a very large increase in revenue was obtained. Walpole in 1733 proposed the extension of bonding facilities and concomitant controls to wine and tobacco. He desired at one blow to discourage smuggling, make London the greatest free port in the world and obtain enough revenue to abolish the land tax. Some confused draughtsman headed the bill " Excise."

The witty Chesterfield said afterwards that a general excise bill would pass if it were entitled instead " an act for better securing the liberty and property of His Majesty's subjects by repealing the most burdensome Custom House laws." Howbeit, the then unpopular word was flaunted, to be taken as an omen of new taxes : the offer to abolish the land tax as a set-off carried no weight, for it was down to 1s. and was paid on absurdly low assessments, and a sceptical age perceived that if it went something nastier would be put in its place. Men also inveighed strongly against the increase of the Government's patronage by a multitude of new Excise officials. The actual number was 126. The Commons therefore killed the proposal. The younger Pitt put it through for tea and tobacco half a century later in 1787 and 1789 for the sake of simplicity, cheapness and efficiency of collection. But habit died hard; even then, the tax of 1s. 3d. a pound on tobacco—it had been fixed at 1d. on colonial and 6d. on foreign tobacco exactly 100 years before—was divided into 6d. for customs and 9d. for excise. A good deal of duplication between the detection services of the two departments was inevitable.

By the end of the eighteenth century the Excise was collecting twice as much a year as the Customs. £585,000 a year before the glorious Revolution had swelled in a century to £7,000,000, while the customs revenue had only risen in the same time six or sevenfold : from £530,000 to between £3,000,000 and £3,500,000. The Excise commissioners had for some time endeavoured to economise by increases in the more responsible staff and greater reduction in the numbers of the lower. Their landing waiters were paid £55, their gaugers £70, their surveyors £90, their collectors £240 rising to £300. The rough-and-ready method of appointment by introduction and recommendation, with a subsequent test, had some human advantages. It enabled a living to be provided for Robert Burns as an excise man, as which he got £90 a year including rewards for seizures. The Board itself consisted of two chairmen at £1,750 each and five other members at £1,250 each, with a secretary at £1,300, who had, however, to expend £480 of his salary on clerks. The secretary handled in this private office, no doubt delicately, letters from Government departments and " persons of distinction." Letters from the country, on the contrary, were left to an officer called the correspondent on a mere £235 a year, with five assistants rising to the same salary and five clerks under them at the fair pay of £50 to £90.

The plums of the department were the post of solicitor (£3,346), whose work was done by a deputy at £500, and of receiver-general at £3,050. But the last had to pay his own clerks over £1,200 a year. The Excise came unscathed through the committees of enquiry of that period.

Three separate Excise Boards, one for each kingdom, were maintained till 1823, when they were united. The huge body of seventeen commissioners which resulted was but modestly reduced to fourteen in 1830, when some of their high officials were also dispensed with. The Board was reduced to seven, with further reductions in the staffs below them, in 1849, when it was merged in the Inland Revenue. The savings were what then seemed the substantial annual figures of £17,000 on the first occasion and £31,000 on the second.

Stamp Office

Separate commissioners were appointed in 1694 to extract revenue from the use of deeds and documents of almost every kind. Their first instructions were to have six dies engraved for impressing or embossing papers and parchments with stamps priced at 1*d.*, 6*d.*, 1*s.*, 2*s.* 6*d.*, 5*s.* and 40*s.* The taxpayer could either take his papers to the Stamp Office to be charged and impressed or buy blank sheets already stamped. The dies were cut by the engraver of the Great Seal, and a sceptical Isaac Newton was consulted in 1704 and 1708 on the possibility of gummed stamps and on elaborations to prevent forgery.

The price of the stamp depended at first solely on the nature of the document. University degrees, for instance, paid 40*s.*, marriage certificates 5*s.*, admissions to a university and most deeds 6*d.*, and a copy of a will 1*d.* But every leaf had to be equally stamped, so that the

Receipt of Custom, 1841
The Long Room, London

Robert Burns
Excise Officer

tax varied with the length of the document, and the provident law prohibited cramped writing or any shortening of verbiage. Stamps began to vary upwards with the values contained in the document from the end of Anne's reign, and their range and amount were continually increased. Heavy probate and legacy duties evolved from their use. The stamp on probate of an estate of half a million was £6,000 by 1804. Ordinary deeds, leases and contracts rose in sixty years from 6d. to 5s. a sheet, and by 1804 paid 30s. for a first sheet and 20s. on each succeeding sheet. Three hundred different stamps were then in use. Receipts for payments over £2 were not required to be stamped till 1783, when they took a 2d. stamp up to £20 and a 4d. stamp above that amount; receipt stamps rose to nine different rates, of which the highest was 10s., before this logical but not very practical system was abandoned in 1853 under the lead of penny postage for a uniform 1d., for which an adhesive stamp was at last accepted. Newspapers and advertisements were made subject to stamp duties—the " taxes on knowledge "—in 1711 and 1714.

Near the end of the century some new impositions were passed to the Stamp Office for collection. It taxed riding- and carriage-horses, and after these were transferred to the window-tax commissioners, it continued to deal with race-horses. At the same time the tax on carriages and coaches was handled by the Excise, while the window-tax commissioners took that on dogs. The Excise extracted the tax on the plate-chests of the rich, but the Stamp Office that on their armorial bearings. The Stamp Office also issued the game licences instituted in 1785 and collected the guinea a head a year which persons who powdered their own or their servants' hair had to pay from 1795; this tax was not abandoned till 1869, when it brought in only £1,000 a year. The Office lucidly called its extraneous tasks " Unstamped duties of stamps."

The Stamp Office was run at the end of the eighteenth century by a comptroller and a registrar under a nominal board. The London office, where impressing was done by hand-presses, had a staff of 123, of whom forty-six were stampers and the remainder clerks of various grades. The stamper's salary was £50; a clerk's was £60; a head clerk's from £100 to £140. Clerks were invariably entered in their bottom grade, and the upper ranks were staffed by promotions. The provinces were provided for by sixty-six head distributors of stamps and a much larger number of sub-distributors.

H

Tax Commission

In 1662, soon after the Restoration, a tax of 2s. a year was imposed on every fireplace in all houses except mere cottages. It had ancient and forgotten precedents in an Anglo-Saxon levy called fumage and in a tax of a groat a hearth levied for 1377 and then dropped. Charles II's hearth or chimney tax, which involved entry and counting by the local assessor, was just as distasteful, so it was farmed out to contractors for thirty-seven years. Though its yield was large—up to £200,000 a year—popular distaste prevailed and it was cancelled at the Revolution.

It was replaced by a tax on windows, which was dealt with by the Tax Commissioners recently created for the land and property tax. These operated through parochial assessors, selected by them from the most substantial inhabitants of the district, and collectors, appointed on the nomination of the assessors. This tax also required close inspections, especially after it was converted in 1747 to a charge on each window, at a rate increasing as the numbers rose—6d. a window up to fourteen; then 9d.; and 1s. a window if there were twenty or more. Skylights, ventilators or coal-chutes were all held to be windows. An inhabited-house duty was imposed in addition to the window tax. The Treasury had to appoint a receiver-general, surveyors and inspectors, with power to surcharge, to supplement the traditional local management. Inhabited-house duty was repealed in 1834 and window tax was retained; the charge was reversed in 1851—window tax was repealed and inhabited-house duty was resumed.

To the Tax Commissioners fell some of the other duties invented in the eighteenth century. They took over in 1785 the tax on carriages, which the Excise had managed for nearly forty years, and that on pleasure-horses, which had been run by the Stamp Office. The tax on domestic menservants was also transferred from the Excise; " domestic " was used rather widely; the number of clerks, porters and shopmen, whose employers were mulcted by the Commissioners, rose to over 200,000, against 80,000 merely household servants. All these taxes developed a cumulative bias against the rich during the war—so much for one carriage, more than double for two. On servants, for instance, a bachelor paid in 1812 £4 8s. for one; but he was charged on a rising scale which cost him £19 13s. each if he kept eleven; a married man was taxed on the same system, but at lower rates.

Pitt tried to convert the aggregate of these taxes (as rough evidences of wealth) into the equivalent of an income tax by his famous " triple assessment " of 1797, which was in fact for the rich a five-fold assessment. A return to the Tax Commissioners was required from each taxpayer of all his taxable possessions. Tax was then imposed on the aggregate on a steeply rising scale. The attempt was foiled by the latitude which men allowed themselves in their returns, and an income tax proper followed.

Income Tax

The taxation of the individual on the basis of his income was tried in the Middle and later ages. Parliament voted the King in 1332, for that occasion only but following earlier grants of the same sort, a tenth of a year's actual or estimated income from property in cities, towns or elsewhere on Royal demesne lands and a fifteenth of the income from property in the shires. Similar grants were henceforth the standard means of meeting all-too-frequent financial crises. It was agreed in 1334 that, in view of past extortions, commissioners should fix with the various communities on behalf of the Exchequer the total due from each, and that this should be assessed and apportioned locally between the taxpayers by their representatives. Local agreement of this sort remained the machinery to the end. As the Exchequer never ventured to reopen the 1334 figure, at any rate upwards, a subsidy of one-tenth and one-fifteenth was converted into a fixed grant of between £38,000 and £39,000. Though the figure did not rise with prosperity, it had to be reduced for calamity, and abatements were made to distressed areas which in the next century came to over £6,000 on each subsidy. An attempt in 1463 at direct assessment by the Crown and at spreading the £6,000 over solvent districts was defeated. When the fall in the value of money or the increase in prosperity persuaded Parliament to larger grants, they took the form of two- or three-tenths and fifteenths. The last grant was made as late as 1623. The Tudors tried a fresh start with a tax of 4s. in the pound in income from land and 2s. 8d. on assumed income from crops and movables of a capital nature, provided that the individual was charged only under one head or the other, and not on both. District commissioners were appointed by the Lord Chancellor and others. They appointed both assessors and collectors; the latter sent one copy of the assessment roll direct to the Exchequer, and accounted for their takings to a head collector, who in turn accounted to the Exchequer.

A tax on income was resumed in 1688. Commissioners of tax were appointed to collect whatever rate in the pound Parliament voted for the year, on all incomes from employment, personal property, money, merchandise and land. Year by year for a century the formulæ repeated the onus on the first four, leaving only a residue of tax on land. But in fact the total of the first and grossly inadequate assessment was accepted as final, and each 1s. in the Parliamentary vote was read as exactly £494,671. It was accepted, moreover, that the local assessors should not replace the first victims in categories other than land, as they died; their task became to apportion the resulting deficit proportionately over the taxed lands in their area. The tax thus became an annual land tax, sometimes, in time of peace, as low as 1s. on the shadowy valuation, but in times of war often 4s. Finally Pitt in 1798 converted the annual tax into a permanent but redeemable burden on the land. Having thus masked the existing charge, the Commissioners of Land Tax were switched to manage a new tax of 10 per cent on all incomes, including landed incomes, over £200, with lower rates down to £60. It was introduced by him as a strictly war measure; it was also strikingly successful. Parliament accordingly declined to continue it beyond 1815. This tax was revived in 1842 at the lower rate of 7d. in the pound, with the same and long-repeated pledges that it was a temporary resort.

Both the nineteenth-century arrangements kept to the age-old tradition that assessment and collection were matters for local and unofficial minds. The tax was divided into the still familiar schedules. The taxpayer might conceal his affairs from his neighbours by making his return under certain of these to the paid commissioners at the centre; otherwise it was the honorary commissioners for his area who received his statements, assessed him and appointed the paid collectors who took his money. The snare was the appointment, as for several recent taxes, of Government-paid surveyors to advise the amateur commissioners. The surveyor supplied local assessors with forms of return, criticised these on completion, compared them with the poor-rate assessments and attended the commissioners' meetings. If he did not like their findings he had power to surcharge. Out of these insidious auxiliaries grew the magnificent apparatus of inspectors and higher inspectors and clerks and super-clerks who left the local commissioners little to do but sign schedules at the foot.

The tax-gathering machinery began to be consolidated in the years between the two impositions of income tax. A direction by the Treasury, which was in ultimate charge of both, united the Stamp Office and the Commissioners of Taxes in 1834, to save £18,000 a year. While income tax was still supposed to be temporary, the joint body was converted into a new Board of Inland Revenue in 1849. As excise was obviously inland, the Excise commissioners too were merged in the Board. In spite of the practical intermeshing of their duties with the Customs, this academic decision was not undone for sixty years, when in 1909 excise was at last taken away from Inland Revenue and joined to customs.

The Excise commissioners, before their absorption, had called chemists into their service and set up a laboratory to test the adulteration of tobacco, analyse other excisable goods and investigate the mystery of brewing. The Customs, still separate, set up another scientific establishment in 1875 to do the like for food and drugs and imported commodities. The two were combined in 1894 and began an independent existence as the Government Laboratory or the Government Chemist, for the service of all departments.

The Excise was clearly a formidable machine from early in the eighteenth century, the Customs by its close and the Inland Revenue from the amalgamation of departments in the middle of the nineteenth. To the joint body of Customs and Excise, the tax on entertainments of 1909, the duty on betting of 1926 and the purchase tax imposed during the Second World War naturally fell, while unrelated work, as in connection with old age pensions, was also attracted by the convenient locations of its officers. The Inland Revenue Board was inevitably used when Gladstone and others grasped at more of the leavings of the dead, and at the expanded income-taxes called excess profits, corporation and super- or sur-tax.

10

THE ADMIRALTY

OUR early conception of war, at sea as on land, was that the nation took to arms. Although Alfred and his sons had to build a fleet in the Danish troubles, Kings of England from the Norman Conquest to the Tudors relied, with small exceptions, on the ships of their merchants. The trading- and fishing-smacks were left to cope on their own, and not always successfully, against the mere pirate. For larger emergencies the King was entitled for one month in the year to fifty-seven ships and crews from the Cinque ports and, later, to a few more from Essex harbours. If these numbers were too small or the month was too short, he fell back on hiring these or other merchantmen at traditional rates. Some successful merchant was appointed to muster and command the fleet.

The immense convoy which took Richard I on crusade to Palestine was chartered from all over England, Normandy and Poitou, and was commanded by Henry of Cornhill, a London trader. The next King, John, being for ever in trouble in Normandy, maintained his own navy, to whose dignity from 1200 onwards he required all private vessels to strike their sails in salute; it comprised fifty-one ships when invasion threatened him from France in 1205. This navy was created and administered by William of Wrotham, Archdeacon of Taunton and Keeper of the King's Ships, who pressed ships and men for the service, and supervised building and repair. On the fleet's putting to sea, one of its three divisions was commanded by the Archdeacon; the other two were under the command of London merchants—Reginald of Cornhill, brother to the foregoing Henry, and William of Furnell. This navy lapsed by the end of the reign.

A merchant, William of Leyburn, was the first man in England to be entitled Admiral; he was designated " Admiral of the English sea " when sent by Edward I in 1297 as envoy to a maritime conference in the Lowlands. The title was expanded for Gervase Allard, a Cinque Port mariner, who was put in command in 1303 of the Channel flotilla, potential or actual, as " Captain and Admiral of the fleet of the Cinque ports and of all other ports from Dover by the sea westwards as far as Cornwall, and the whole of Cornwall." A second Admiral was shortly appointed for the coast north of the Thames, with deputies for particular ports.

The two offices were united and transferred in the middle of the fourteenth century from sea-going folk to eminent landsmen. John de Beauchamp, brother of the Earl of Warwick, was put in sole charge in 1360 of the gathering and running of the fleet, but the title " Admiral of England " did not appear till a generation later, when it was conferred in 1391 on Edward of York. It became indifferently " High Admiral " or " Lord Admiral " under Henry VIII; the two adjectives were only combined in the proud style of Lord High Admiral of England on the appointment in 1618 of a King's favourite, George Villiers, Duke of Buckingham. The eleven Admirals whose offices covered the century from 1435 to 1536 were all dukes or earls; they included Thomas of Lancaster, son of Henry IV; Warwick the Kingmaker; and Richard III until his accession. John de Vere, first Earl of Oxford, Admiral throughout Henry VIII's reign and until his own death in 1513, was also Constable of the Tower, and the next Admiral, 1513–25, Sir Thomas Howard, Duke of Norfolk, was a commander of land armies, Lord Lieutenant of Ireland, Treasurer and Earl Marshal. Then came Henry VIII's illegitimate son, Henry Fitzroy, Duke of Richmond, who was six years old on his appointment and held it till he died at seventeen.

Until the Tudors, when the duty of command at sea was re-imposed, the main interest of these magnates was the profit and fees of an extensive criminal and civil jurisdiction. This jurisdiction was conferred not many years after the naval battle of Sluys. Edward III based on his great victory a claim to be master of the seas, and was compelled to set up some machinery to deal with the buccaneers amongst his own subjects, as well as with the violence and crime with which the Channel was rife. So the admiral became a judge as well; the scope of his court was steadily extended to almost every matter below high-water mark and up to the first bridge on each river, not without many disputes about the marginal cases with existing port authorities. Not only piracy, mutiny and murder, whether on the high seas or on a " great " ship below the bridges, were tried in this court; it also dealt with commercial disputes on such matters as contracts that were made or were enforceable abroad, or on charters, insurance, collisions or salvage; suits about seamen's wages had to be taken there. The Admiralty Court decided the disposal of loot or prizes taken from an enemy, and naturally managed the rights of the Crown to wrecks, flotsam, jetsam and stranded whales. Both droits of Crown and of Admiralty, at first shared, ultimately became the Admiral's perquisites until the post was turned into a board, and with the fees for actions constituted his practical interest in these legal complexities.

The Admiral was empowered to act by deputy; his juridical work was entirely delegated from the outset to lawyers, and to that branch of the profession which specialised in the code called the civil law. Their chief, the Dean of the Arches, was commonly appointed the Admiral's deputy, and so the effective judge. In commercial matters the civil law had the advantages over the common law of England that it was west European in its principles, and so better fitted for proceedings in which foreigners were involved; that it could take evidence outside the realm, out of which the insular courts could not stray; and that the Admiral's marshal could arrest a ship till the case was settled and the damages paid. But it had the weakness, or humanity, of requiring direct and oral evidence of criminality; pirates, for example, were seldom hanged by it, because they had disposed of all hostile witnesses. Statutes of Thomas Cromwell's time, in 1535 and 1536, compelled the Admiralty court to comply with English common law in all criminal cases; by a further delegation of jurisdiction, criminal work was passed to a commission of common-law judges, and the number of hangings went up to a gratifying extent.

Coke, an enthusiast for the common law and contemner of the civil, paralysed much of the Admiralty court's jurisdiction by ingenious and unworthy fictions under James I and shifted it to the ordinary courts; whence it was transferred back by Victorian legislation. The entire functions, civil or criminal, of this offshoot of the Admiral were, however, transferred in the nineteenth century, with those of other courts that used the civil law, to the Probate, Divorce and Admiralty division of the High Court and to the Prize Court, except for questions of discipline in the Navy and courts-martial, which had been passed down under the Commonwealth to naval commanders.

To make admirals of military men was sensible as long as sea battles were fought by grappling and boarding and won or lost by arrow, sword and spear of yeomen, as on land. The growth of cannon

altered both fighting ships and fighting men. The change at the last
was sudden. The victory of Lepanto was won in the old style by the
Spaniards in the Mediterranean in 1571; in 1588 the invincible
Armada was defeated by the new style of manœuvre and gunfire.
The office of Admiral continued to be filled as before. Charles
Howard, Earl of Effingham, in supreme command against the Armada,
had been Lord Chamberlain, like his father, an earlier Admiral, and
so continued for thirty years more. He was followed by the courtier,
Buckingham. On Buckingham's murder in 1628, Charles I did not
appoint an individual as successor, but created a board of commissioners to see to the duties of the office. But executive command of
ships in action was hardly suitable for a committee, and commanders-
in-chief had to be found outside the board, else the Bishop of London,
as a First Lord, might, like some mediæval prelate, have had to lead
the fleet into battle. The experiment, of which the purpose was merely
to set free the fees and profits of the Admiralty Court for the comfort
and succour of the Duke's widow, was not final. James, Duke of
York, afterwards James II, was appointed Lord High Admiral at the
Restoration, and in the active discharge of his command narrowly
escaped death in a major naval action.

The Admiral had long before been relieved of material cares by a
new department, and took no part in the building of ships for the King.
When Henry V required ampler transports of 400 to 500 tons' burthen
for his invasion of France, William Soper, draper and shipowner of
Southampton and Keeper and Governor of the King's Ships from 1414
to 1442 at, ultimately, £40 a year, oversaw construction and undertook
management after completion. Individual ships were built by clerks
of ships, of whom Richard Bird at 12d. a day built the unseaworthy
Grace à Dieu of 1,400 tons, the biggest English ship for 100 years. The
Statute of Labourers was set aside and a carpenter got up to 8d., a
labourer up to 4d. a day. Actual costs, artificers' wages and their food
and outlays on materials were paid by the Household; timber was
drawn from the Royal forests, supplemented by gifts from abbey
woods. Such was the usual arrangement for adaptation to war of a
merchantman or for new construction; a merchant in the coastwise
or overseas trade was appointed Keeper of King's Ships either for
a single vessel or for a port, and either for one occasion or for a period
of years.

What was not sold of Henry V's fleet, such as it was, rotted away under Henry VI for lack of funds; though a grant of £11,000 extorted from the Commons in a desperate crisis of 1443 was enough to equip twenty-eight ships and keep them at sea for fourteen months. Edward IV left a Royal Navy of four ships. But now the coming of great guns began to separate the design of men-of-war from mere merchantmen. Henry VII, who disputes with Henry VIII the name of " father of the Navy," added six large vessels of his own building—mainly used by him for commerce—of which two were 1,000-tonners, and his special pride. These too were built not under contract but by direct labour, under the supervision of Sir Reginald Bray, in part charge of the King's finances, and of Sir Richard Guildford, Master of the Ordnance, a famed civil engineer. This King built also at Portsmouth in 1495 the first dry dock in England for his Navy.

Henry VIII, by the time he died, had increased the fleet to fifty-three vessels, small and large, in all only 11,268 tons, though the biggest, the *Grace à Dieu*, launched in 1513, rivalled its predecessor of that name. He established further dockyards at Woolwich and at Deptford between 1509 and 1512, and in 1540 he enlarged Portsmouth on the dry-dock site. Chatham followed in 1550 and Sheerness under Elizabeth I; Plymouth dockyard not till 1698. Rosyth was started in 1903. Each dockyard had its permanent, but not necessarily full-time civilian officials—a superintendent, a master shipwright, a master carpenter, a master mast-maker, masters of other trades, a clerk of the cheque and other clerks. The heads of the various trades each hired what workmen he required at the King's cost, or impressed them even up to the middle eighteenth century—though fantastic overtime payment without additional labour was then customary to bring traditional dockyard pay up to current private earnings.

Henry VIII created the Navy Board to deal, under the Lord Admiral, or his vicegerent the Lieutenant of the Admiralty of England, with the proliferation of docks and ships, by adding to the clerk of the ships in 1514 a keeper of storehouses, who was soon converted into a financial officer and treasurer; a comptroller in 1524, as a check on the treasurer; and a surveyor and rigger in 1544. These four " principal officers " are first recorded to have met in 1545 as the Board which was destined to administer the Navy for almost three centuries. The treasurer estimated the cost of programmes, extracted funds from the Palace treasurers or Lord Treasurer, disbursed and accounted for them, and came to be regarded as the head of the board. The comptroller was in charge of victuals and materials and had a roving commission to detect waste or fraud; the surveyor was responsible for design and construction of ships; the clerk of the ships, or of the records, or—his final title—of the acts, was the secretary. The treasurer got £66 13s. 4d. a year plus 6s. 8d. for each day he worked and a commission of 1¼ per cent on all money that passed through his hands; the comptroller and the surveyor each got £50 a year plus 4s. a day duty pay; the clerk of the acts £33 6s. 8d. plus 3s. 4d. duty pay. The first three were each allowed 16d. a day for the hire of two clerks each; the comptroller had also under him a clerk of stores at £26 13s. 4d. plus 2s. 6d. duty pay, and by 1560 a surveyor of victualling; the clerk of the acts did his own writing. All had allowances ranging from £10 to £6 a year for boat hire.

Guns and powder were obtained from the master of the ordnance. The Board included for a time a master of the ordnance of its own for the ships, better paid and clerked than the treasurer, to prevent abuse and waste; this post was first absorbed by the comptroller and then dropped, after which the Navy continued to depend on the Ordnance for its equipment.

The Tudor principal officers were almost all selected from men who had proved themselves at sea, often in command of Royal ships; the higher-paid posts were frequently filled by promotion from the lower; the unpromoted remained till death. Almost all members of the Board, even some of the clerks of the acts, continued to go to sea in command of Royal ships or squadrons. The first comptroller, Sir Thomas Spert, was also the first Master of Trinity House. Many of them were made grooms or ushers of the King's Chamber, and above the rank of clerk of the acts knighthoods were usually conferred. Only once did a clerk, Peter Buch (1600–25), receive the accolade.

Appointments in the dockyards and on the Board tended to run in families. The Petts were the prevailing clan in the dockyards round the Thames. They had been architects of ships for a hundred years when Peter Pett was appointed, some time before 1550, master shipwright of Deptford, where he built most of the naval vessels. He was succeeded in the post by his two sons, Joseph and Phineas, in turn. Phineas moved to Woolwich as master shipwright in 1607; in 1630 he was put on the Navy Board with special responsibility for the dockyard there and at Deptford, where he was succeeded by his son Christopher. A great designer, Phineas launched the first three-decker in 1637.

Christopher remained master shipwright of Deptford till he died at what must have been a very advanced age in 1688. Another Peter Pett—he of Pepy's diary, a cousin of Phineas—was master shipwright of Chatham yard during the civil wars, and was advanced to its commissioner or superintendent in 1648 after their conclusion. His services to the Commonwealth did not prevent his being raised to the Navy Board, with continued responsibility for Chatham, at the Restoration. Many others of the family were employed in the dockyards round the Thames then and later, and Petts continued in this service till 1800.

At the Navy Board, the second man to be treasurer was William Gonson, who after twenty years of the duty committed suicide in 1544. His son Benjamin, a clergyman, was then clerk of the ships, in 1546 surveyor, and in 1549 treasurer in his father's place. His death in 1577 freed the post for his daughter's husband, John, afterwards Sir John, Hawkins, a privateering, slave-trading, fighting merchant, son and brother of like forcible sea-captains, and one whose enterprises suffered bitterly from the Spaniards at San Juan de Ulua beyond the Atlantic.

The new treasurer laid it against the honesty of his colleagues, perhaps even before his appointment, that the fleet by their contrivances cost half as much again as it should, and clinched the point by twice contracting to do all the maintenance, repair and replacement for a fixed annual payment. The contracts covered the nine years preceding the Armada; under the second, £5,700 a year covered all repair of ships and docks, including 'extraordinary' or heavy repairs, labour and material alike, and the payment of harbour and gunner staff. It was a saving of about a third. Nevertheless, he was accused of feathering his nest by collusive sub-contracts with relatives and shipwrights, and Burleigh at least considered issuing a ukase against the conduct by principal officers of private shipbuilding or of merchandising of commodities in which they dealt officially.

A larger matter was that Hawkins, knowing the Atlantic better than the narrow duty of a treasurer, forced through a revolution in ship design. The towering castles on bow and stern were discarded; the ships, relieved of the over-burden, were made longer in proportion to their beam, faster, easier to manœuvre and more sea-worthy; some ships were even cut in two and lengthened by the insertion of a middle section; finally, the vessels were equipped with new inventions, from chain-pumps to improved boarding-nets. A little later, since ships were meant to fight at a distance, he cut down the personnel and raised the pay by a third. Thus, with fewer mouths to feed, more space and sounder vessels, they were enabled to keep at sea for much longer, even up to six months; the continuous blockade was in sight. These changes were bitterly fought by his colleagues—experienced men, but with knowledge mainly of home waters—but Hawkins had served his country well. Though two-thirds of the fleet that opposed the Armada were still private vessels withdrawn for the emergency from trade, his low, fast warships were the spearhead that beat the Spaniard.

When two deaths occurred on the Board next year, Hawkins was made comptroller as well as treasurer, and another Benjamin Gonson, son of the old treasurer, became clerk of the ships. Like others of the Board and their subordinates, Hawkins commanded as rear-admiral one squadron against the Armada; in 1590 he commanded an expedition against Spain; in 1595, being then sixty-three, he sailed in joint charge with Drake on one against the West Indies and died at sea.

The Navy Board was replaced during the Commonwealth by more numerous commissioners; three extra commissioners were added to the four principal officers on its reconstitution at the Restoration. A nice balance was kept between the claims of loyalty and of usefulness in the new Board, whose names are made so familiar by the accident of a diary. The pre-war comptroller, Sir George Carteret, came back as treasurer; the pre-war surveyor, Sir William Batten, though he had served the republicans till 1648, resumed his post; Captain Robert Slingsby, a naval man who had been secretary to the Duke of York, who was made Lord High Admiral, became comptroller; a Cavalier officer, Lord Berkeley of Stratton, was one of the additional commissioners. But the other two were Peter Pett, who had served the Commonwealth and the Protector at Chatham, and Sir William Penn, father of the founder of Pennsylvania, who had been one of their generals-at-sea, the equivalent of rear- or vice-admiral. The pre-war clerk of the acts, Thomas Barlow, might have been reinstated, but he was bought off for £100 a year by Samuel Pepys, then a substitute clerk at the Exchequer.

Pepys, on coming down from Cambridge, had been employed about February 1656 as a private factotum by Edward Montagu, Earl of Sandwich, one of the Commonwealth commissioners of the Admiralty, and his cousin once removed. Two years later he added an engagement by Sir George Downing to do his work as a teller at the Exchequer for £50 a year, and by Sir George's favour a third concurrent job in January 1660 as a clerk of the Council. He was twenty-seven when Sandwich got him made Clerk of the acts at the new salary of £350 plus a house. A month later Sandwich, having acquired a clerkship of the Privy Seal, appointed Pepys as his substitute. Pepys called in Henry Moore to assist. Even deputies only attended at the Privy Seal in rotation for one month in four. They, like their principals, were unsalaried; Pepys collected in his first month (August) £532 in fees —£400 for Sandwich, £107 for himself and £25 for Moore. The fees were inflated at that time by the reversal of Commonwealth grants, and when they fell Pepys gave up his deputyship. He acquired the treasurership of Tangier in March 1665 by a promise to Povy, the holder, of half the profits, a promise which was broken. That year he reorganised the arrangements for victualling the Navy and created, in October 1665, the Board of Victualling Commissioners, with the top post of surveyor-general and £300 a year for himself.

Without meagre living, Pepys put by £200 a year in his first years at the Board and £2,000 a year from 1664, when he had found his feet, to mid-1666, so profitable were his side-lines from fees and dubious gifts for favours done. One case among many: a business firm offered him £150 a year if the contract for victualling the Tangier was awarded to them at 3s. 1½d. a head, and £300 a year if the price was 3s. 2d. They got the contract at the larger figure. How soon afterwards a fastidious probity was acquired by the Civil Service cannot be declared, but some groups would have recoiled from Pepys' ways in 1700, and by 1800 most would have thought him impossible.

Pepys, its junior member, dominated the Navy Board by this time. He was assiduous in seeing things for himself and in the perusal of records; he was lucid and pertinent in presentation of facts; and his ways had won the confidence of the Admiral and the King. How completely care and maintenance of the Fleet fell to the Board was shown by the reaction to its annihilation, while laid up in the Medway, by the Dutch in June 1666; the blame for the disaster was fastened on Peter Pett, who was discharged in September. "His name alone seems fit to answer all." But it was Pepys who was chosen to defend the Board in the committee rooms and at the bar of the House of Commons.

The Duke of York was forced out in 1673, and the Admiralty was placed under a commission to which Pepys was transferred as its secretary at £500 a year. He brought over Thomas Hayter of his old office to strengthen the clerks and appointed his brother John as another. Six months later Pepys got himself a seat in the Commons, an honour and useful, but not essential, to his place. What was more important, he brought back with him to the Admiralty active supervision of the Navy Board. Periodic inspections of dockyards were instituted; the Admiralty at need communicated direct with subordinates at the yards. Under Pepys' stimulus and directions, and by his persuasiveness in getting funds, the Fleet had been rebuilt by 1679. Parliamentary attack then caused his dismissal. Hayter was appointed secretary in his stead, but soon found a job in Chelsea Hospital and was replaced by John Brisbane.

Political stress had relaxed enough to enable the commissioners of Admiralty to be disbanded in 1684. The Duke of York returned to the role but not the title of Admiral. The King kept much of the control in his own hands. Pepys was recalled to be secretary at a salary quadrupled to £2,000. The effective Fleet was found to have fallen to a quarter of its strength in the interval of five years, although 1,500 hands hung about in the dockyards. It took the restored secretary exactly two years of enquiry and manœuvring to dislodge three out of the four principal officers and effect their replacement by a new and more vigorous Navy Board. The superseded men were secured their salaries under a pretence of work. The King signed a warrant for the pay of the new Board on 17th March, 1686; Pepys assembled and instructed them on the 20th; but at this stage the chief clerk in the Secretary of State's department imposed an embargo on all the proceedings, on the ground that the documents should have been presented through his master for the Royal signature. A month elapsed in overcoming the constitutional difficulty, which disappeared when the Admiralty paid the Secretary of State's usual fees; the Great Seal enabled the Board to come into existence on 17th April.

The Navy was repaired and rebuilt in the space of two years; the new Board was dissolved on 12th October, 1688. The displaced officers resumed their seats; the new were also kept on as superintendents of the three dockyards at Chatham, Deptford and Portsmouth or as supernumeraries, while two admirals on the active list were added to the Board as comptrollers of victualling and of storekeeping.

The Board was indeed closely linked by its personnel not only with the shipyards but with the Navy.

Pepys resigned in February 1689, as soon as the Government of William and Mary was well established, and was succeeded as secretary by Phineas Bowles, one-time storekeeper at Tangier and latterly private secretary to Admiral Lord Dartmouth. The diminished importance of the post was shown by the reduction of its pay to £500.

Pepys was the greatest administrator of his century. Not only was the Navy twice rebuilt and the Navy Board reorganised, but paper became a controlling force; standing orders were substituted for ad hoc decisions; cadres of men, guns and stores of every description were prescribed for each class of vessel, from guardship to first-rate man-of-war; and written rules governed everything from the keeping of watch and use of flags to the transport of bullion. Ships on cruise were required to report at every point of call and, on their return to England, send their journals, properly kept, to the Admiralty for scrutiny. The recruitment of officers was strongly influenced by the introduction of a low age limit, and a school was started for their training; Pepys laid the foundations for the corps of naval officers of the next century. Honours were showered on the lecherous little man. He was twice Master of Trinity House, Master of the Clothworkers' Company, Baron of the Cinque Ports, a Deputy Lieutenant, President of the Royal Society.

Nearly the whole administration of the Navy returned once more to the Navy Board throughout the eighteenth century. As the Navy became professional, the Board grew less nautical. Treasurers, always laymen, seldom even attended meetings of the Board after the beginning of the century; before its end their office was regarded as a sinecure and was used to reward some such politician as the unpaid President of the Board of Trade. Surveyors were always selected from master shipwrights at the dockyards; none after Admiral Sir William Batten (1638–48 and 1660–7) had sea-going experience. Clerks of the acts after Pepys were usually promoted from clerks in the Navy Office or the dockyards. The comptroller alone was invariably a naval officer, often a distinguished one. The personnel is believed on the whole to have deteriorated. Once in, they stayed there into senility. One surveyor, not an isolated example, Jacob Acworth, who entered Government service in 1682, retired in 1755; his work was done in his later years by proxy. Yet, with all their defects, there were always enough men of quality among them to keep the Fleet more or less fit for battle in time of war. But advances in design depended on the capture of French ships, except for Sir Robert Sepping's inventions about 1805, and were not systematic till the creation of the School of Naval Architecture in 1810, which in the end evolved the civilian Corps of Naval Constructors.

The Board, almost independent of the Admiralty, lost control in turn of the inferior Boards which were created for particular services. Naval business towards the end of the eighteenth century, when the Navy Board had itself swelled to eighty-four clerks, was dispersed over thirteen offices, remote from each other, of which the several staffs went their self-contained ways with no liaison and as few contacts as might be. These scattered and unworkable bodies were amalgamated early in the nineteenth century, and only two formations besides the Admiralty remained in 1832—the Navy Board, and the Commissioners for Victualling the Navy, who had quite recently absorbed the commissioners for transport and those created in 1653 for the care of the sick and wounded.

The original headquarters of the Board were in Seething Lane and Crutched Friars, near the Tower and river; the members had travelled thence, at first weekly, in Pepys' time monthly, afterwards more rarely, to report at the Admiralty and receive directions. In 1781 it moved to Somerset House.

In the days of the Lord High Admiral, his secretary and the secretary's two or three clerks were accommodated in the Admiral's own house. Pepys, as secretary, was able to move the entire office and staff into the house which he hired at the public expense for his own residence. A new and capacious office was built on the site of Wallingford House for the residence of the First Lord, the Board's meetings, and the accommodation of the clerks, and was occupied in June 1695. It was pulled down as early as 1726, and was replaced by a larger edifice, which, immensely extended, is part of the present building. The staff remained small; at the end of the Napoleonic wars the Admiralty employed only fifty-five clerks, whom ten years of peace reduced to twenty-two.

James II was the last effective Lord High Admiral. Lord Pembroke and Prince George of Denmark, Queen Anne's husband, were but puppet holders of the title, and the appointment of the Duke of Clarence, before he became William IV, for eighteen months in 1827–8 was a

I

compliment which all were relieved that he took as idle. Apart from him, the high office remained in solution as a commission or board from 1709 onwards. Eighteenth-century Boards of Admiralty became political bodies, liable to change with governments; they consisted mainly of civilians, whose appointment turned on their connection with leading politicians, but often included the leading admiral of the day, either as chief naval adviser or as First Lord. Anson, Hawke, Keppel, Howe and St. Vincent all occupied that chair. In the nineteenth century the First Lord, on the contrary, was invariably a politician of the first rank; naval lords were restored, and officers, having ceased to be politicians, were appointed for fixed terms of years from 1886.

The Admiralty decided policy and the size of the Navy, in the Cabinet, if need be; dealt with political and parliamentary issues, collected intelligence and directed the movements and operations of the Fleet. From it emanated the innumerable general regulations entailed over the years by the task of administering a large body of men. The training, posting and promotion of commissioned officers were the concern of the Board of Admiralty, but they were in the main selected by the generation previously commissioned. Each captain or admiral was entitled to carry on board a large retinue, up to fifty, of his own choosing, nominally his servants, actually part of the ship's company; and it was in this that the budding officer secured inclusion. Promotion depended partly on captains, who could up to a point choose their own subordinates, partly on Admiralty regulations on qualifications, and largely on the increase or decrease in the number of ships in commission. Once the rank of captain was reached, promotion was in theory by strict seniority. The Admiralty entered the picture at the end of the seventeenth century by securing some direct entry, and very slowly reducing the size of retinues. The " Admiralty letter boys," however, were probably only one in ten till the end of the eighteenth century, and it was 1914 before the Civil Service system of open competitive entry was fully adopted.

The Board also organised the various training-schools. In the long run it controlled promotion; it invented some indirect devices for this, rather than alter the rules. A worthy commander could only be promoted to a vacant captaincy; accordingly he was formally appointed to a newly commissioned ship and moved back next day to his own, retaining the step in rank. The method of advancing a junior captain to flag rank was to clear the list by appointing his seniors to be admirals but omitting to specify the squadron; this promotion, in reality retirement, was obviously not to the known red, blue or white squadrons; the non-existent squadron was accordingly dubbed the yellow.

As secretary after Pepys's successor, Josiah Burchett and Philip Stevens almost covered between them the eighteenth century. Burchett, a man of humble origin, was in his teens Pepys's personal servant and clerk till he was summarily dismissed; he found further employment in the Navy and then as private secretary to Admiral Lord Russell. In 1695 he was made joint secretary and in 1698 sole secretary to the Admiralty, and such he remained till 1742. Stevens, who had many relatives in the Navy, entered the Victualling Office as a youth, was moved to the Admiralty in 1744 to be Anson's private secretary, promoted presently to assistant secretary and in 1763 to permanent secretary. He resigned, now Sir Philip Stevens, Bart., F.R.S., in 1795, and was placed on the Board as a Lord Commissioner till 1806, when he retired with a pension of £1,500.

Burchett was M.P. for Sandwich, an Admiralty borough, for eighteen out of his forty-four years as secretary. Stevens sat for the same place after his first three years as secretary; there was not a family in Sandwich which had not to thank him for employment in the naval or civilian service. These two owed their places in the Commons to their positions in the Civil Service. The line between the continuous and the political appointment was settled a little later.

Lord St. Vincent, the great admiral, on becoming First Lord of the department in 1801, transferred his personal secretary, Tucker, from the Navy Board to be second secretary of the Admiralty. On that government's fall in 1804, Melville, the new First Lord, turned Tucker out, as a strong partisan of his opponents, without a day's notice, and appointed his own protégé, (Sir) John Barrow, who had done good administrative service in the Cape. The party tide turned; the next First Lord as promptly discharged Barrow in 1806 with profuse apologies and, after consideration, a pension of £1,000 a year. Barrow agreed that his discharge was reasonable and " almost imperative." On the next change of party in 1807, Tucker was again discharged and Barrow was reinstated to survive all further play of party until his resignation in 1845. But a Whig minister was agreeably surprised that Barrow was willing to continue under him. The first secretary, William Marsden, F.R.S., a famous orientalist, who had been induced to enter Admiralty service in 1795, resigned at the 1807 change of government with a pension of £1,500. The Cabinet decided that first secretaries must in future have seats in the Commons. Barrow presently refused advancement at this price, although the pay of first secretary had advanced to £3,200 plus a house, and the post was conferred on John Wilson Croker. He became an almost permanent officer and held that position from 1809 to 1830, refusing all offers of higher posts. Most famous for his forthright criticism of Keats, for he remained a writer, Croker greatly improved the organisation of the Admiralty; " all that is best and most businesslike in that department " was held to be his doing. The two secretaries dovetailed their holidays, in order that one should always be present to open the letters; both attended the Board's meetings.

The Navy Board, the Victualling Commissioners and the Admiralty were amalgamated in 1832, though the departments were not brought into physical proximity till 1869. A further reconstitution and closer union in 1886 produced the present arrangements. The First Lord, the Civil Lord, who is responsible for maintenance of buildings, and the original secretary, who is now the parliamentary and financial secretary, are members of the Government and change with it. The Navy is represented by naval officers on the active list who are appointed from different branches to be Sea Lords for set terms of years. The Board of Admiralty is completed by its secretary, the former second secretary, who is the head of and responsible for the large civilian staff.

11

THE WAR OFFICE

U P to the Civil War, English armies consisted of the militia, mustered from Edward VI's time by the new lords lieutenant and previously by the sheriffs, war bands of great nobles which were put down after the Wars of the Roses, and bands of ill-disciplined volunteers raised for an occasional foray abroad and at once disbanded. The one regular duty was the production and preservation of heavy equipment—the great machines for battering fortresses; pontoons for bridging of rivers; cannon, when these came in, both for ship and shore; and reserves of minor weapons, such as bows and lance-heads. This need produced a civilian department. A Master and a Clerk of the Ordnance, Nicholas Merbury and John Louth, were appointed in 1414 by Henry V for his invasion of France. Continuity begins with Edward IV, who appointed soon after his accession a Master of the Ordnance, John Wood, at 2s. a day for life, and a Clerk of the Ordnance, Thomas Bowes. The Tower of London was their main arsenal, and appointments as Warden and Deputy Warden of the Mint within its walls helped to swell their remuneration. Wood dying in 1485, the new King, Henry VII, gave the post on the same terms to Sir Richard Guildford, who had fought beside him at Bosworth, with a further 1s. a day for charge of the armoury, besides a number of other high posts in the Exchequer and in the Palace. Guildford was an engineer whose name is preserved by the Guildford level in Kent, which he recovered from the sea. A corporate Board was established under the master in 1518 and steadily expanded to five principal officers and many subordinates, who looked after Navy as well as Army supplies.

Masters became professional military men, but the Ordnance remained outside the later Army till the mid nineteenth century. Its master-general was not subordinate to the Commander-in-chief in peace or war, and he took his place in the Cabinet till 1828 as an independent minister. The men who operated his guns and moved the Army's impedimenta, growing into the Royal Artillery and Royal

Engineers, remained dissociated from the infantry and cavalry commands. Their corps even had separate finance and medical branches. A civilian flavour clung to the Ordnance. Civilian supplementaries were freely hired during a campaign. Erection and maintenance of fortifications and of barracks when public opinion at last permitted them fell automatically to the Master of the Ordnance, and as soon as Army postal services were inaugurated, the men needed were nominally enlisted as Royal Engineers.

The Royal Engineers were forerunners of the Ministry of Transport in their construction of the Highland road system. The rough mapping of England was begun for the Surveyor of Wards and Liveries by Christopher Saxton in the reign of Elizabeth I. It was resumed and completed scientifically by the engineers of the Ordnance, who undertook this work in the Highlands in 1747 after Culloden. A Post Office boy, William Ray, was put in charge of the work as an assistant quartermaster-general, and, in the intervals of campaigns, continued till his death in 1790, a major-general and a Fellow of the Royal Society, to organise its development over the entire island. Several artillery officers were then assigned to the Ordnance Survey and the general one-inch map was begun. The mapping business branched out, in 1832, into the Geological Survey, which passed through the departments of Woods and Works (1845) and Science and Art (1853) into that of Scientific and Industrial Research (1919).

The Survey's headquarters were in the Tower of London till the great fire of 1841 drove them out to Southampton. The service remained under the Master-general of the Ordnance and after him under the Secretary of State for War until 1870. It was transferred to the Office of Works in that year. Thence it was removed to the charge of the Board of Agriculture in 1903, as that new department got into its stride. Under these changing chiefs, the Ordnance Survey has continued to be officered and manned by Royal Engineers. To confuse civil and military service further, the Royal Engineers have been called on to fill all sorts of miscellaneous appointments. Colonial governors, consuls-general, a commissioner of police, inspectors of railways and of scientific education, directors of works and of prisons were among the posts filled by members of the corps in 1869.

Two fossils also are a century older than the Regular Army. Henry VII retained as a bodyguard, like any feudal lord of the earlier time, a body of some fifty archers from his invading force—the Yeomen of the

Guard. He formed later another guard of gentlemen which disappeared momentarily under its first name of the King's Spears but was
revived by Henry VIII as the Gentlemen Pensioners. Under Mary,
the first rose to 440 strong, the latter to about seventy-five gentlemen
with three servants each—300 in all. The pensioners constituted for
quite a time a reserve of officers from which commanders were drawn
for operations at sea as well as on land; then it too sank or rose to a
ceremonial body about the Court.

The standing Army dates from the preservation at the Restoration
of certain regiments from disbandment. Its civil organisation is
slightly older. In September 1642, immediately before the outbreak
of hostilities, Charles I assigned Sir Edward Walker of the Earl
Marshal's office, afterwards Garter King of Arms and a secretary of the
Council, to be his Secretary at War and the channel for his military
measures. The Commonwealth appointed to a like post in its later
years (1657) Sir Edward Nicholas, who had been one of the King's
principal Secretaries of State before the war. When Charles II came
back in 1660, he restored Nicholas to be Secretary of State again, and
bestowed his post of Secretary at War, which always remained quite
distinct in spite of the similarity of titles, on Sir William Clark, who
for the last six years of the Commonwealth had been military secretary
to General Monk, the Commander-in-Chief. Naval, military, and
civil positions were still intermingled. Clark was killed at sea in the
great naval battle of 1666; his clerk, Matthew Locke, was promoted in
his stead.

A Royal warrant ten years later, on 7th September, 1676, emphasised
that all documents that would have issued from Monk as Commander-
in-Chief, and which would for the present issue from the King, must
pass through Locke's hands for his countersignature. Locke sold the
post in 1683 to William Blaythwayte, who had started at nineteen or
twenty as a diplomatic secretary at four successive capitals, and on his
return to England in 1676 was appointed a clerk of the Council and
secretary of the Board of Trade. Besides retaining that post, he
managed almost the whole domestic business of the Army till 1704.
He was accommodated with his tiny staff in the old Horseguards,
which had been built just twenty years before to accommodate the
horse- and part of the foot-guards. It was demolished in 1750 and
replaced by the present building of very similar appearance.

Blaythwayte was frequently taken abroad by William III and his duties at home were performed by a substitute. The importance of the secretariat was vastly enhanced under Anne by the continual absences of Marlborough at the wars, and was still further advanced by the Kings themselves being the Commanders-in-Chief, except in special seasons of stress, from 1670 to 1793. The office was charged with some aspects only of the administration of the horse and foot; it was responsible for estimating costs and procuring finance, for civil contracts, for directing the movements at home and the quartering of troops, for fixing rates of pay and allowances of officers or men and for the organisation of home defence. It dealt with grievances of civilians against the troops, and in internal management even such a question as the grant of special leave to an officer was reserved to it, as indeed in Pepys's time it was reserved for naval officers to the secretary to the Admiralty.

All this work had descended in practice as early as the first years of George I on to the head of the Secretary at War's subordinate staff. At that time this head was one Theophilus Blyke, who carried enough influence for his son to be made both deputy auditor of the imprests in the Exchequer and clerk of the journals of the House of Lords. Blyke had only eight clerks under him in 1717. The Army at home was, of course, very small.

The post of Secretary at War was a political office from 1704 onwards, but the holders, though they sat and spoke in the Commons, repudiated any responsibility for decisions or for their defence till near the end of the century, on the ground that they were not " ministers."

The office, however, was excluded from large parts of the military field besides the Ordnance. The Southern or Home Secretary handled all policy in the employment of troops at home or abroad, and their movements overseas. He entirely controlled the militia, and his office handled the grant of officers' commissions and kept the prescribed fees, which were on more than double the Navy scale. The Treasury developed a Commissariat branch to take control of Army victualling and fuel. A board of generals with a separate office took over the management of the troops' clothing. There were also independent bodies to look after the sick and wounded and the pensioners. The richest of all the detached and independent functions was the transmission of funds. One, later two, paymasters of the forces, housed at the north of the Horseguards, received from the Treasury well in advance the lump-sum issues for Army supplies and pay of troops.

Six, or it might be twelve months later, they settled with contractors and sent sums for the soldiers' pay in arrear to the agents of the different regiments. The paymasters were not only paid substantial salaries; they were also entitled to a commission of ¼ per cent on all sums remitted, which could be very large when foreign troops or the Army were employed abroad. They were also entitled to employ the big balances in their hands to the best advantage. Why should they, like the slothful servant, bury the money in the earth, or why should they, as one asked, leave it with a banker to earn him, rather than themselves, interest? The paymaster's income could run to £27,000 a year during an eighteenth-century war. The posts went, of course, to rising or risen politicians, and, as they had not established a tradition of life tenure, changed hands on a change of Government. All the work was left to their office clerks. The attack on political largesse which began in 1782 crushed the paymasters and transferred their work to the Secretary at War, who at length found himself answerable to the House of Commons.

The position of Commander-in-Chief was revived in 1793 in consequence of the war with revolutionary France. The Secretary at War, however, would not abate his independence, and co-operated so poorly that an appeal body of Cabinet ministers had to be set up to keep the domestic peace. A new Secretary of State was created for the Army in 1794, but little came of him in this field. In spite of the two appointments, the head of the Secretary at War's office, or Deputy Secretary, so increased in importance that his pay was raised from £320 to £2,000 in 1798 and £2,500 in 1806.

Army work was still split up between six major bodies when the Crimean War broke out. The Home Secretary controlled numbers and operations; the Commander-in-Chief handled promotions and discipline of horse and foot; the Ordnance Board all arms and stores, barracks and fortifications, and pay and discipline of artillery and engineers; the Treasury Commissariat dealt with provisions and fuel, and the Board of General Officers with clothes. There was no controlling body, and each went its own way and made as few grudging contacts with the others as possible.

In spite of this, and of elderly generals, discordant allies and a mammoth foe, the war was won. Army management in London was quickly concentrated. A Secretary of State for War was again appointed within three months, in June 1854. In December he had taken over the vital Commissariat. In the following February the Secretary *at* War was absorbed by the simple expedient of appointing Lord Panmure to both offices. In March the militia were taken over from the Home Office. The Clothing Board was absorbed, and medical services, which had been purely regimental, were centralised. The Board of Ordnance was abolished; its military functions went to the Commander-in-Chief and its civil functions to the new Secretary of State.

Ordnance headquarters had been moved from the Tower, to make more room for forces swollen by war, and settled in Pall Mall in 1806. The new civilian side—the War Office, as it was called from 1857— took over that house, acquired the neighbouring dwellings, knocked openings at odd levels in the party walls, and occupied the block, 80 to 91 Pall Mall. The military side concentrated in the Horseguards under the Commander-in-Chief, the Duke of Cambridge. The Duke, being the Queen's cousin, and his men naturally opposed the politicians who had thus diminished the prerogative, and a deal of testiness developed. Communications between the two sides were confined to writing; they faced each other with levelled quills for a dozen years. An Act of 1870 then formally put the Duke under the Secretary of State, who forthwith compelled him to move with his staff into forced fraternisation in a joint establishment in Pall Mall. 30,000 letters a year, 100 each working day, ceased to be written.

The first Civil Service head of the new War Office was found from the Secretary at War's old staff. Sir Benjamin Hawes was a man of very varied interests; he had an early ascent of Mont Blanc to his credit, as well as such minor social achievements as the Sunday opening of the British Museum. After fourteen years in the House of Commons, he was appointed Permanent Secretary of the Colonial Office in 1846, and was transferred thence five years later to the like position of Deputy Secretary at War; so far he had retained his seat as an M.P., but he resigned it next year (1852) and became the complete Civil Servant. In 1857 his title was changed to Permanent Undersecretary of State to the War Office.

The difficulty of remodelling ancient ways is shown by the labour spent on the shape of Army administration. 567 commissions and committees poked the problem about in the seventy years between 1833, when the lack of contact and the multiplication of correspondence between its units already provoked remark, and 1904. The solitary

Secretary-of-State conception was abandoned in that year. The Board of Admiralty was taken as a model; an Army Council was set up which consisted of a Secretary of State as head, two other politicians, four military members and the Permanent Secretary of the War Office. The new unit received a new home; the War Office moved from Pall Mall in December 1906 to the great building in Whitehall which had been slowly growing for it since 1899.

Immense as this building was, and immensely as the War Office had already swelled since Blaythwayte's eight clerks, it proved all too small. At the time of Cardwell's reforms, in 1873, the War Office comprised eighty-two Army officers and 673 clerks; immediately before the war of 1914 it held 550 uniformed personnel, some serving, some retired from the forces, while the number of civilians had dropped a little to 580. Expansion passed manageable limits during the war; after the painful concentration of services sixty years before, dispersal among new-born departments began again. The Ministry of Munitions was budded off in 1915, the Ministry of Pensions in 1916, the Ministry of National Service and the Air Board in 1917. Even so, the staff at the War Office at the armistice numbered 22,000, who for lack of room were scattered over fifty-nine buildings.

The Air Board became in 1918 the Air Council, again modelled on the Board of Admiralty, and again weaving into co-operation the politician, the professional service officer and the professional Civil Servant.

In all three cases peace brought contraction and concentration; in all three a fresh war forced new expansion and the transfer of large services to new departments.

12

THE POST OFFICE

Iɴ the old days, when middle-class folk depended for the conveyance of their letters upon the chance of a traveller bound the right way, Crown departments, and especially the Palace, had couriers on their staff to carry despatches. King's home-service and foreign-service messengers continued from mere habit to be borne on the strength of the King's Chamber until 1824, long after the independence of the Home and Foreign Offices whom they served. The silver greyhound of the latter seems to have been adopted as an emblem of speed under Anne or George I. Burleigh's sign for hurry was the picture of a gallows.

When speed was paramount, as when Richard III awaited news of Henry VII's landing, relays of men and horses were spaced out beforehand. A permanent service on these lines was laid down about 1516 under Henry VIII. Sir Brian Tuke, one of the four clerks of the Signet, afterwards also secretary to Wolsey, French secretary to the King, clerk of the Parliaments and treasurer of the Chamber, appointed persons, mostly innkeepers, ten or fifteen miles apart on several routes, at retainers of 1s. to 1s. 4d. a day, to carry the Royal mail, night or day, by their mounted servants to the next stage. The engagements required them also to maintain three or four saddle-horses to carry to the same point, for 1d. a mile, the King's messengers or private persons with an official permit. Tuke remained Master of the Posts till his death, when he was succeeded by Sir John Mason, son of a cowherd, who was also made French secretary, and later Dean of Winchester, Master of Requests, clerk of the Parliaments and treasurer of the Chamber. Mason, dying in 1566, was followed by John Randolph, and Randolph on his death in 1590 by John Stanhope, Lord Harrington and his son Charles. This is the Harrington who was given the licence for " Harrington farthings," the first coinage of copper, which was deemed beneath the dignity of the Crown. Both Mason and Randolph were often out of the realm on diplomatic missions; probably the

Harringtons also left their postal work to deputies. Mason's pay as Master of the Posts was but 1s. a day. Five routes were regularly staffed : the Great North Road to Berwick, where it connected with the Scottish system; the Dover road, for communication with the Continent; the West road to Plymouth and Falmouth; the Bath road, prolonged to Milford Haven for Ireland; and the Holyhead road, also for Ireland. Four of these routes still take pride of place as numbers 1, 2, 4 and 5 in the Ministry of Transport's road classification. An average speed of seven miles an hour in summer was commanded; five miles an hour was hoped for, and three miles an hour was accepted.

Royal Mail carriers conveyed also private letters by the reign of Elizabeth I. Two London groups, however, the Merchant Strangers and the Merchant Adventurers, ran private and rival postal services to the Continent from at latest early in that reign. Examination of letters was so important a source of intelligence that the Queen's Government brought the nomination of the directors of these services under the Master of the Posts. James I took the foreign services from him and put in charge, in 1612, two natives of Bruges—the de Questers —as the permanent postmasters of England for foreign parts. These, in 1632 under Charles I, ceded their rights to Thomas Witherings, with a colleague, William Frizzell, who soon disappeared.

Having organised his foreign service, Witherings was also given, in 1635, the inland service, which cost the King £3,400 a year, for its conversion into a paying concern by an official instead of an unofficial charge for private letters. He provided a weekly service on each main route, and undertook that a letter to any terminus and back should take only six days; threw out branches to important towns; and charged 2d. for eighty miles, rising to 8d. to the borders of Scotland for a single sheet, and proportionately more for two or more sheets or a letter and envelope. He was granted a monopoly, though in practice this was much infringed by unlicensed undertakers. When Charles I removed Witherings on the outbreak of war, the legal position was further complicated by the King's having conceded conflicting rights to different persons. Edmond Prideaux, the Attorney-General, got round the difficulties by himself, in 1644, assuming control which he retained during the wars and the earlier Commonwealth; he paid a rent of £5,000 a year, bore all the expenses, took all the receipts and was thought to make an annual profit of £15,000, notwithstanding trespassers, of whom one offered to run a penny post throughout England.

Witherings had certainly turned the service into a profitable under-taking. The future of the Post Office was to depend on such zealous intruders.

The Office was put up to tender in 1653 and was secured by John Manley for £10,000 a year, notwithstanding that at this point the profligate concession of exemption from postal charges was made to members of the Commons and high Government officials. In the later eighteenth century franking by members had so grown that nearly half the letters in the country were said to go free; one Member made £300 a year from a single firm by lending it his services, and the privilege brought many others directorships.

The Commonwealth Secretary of State, John Thurloe, took over Manley's contract in 1655 and sublet it at a profit to himself, but retained control of the detective work. Sir Samuel Morland, one of the Clerks of the Signet, and the ingenious originator of the ear-trumpet and many other gadgets, invented for him four machines, which would respectively open a sealed letter and leave no trace, copy a seal exactly, imitate any handwriting exactly, and copy manuscript at a tremendous speed. Morland continued his labours under Charles II, and was rewarded in 1661 with £500 a year for life. His machines perished, perhaps fortunately, in a fire, and no more trace remains of them than they left on the letters subjected to them.

At the Restoration many royalist postmasters were reinstated; many more were disappointed. The Post Office continued to be farmed; it cost Colonel Henry Bishop, the inventor of date- or post-marks as a check on service delays, £21,500 a year to be made Post-master-General in 1660 for seven years. Possibly he was a mere cover for that underground man, Major John Wildman, an extreme plotter of the left under the Commonwealth, who put up at least part of the money. Bishop's contract was transferred, however, in a couple of years to a Groom of the Bedchamber, Daniel O'Neile. In his time the total London staff, including twenty-eight postmen, numbered forty-five, of whom between twenty and thirty died of the Great Plague, while the Great Fire in the following year destroyed first the foreign and then the inland letter offices. They were rehoused close together in another building in Bishopsgate, but ten years later removed to Sir Robert Viner's house in Lombard Street, where they stayed till their removal in 1829 to St. Martin's le Grand. But the two continued separate, each with its own force of letter deliverers.

When the seven years' contract expired in 1667, the farm went to Lord Arlington of the Cabal at £25,000, which was raised on the next renewal in 1674 to £43,000; drastic cutting of salaries and wages was required to produce a profit as well. With Arlington's appointment the administration definitely passed to a subordinate, at first called deputy, but soon secretary of the Post Office. Farming out the main Post Office accordingly ceased with Arlington in 1685, except that services in certain towns were leased to the postmaster on the spot (that of Hull, for example, for £50 a year) owing to the common interception of the postage on local letters. The profits from the Post Office were added to the hereditary revenue of the Crown.

Letters at that time were neither collected nor delivered by the Post Office, even in London, but private messengers earned a living by carrying local correspondence at 6*d.* a time. In 1680, William Dockwra, a City merchant, opened several hundred receiving offices from which he delivered letters for 1*d.* each at hourly intervals to offices or homes in London or the suburbs or to the central Post Office if they were addressed to other towns or abroad. As soon as this new service began to pay, the authorities called in the courts to defend the Government monopoly. Dockwra's penny post was stopped after two years' operation; four days later the Post Office opened an identical service, except that parcels were omitted. It employed fifty-seven messengers; the same number was still employed and the receipts had only risen from £5,500 to £10,000 in 1794, when an ex-postman, Edward Johnson, reorganised the service, and increased the delivery staff to 217, with further increases to come. Dockwra was awarded ten years' compensation of £500 a year after the Revolution and was later given charge again of the penny post for four years from 1696 to 1700. The London penny, later the twopenny, post kept its separate identity and delivery staff, so that with the inland and foreign departments there were three independent groups of postmen perambulating London. They were not amalgamated till 1856.

Major John Wildman completed his career by being made Postmaster-General after the Revolution. He had to be discharged in two years' time and was replaced by a pair of business men. The precedent, once set, was followed for 130 years, during which time there were always two Postmasters-General to leave management to the secretary and enjoy the fruits of office. The Marquess of Salisbury, dying in 1823, was not replaced; one Postmaster-General sufficed thereafter, and took more part in the business. Peers were invariably appointed from 1765 to 1871. Of the secretaries, two covered seventy years; Anthony Todd entered the secretariat as a clerk, and was promoted in 1762 in place of the then secretary, Henry Potts, who had reached the headship after long service in charge of the inland section; Potts superseded him again for three years from 1765; Todd then became secretary again till his death thirty years later (1768–98). He was followed by Sir Francis Freeling, who entered the service as an employee at Bristol of John Palmer, the postal reformer, in 1785, was advanced almost at once in 1787 to principal and resident surveyor, and was promoted in 1797 to assist the aged Todd as joint secretary. He was secretary for thirty-eight years till his own death in 1836. His son, Sir George Henry Freeling, then an assistant secretary at £800, did not succeed him, but was found a place on the Board of Customs.

The two Postmasters-General had in theory the sole right to appoint staff; in practice staff were selected by the secretary, surveyors, local postmasters or others. Educational tests for necessary qualifications were instituted, and if the views of the patronage secretary to the Treasury or of a member of Parliament were met on occasion there is no reason to suppose that the recruits were not up to their work.

The next great reformer to plague the Post Office after Dockwra was Ralph Allen, the Squire Allworthy of *Tom Jones*, who, starting as a boy in his grandmother's sub-office, was made postmaster at Bath in 1714. The inland post was then organised from London along six main roads, the Yarmouth road having been added in 1653, each under a headquarters clerk of the road. The main roads had a number of branches to important towns but there were few complete cross routes, though Exeter was linked to Bristol in 1696, and both to Chester about 1700. Letters in other cases had officially to travel via London, take so much more time and pay so much the more. The main routes also carried letters posted along their course which need not reach London— bye-letters, as they were called. Postal revenue on all letters that did not touch London was freely misappropriated; even the appointment in 1711 of one surveyor or inspector for each road could not overcome the ingenuity of postmasters and postboys. The country letters routed through London brought in only £900 in 1719, and the cross-road and bye-letters only £4,000, out of a total gross income of £150,000. Allen obtained in 1720 the management of all three services, on a seven years' contract, six times renewed till his death in 1764, at stated rents.

Any profit above the contract payment was his. By new rules, records, inspections and, when need be, dismissals, he stopped the leaks and went on to create at his own expense an elaborate network of cross routes throughout the country. Allen left a fortune of over six figures, but the Post Office had gained a sum of well over seven. It took over the business and kept it as a separate section, the Bye-letter Office, under Allen's nephew.

So far the mails had been carried on horseback. When Allen died, turnpike trusts were rapidly making roads fit for the flying stage-coaches which presently tempted away letters by their celerity. John Palmer of Bath, an owner of theatres, propounded the use of the new vehicles to the Post Office, to cut the mail times by half, and, by carry-ing an armed guard, to save them from the incessant robberies by high-waymen. Todd, his surveyors, and other officials, were unanimously against the change. They mistrusted the inhuman, perilous and unprecedented speeds; saw no merit in mere saving of time; and certainly no advantage which could balance the complete disruption of the intricate office schedules. Palmer in two years' time got round them to the ear of the Prime Minister, and the first coach to carry mail ran from Bristol to London on 2nd August, 1784. It did the 114 miles in seventeen hours; in spite of continued opposition by the Post Office, many routes were converted during the next twelve months. Palmer's reward was appointment as Surveyor and Comptroller-General of Mails at £1,500 a year and 2½ per cent of any increase in net revenue. He asked for complete independence of the Postmasters-General and the secretary in running the mail-coach service, which could not legally be granted; and brought on his own dismissal in 1792 by treating as obvious ciphers those worthy ministers, of whom one was anxious to show that his office was not the sinecure which it had just been acknowledged to be. A pension of £3,000 a year seemed to a later Parliament so much below his merits that a special Act twenty years later gave him an award of £50,000.

Riding posts had latterly cost 3*d*. a mile. The new coaches of special design were built and put daily in order for the Post Office by the same firm for 1½*d*. a mile till 1836, when Parliament insisted on competitive tenders. Horseflesh and drivers were obtained from contractors for suitable lengths of road for another 1½*d*. a mile, which those contractors passed back to the coach-builders. The contractors' own remunera-tion was the fares of the four to eight passengers which the coach was

K

allowed to carry. The mail-coach was exempted from the usual turnpike tolls, which would have averaged another 3*d*. a mile. Thus passengers and road-makers in effect paid the extra cost of postal speed. Nevertheless, postal charges were substantially increased in 1784. The guard, however, was a Post Office servant and was paid by it; an innovation which stopped mail robberies entirely.

Overall speeds of mail-coaches, without deducting stops for meals, exceeded ten miles an hour when the steam railway came in and outpaced them. Train conveyance of mails was much more costly, but Freeling was Palmer's pupil and more open-minded than Todd. The first post went by train in 1830. In 1838 the first travelling post office —a special carriage in which the postal staff could continue the work of sorting—was attached to a train. The last mail-coach was run in January 1846.

For carriage of mails beyond the seas, though much correspondence went privately by merchant-ship, the Post Office used six ports. The Dover–Calais service, by far the oldest, ran twice weekly in Charles II's time, as did a Dover–Nieuport service, and a bi-weekly service from Harwich to Helvetsluis was set up soon after 1660. Mail-boats were run regularly to three Irish ports from Portpatrick, Holyhead and Milford Haven. Falmouth, the ocean-going Post Office port till the establishment of steamships, was the base of packets that ran to Corunna from 1688, to the West Indies from 1702, to Lisbon from 1704, to New York from 1755. Packet-boats were specially designed for the Post Office; some were owned outright; more were hired, though the crews were regarded as temporary Post Office servants; all were armed, but forbidden—in vain—to delay the mails by seeking to capture prizes at sea. The secretary of the Post Office was entitled till Todd's death in 1798 to $2\frac{1}{2}$ per cent on all expenditure on the packet services. With other Government officials he was entitled to the charges made for conveying newspapers abroad; and a number of high postal officials had profitable shares in the packet-boats that were hired. These perquisites were ended round the beginning of the nineteenth century, but the cost of the packet services still seemed high beyond comprehension. The Falmouth services were therefore transferred for more expert management to the Admiralty in 1823, and the rest of the ocean services in 1837. The Admiralty, having made a number of very expensive contracts with the new steamship lines to obtain the construction of vessels to suit naval needs in war, passed them back in 1860.

An activity of a novel type began in 1792. To send money through the post was most unsafe; the public were officially advised to cut bank-notes in two and send the halves at different times. The clerks of the roads could not persuade their superiors of the legality or even usefulness of a scheme which they evolved for sending remittances by official machinery, but were allowed to adopt the plan as their private affair. So the Money Order Office started. Cash was handed to a clerk in London; the postmaster in some distant town paid out the amount less a commission of 6*d*. in the £1 to the payer's nominee and recorded the transaction in his headquarters account; the clerks got the commission less a percentage. As the business proved successful, it was taken over by the Post Office in 1838; forty-three years later, in 1881, the simple methods of the postal order were grafted on to it.

The easy old times had come to an end when Freeling died in 1836. Eighteenth-century staff had many guerdons. Allen in the eighteenth century had repaid the extra work entailed by his contract with allowances of £300 a year each to the secretary and all the surveyors, with smaller gratifications to other officers and many of the county postmasters. Lloyd's Coffee House gave £100 a year each to the secretary and others. Then there were the newspapers; so long as they paid stamp tax, the Post Office circulated them free at home, but the staff divided charges made for carrying them abroad. Christmas boxes and feast and drink money added a trifle. The salaries of the six clerks of the roads were £60; they took £250–£300. The salaries of comptrollers were £200; they drew from £800 to £1,250. The salary of Mr. Secretary Todd remained £200; his actual income was about £4,000, while Sir Francis Freeling's was £4,565, and both were allowed in addition a free house, candles and coal. The two Postmasters-General were supposed to divide a salary of £2,000; at the end of the eighteenth century they were sharing £5,200; the cost of their free candles and coal alone came to £930 in 1782.

All these additions were withdrawn as vacancies occurred about the turn of the century, with some adjustments of salaries. On Freeling's death in 1836, William Leader Maberley, a half-pay colonel who had seen good army service, an M.P. and latterly a Commissioner of Customs, was made secretary to carry out the many retrenchments and rearrangements recommended by the Duncannon commission. He habitually reached the office at 11 a.m., and at once rang for his breakfast and a man to change his boots. On his appointment, the emoluments were reduced to £1,500 plus £400 in lieu of a residence and its perquisites. These changes were trivial in comparison with the blow to the Exchequer which was impending.

The profit on the Post Office fluctuated round half its expenditure from 1750 to 1790. Postal rates were increased from 1795 to 1815 to meet war expenditure and were not reduced afterwards; a single sheet cost 6*d.* for thirty miles in 1815 against 3*d.* a century earlier; a single sheet to Edinburgh, the charge for which had dropped to 4*d.*, rose to 13*d.* The proportion of profit increased to two-thirds; the figure was £1,500,000 to £1,600,000 a year from 1815 to 1840. The penny posts of many towns and their environs had likewise been gradually doubled by the Post Office, following the alteration of the London service to twopence. This logical action was found to have been illegal, and after a great many years provincial towns, some 600 of them in the United Kingdom, had their penny post tacitly restored. Newspapers also were carried throughout the kingdom for a penny, paid as a tax and not as a postal charge.

Sir Rowland Hill, K.C.B., F.R.S., as he became, who had been a schoolmaster, then secretary at £500 a year to the Commission for colonising South Australia, turned to universal penny postage as a promising field. The extravagance of collecting variable charges from individual recipients of letters was obvious, while enquiry showed that total costs varied little with length of transport. The Post Office objected to the huge loss of revenue if only a penny was charged; Hill maintained that the growth of business would obviate any loss, or at worst make it good. A committee of both Houses decided on a uniform 2*d.*; they were probably wise, though the Government threw them over because public sympathy was naturally with Hill. General penny postage began on 10th January, 1840, after a tentative five weeks at 4*d.* The public were left three options—to pay in coin at the time of posting, to use the new gummed stamps or stamped envelopes as soon as these could be made, or to let the recipient pay as before at a rate reduced to 2*d.* The Civil Servants were correct and Hill was wrong in their forecasts; net revenue was cut to less than half and did not again reach its 1839 level for thirty-five years. The economies of uniformity and pre-payment were what mattered, and these, not the penny rate, were copied by foreign countries.

Hill was given a two years' appointment, not in the Post Office but in the Treasury, at £1,500 a year to organise the change, with, as assistant, (Sir) Henry Cole, a Record Office official who had been an active propagandist for the reduction. After a short extension he was forced out, and became chairman of the Brighton railway, whence he intrigued continually for a job in the Post Office. He was made a sort of parallel secretary in 1846, and, on Maberley's removing to the Audit Office, sole secretary in 1854. Vain, self-seeking, obtuse, he quarrelled with his ministers and immediate subordinates and was threatened with physical violence by the rank and file. His retirement in 1864 brought him a special grant of £20,000 and his full salary for life. Four of his immediate family had been found Post Office employment.

Until the 1850s all major changes were forced from outside on a complacent Post Office; thereafter, its staff took the initiative. The Post Office had spread itself by then over 11,000 offices, of which far the greater part were private shops whose owners took the Government business under contract, as Civil Servants had done in all ages. When some areas were observed to be provided with savings banks, while others had none, the plain course for a philanthropic State was to provide the service at these widespread counters. The Post Office Savings Bank was started in 1861. By a natural development, the department became in the fullness of time the banker for national savings certificates, the vendors of wireless telegraph, gun, dog and other licences and the agent for paying weekly allowances to the aged, the widow, the orphan and the soldier's dependant.

Analogy with letters gradually drew in later modes of communication. Telegrams were developed in the eighteen forties and fifties, wherever they paid, by commercial companies. Districts where profit was unlikely and persons who hoped for a lower charge or better service invoked the more squeezeable Post Office. Its officials favoured a Government service. F. E. Baines, who had transferred from a telegraph company, urged as early as 1856 the assumption of a monopoly and a service to every main post office with a flat charge of 6d. for twenty words. Frank Ives Scudamore, second secretary, after twenty-four years' service, who had organised the Savings Bank, strongly recommended the same course in 1866, but with a charge of 1s., and anticipated an ultimate profit of £600,000 a year. Acts of 1868 and 1869 made telegrams a monopoly of the State; the existing installations were bought for £8,000,000, the staffs were transferred and Scudamore was put at the head of the new organisation, where Baines succeeded him on his retirement in 1875. The golden profits did not emerge; on the contrary, the system, handsomely extended to villages, showed increasing losses. A private member in 1883 carried a motion for sixpenny telegrams; both the Postmaster-General and Baines thought that the halved charge would stop the rot; the Treasury gave way, and the loss on telegrams mounted slowly into the millions.

Telephones were one of the causes. The first small telephone exchange was opened in London by a commercial company in 1879. Next year the Post Office was given dominion over the new facility by a High Court decision that a telephone call was a telegram. Private enterprise was still allowed to develop the device further; the department merely compelled the various companies as they were formed to operate under a licence from the Post Office and pay it 10 per cent of their gross takings, though the Post Office opened some exchanges of its own to give it a better bargaining position. The telephone companies combined; the telegraph losses increased; the Post Office bought the trunk telephone lines in the early 1890s for under half a million pounds and the whole of the installations, except the municipal services maintained by Hull and Portsmouth, for $12\frac{1}{2}$ million on 31st December, 1911.

The Post Office was in close touch from the start with wireless telegraphy, which it used in place of a broken cable as early as 1882. Its monopoly was duly established; all transmitting or receiving apparatus required its licence. The stations of Marconi and Lloyd's were bought in 1910. Long-distance stations were later constructed to Post Office order and for its use.

These were enormous extensions, and all the time the postal service grew. The department had 1,500 employees in 1797; they had risen by 1850 to 20,000, including 11,000 postmasters and sub-postmasters; but in 1890 the staff numbered 100,000, in 1914 a quarter of a million. This immense multitude for the carrying of messages must be small compared with that needed for the labour of composing, destroying, or preserving them, but it is large enough to entail the creation of large internal departments of specialists in its management, procedure and emoluments. This secondary growth, beginning in the Post Office, now bulks large in all major departments. Its title of " Establishments " is the plainest term in the esoteric vocabulary evolved by the new Civil Service calling.

As in the French and Napoleonic wars a century before, the German wars pushed postal charges up; the sixpenny telegram went in 1915, the penny post in 1918; but still the traffic grew. But though overseas cables and external wireless communications were removed to an Imperial consortium in 1928, the monster was thought to require a different nervous system. In 1934 the overladen and too powerful secretary was replaced by a board of officials representing the diverse duties, and under its ægis administration was divided and decentralised into regional groups.

13

PRIVY COUNCIL DEPARTMENTS

THE trouble of the Privy Council was its unconscionable tendency to swell. The convenience of thus paying a compliment, or the needs of business, kept up an unrelenting trickle of additions. The members of a revived Council rose in number from a dozen to a score in the decade before 1540, and to twenty-six, of whom all but four were officials, on the accession of Edward VI. The rivalry of Somerset and Northumberland was fought out on the Council; packing by the victor raised the membership to forty. The division into five committees of this unwieldy crowd was mooted on the accession of Mary; it was cut down instead to six men. This personal Cabinet of the new Queen was made up of:

The Lord Steward, Henry Fitzalan, twelfth Earl of Arundel, the only member of ancient family;
One Principal Secretary, Sir William Petre, who had held one office or another for eighteen years past;
The Comptroller of the Household, William, Lord Paget, who had been in office for twenty-one years;
The Chancellor of the Duchy of Lancaster, Sir Robert Rochester, who had been in Mary's employment before the accession;
Sir William Herbert, ennobled by Edward VI; and
The Bishop of Ely, Thomas Thirlby.

The dignity of Councillor could not be confined to this handful for long. Elizabeth's Council was nominally seventeen or eighteen strong, but the number of active members was fewer; they met three times a week in the early part of her reign, but in her later years had to gather almost daily, Sundays included, both morning and afternoon. All the business of the State was concentrated in their hands. Dilution did not cease; the Council numbered thirty-five at the end of the reign of James I, fluctuated between thirty-five and forty under Charles I, and soared to fifty after the Restoration.

" The councils at this day," wrote Bacon under James I, " in most places are but familiar meetings where matters are rather talked on than debated," and he recommended standing committees " as for trade, for treasure, for war."

Work had therefore to be split up and developed in sections. A standing committee of twelve was set up in 1615, primarily for foreign affairs, though it felt free to usurp other topics, and the same reign saw the creation of committees, amongst others, for the Navy, for Scotland, for Ireland and for trade. The last-named was a body of six named by the Council in 1621 to examine the causes of the decay of trade and the scarcity of coin in England. At first temporary, it was followed by a standing committee of six, which Charles I raised to eighteen, to advise on all questions of trade, the exchanges and the customs duties at home or abroad, that might be referred to them. These " Commissioners of Trade," as they were called, were only thrown out of action by the Civil War. Similar committees with terms of reference expanded to include the welfare of the plantations were appointed under the Commonwealth from 1649.

The total number of committees of the Privy Council appointed in the years immediately after the Restoration is estimated at seventy-two. Most of these were formed by the Council to deal with a single question and their lives were short; but four at least—those for Parliamentary business and for Irish, trade and colonial, and foreign affairs—were important standing committees. Separate clerks were lent to the Council for each.

Trade

Destiny chose the trade and colonial committee to grow into the department now called the Board of Trade. It started with the appointment of two Council committees in November 1660. One, of sixty-one members, was to look into commercial treaties, to regulate weights and measures, to restore the old high standards of British workmanship, to encourage fishing and coinage and to develop the trade of the plantations by suitable preferences. The other was a committee for the inspection and care of the plantations. The two, which were told to keep in touch with each other, were fused in 1672 into a single, much smaller and more highly paid, Council of Plantations. The president, the Earl of Shaftesbury, received £800 a year; the vice-president,

Lord Culpepper, £600; eight paid members £500 each; the secretary, Benjamin Worsley, who had been secretary previously to the Commonwealth Committee, was taken back at £500 instead of £200, and £1,000 was allowed for clerks, of whom one was John Locke. But this expensive body was dislodged two years later in favour of a committee of eight Privy Councillors; William Blaythwayte, a clerk of the Council and later Secretary at War, received £150 extra as its secretary. In spite of his Army work, he remained secretary till 1696 and retained his connection with trade and the plantations as a paid commissioner till 1706.

When a more presumptuous Parliament showed signs of creating an Empire development board, William III reinaugurated the Privy Council committee in 1696 as the " Lords commissioners for promoting the trade of our Kingdom and for inspecting and improving our plantations in America and elsewhere." The new body was still a committee of the Council with certain unpaid members, six paid commissioners again, a staff and a secretary. Four individuals called Popple, representing three generations of that family, held this last-named post from 1696 to 1745. The last was a dramatist; not trade but stage boards were linked in the *Dunciad* with " Popple's brow tremendous." Both he and his father, also a trade secretary, were promoted to govern the Bermudas.

This committee devoted most of its attention to the plantations. Nominally advisory, and bound to act through older departments, it usurped for a time in the interests of efficiency a good deal of power, even the nomination of governors and secretaries in the colonies. It was shaping into a Colonial Office when a Secretary of State retrieved the losses of his department and reduced the committee to impotence. Constitutional routine was restored also in commercial matters. Merchants were required to apply for redress circuitously to department A, which then requested department B to move the committee, which reported back to B and A; they soon preferred not to start hares rather than chase correspondence round the leisurely bureaux.

During the next revival of its fortunes, the committee organised the colonisation of Nova Scotia. Parliament voted £40,000, which they disbursed in gathering, equipping and conveying the emigrants to their new home. Their transport was impeded at the last by a smug Admiralty. Their Lordships, the Admiralty secretary wrote, would be pleased to attend to the question of ships when instructions were communicated through a channel that had the right to express the King's pleasure.

The committee's authority was confirmed in 1752; the square-toed constitutional view again prevailed against it in 1766, and the order was given that every executive function that it had gradually usurped should at once revert to its proper office. The committee forthwith loosed such an avalanche of accumulated paper on Treasury, Secretary of State and Privy Council, that it was at once requested to carry on as before. The constitutional difficulty was temporarily solved by creating in 1768 an additional secretaryship of State to be conferred on the president of the committee, and its acting secretary was made an Under-Secretary of State. But in 1779 the presidency was isolated again to make a job, at doubled salary, for the Earl of Carlisle, after his failure in America. This grossness touched off the Whig campaign for retrenchment and Burke's plan for economic reform, in which special fun was made of the committee of trade and the 2,500 volumes of reports which were the fruit of their industry. The first attack was defeated, but when the Whigs came into power in 1782 both the committee and the new secretaryships of State were promptly abolished.

The resulting vacuum had to be filled. The transfer of some of the staff to a plantations department under the Home Secretary proved so ineffective that within two years a new committee for trade and foreign plantations—a title soon shortened to the Board of Trade—was created by an Order in Council, which was amended by another on 23rd August, 1786. The Board remained, as before, a committee of the Privy Council, and its composition is still governed by this Order* of 1786. The Order prescribed a membership of some twenty-five; a number of the offices enumerated have vanished with effluxion of time, leaving as members of the Board the Archbishop of Canterbury, the Speaker, the Chancellor of the Duchy of Lancaster, the First Lords of the Treasury and Admiralty and all the Secretaries of State. None of the new board was paid. The President, even, remained unpaid till 1827, and the Vice-president till 1817; they were remunerated by appointment to the sinecure offices of Chancellor of the Duchy, Master of the Mint or Treasurer of the Navy. The Board has not met since 1850, and a single member formed a quorum at its meetings from about 1800. It started with a chief clerk at £500 a year, George Chalmers, who so continued for nearly thirty-nine years, and seven under-clerks. Two clerks of the Privy Council, at £500 a year each till 1808, were attached to the board as secretaries and continued nominally as unpaid secretaries till 1845. The staff had risen to thirty in 1840, to sixty-six in 1853, and to 7,500 in 1914.

The governance of such colonies as remained after the American War of Independence was solely the concern of a Secretary of State. In spite of the word " plantations " in its title, the business of the new Board was commerce, industry, economics and, eventually, welfare work. It played an indispensable part in the negotiations of commercial treaties and in the revisions of the home tariff by Huskisson and Peel, until in the mid-century the Treasury claimed tariffs as a Budget matter. But commercial negotiations and the collection of foreign facts and figures had to go on. After much confusion and movement to and fro, during which the Foreign Office argued for the responsibility and competence of the Board of Trade, and the Board for the superior suitability of the Foreign Office, a new Department of Overseas Trade, which was common to both, was created in 1917.

The duties of the Board were multifarious and became more so. It retained throughout the Privy Council tradition of close contact with industry. In 1787 it bought cotton seed from Bombay and ran experimental plantings in the West Indies, and it organised experiments at home in new dye-stuffs. In 1792 it probed a copper " ring ". As early as 1795, in view of the state of war, it investigated thoroughly the home stocks and probable supplies of coin. Despite the ridicule of the 2,500 volumes, statistics of many kinds—for example, corn prices from 1789— continued to be kept; they began to be digested and published in the Courtney tables in 1830 and in the Statistical Abstracts from 1832.

The old task of improving the quality of goods was reflected in the foundation under the Board of a Government School of Design in 1837 and thereafter of local schools of art; the Victoria and Albert Museum was one result. These activities were transferred to the new Board of Education in 1856, but the Board of Trade retained the function of staging exhibitions.

Improvements by inventors were encouraged by Tudor and even Plantagenet monarchs by the grant of monopolies. When these were perforce restricted in 1624, a proviso allowed exceptions to be made for new manufactures by the application for letters patent. The elaborate ceremonial needed for such applications lasted for more than two centuries. In the mid-nineteenth-century an application went through thirty-five stages, and documents had to go twice to the monarch for personal signature. The hapless inventor toiled to and fro between Law Offices, Home Office, Signet, Privy Seal and Chancery Offices, buying stamps and paying fees at each stage to a total, if he was unopposed, of over £100. This archaic machinery was swept away in 1852, and a single office of legal luminaries acting as commissioners for patents was created; the Patent Office, under the Board of Trade, was substituted in 1883.

Though identity of weights and measures throughout the country had been monotonously ordered from the times of the Saxon Kings, towns, counties and trades had been adamantine in sticking to custom. National standards were effectively prescribed at last in 1824; the duty of keeping and enforcing them was assigned to the Board of Trade in 1866.

The first railway for use by the public—the Stockton and Darlington —was authorised in 1821. In 1840 the supervision of railways was conferred on the Board of Trade, and extended by stages to include inspection of accidents, control of developments and amalgamations, railway charges (transferred later to railway and canal commissioners) and the welfare of workmen.

The administration of the navigation laws to promote the use of British ships was vested in the Board from the first, but the registration of ships lay with the Customs, and when the General Register of Seamen was instituted in 1835 it was placed under the Admiralty. Other dealings with ships raised the number of interested departments to nine by the mid-nineteenth century. These activities, ranging from measures against crimping (the forcible pressing of seamen into service) and the granting of certificates of competence for mercantile marine officers, to the oversight of Plimsoll lines and of lighthouses, were concentrated under the Board from 1845 and 1850 onwards; for full measure, control of foreshores was transferred to it from the Office of Woods and Forests in 1866. Transfer from the Admiralty of the arranging of sea transport for all Government departments and of the coastguard in 1921 and 1923 completed this picture.

In 1883 the administration of the Bankruptcy Acts was transferred from the Law Courts, which had proved themselves incapable of coping with collusion, to a judicial department formed by the Board.

Entry of the Board into the world of labour began innocently enough in 1886 with the collection and publication of statistics of strikes, lock-outs, trade unions and wages. Presently, from 1893 onwards, the Board's officials were settling wage disputes; the Acts of 1909 and 1911 gave them charge of labour exchanges and insurance and of trade boards for fixing minimum wages.

Supervision of coal and other mines was taken by a separate department created under the Board in 1920.

Agriculture

Old-time farming made substantial advances in certain counties in the course of the eighteenth century under improving landlords, not least among whom were " Turnip " Townshend, a Secretary of State who thought more of soils than seals, and Farmer George upon the throne. It was evident that much more could be achieved by taking thought and spreading information. But action did not, as might have been expected, centre on the department of Crown Lands; Sir John Sinclair, Bart., M.P., a great landowner and voluminous writer, petitioned the Prime Minister for a new organisation. A Royal Charter on 23rd August, 1793, set up a Board for Agriculture and Internal Improvement, to which Parliament voted a grant-in-aid of £3,000 a year. That eminent amateur of agriculture, Arthur Young, had laid a wager with Sinclair against the Board's being set up. " Your Board of Agriculture will be in the moon," he said; but he hedged with, " If on earth, remember I am to be secretary." Secretary he was duly made at £400 a year—at which salary he grumbled much —with an under-secretary and a few clerks. All worked together in Sinclair's private house. In the field the new body made immense, detailed and inaccurate surveys of crops and soils, engaged Sir Humphry Davy at £100 a year to lecture on chemistry, and ran a small experimental farm at Brompton.

Though the Board had an immense superstructure of official personages—all the great officers of State, the two Archbishops, two Bishops, the President of the Royal Society, the Surveyor-General of Crown Lands and his opposite number in the Woods and Forests—it was not a Government department, but remained a private society, whose Government grant was supplemented by the subscriptions of its ordinary members. Having trodden on many toes, it was dissolved in 1822, not long after its secretary, Young, had gone blind and retired. Its lineal successor after many years' gap was the Royal Agricultural Society created in 1838.

Three official bodies were next called forth by concrete problems.

A Tithe Commission was set up in 1841 to finance the commutation, and the abolition in suitable instances, of this payment by landowners to the Church. Copyhold, a mode of entitlement to land by inscription in the rolls of the manor, with vexatious fines and doubts on the validity of its transfer, had no longer much virtue apart from antiquity, for the system ran back beyond the Conquest, and had many inconveniences. To facilitate conversion to freehold tenures, there were set up in 1841 copyhold commissioners, presently converted to land commissioners, under the Home Office. Virulent diseases of sheep and cattle, which had seemed for long years to have been stamped out by slaughter, were brought back by free trade. After various sufferings, a great outbreak in 1865 caused the Home Office to set up a cattle-plague department, which was transferred in the following year to the Privy Council and became its Veterinary Department.

A demand then arose for an additional Secretary of State to draw these activities together, or, failing him, at least a special minister, but the Government held that to create a post of minister out of the void was an unconstitutional innovation. Minister of State, and minister without portfolio, were still unimaginable. Accordingly, a new body of leading Privy Councillors was created under the authority of an Act of 1889. All the Secretaries of State, with others of suitable eminence, were formed in 1889 into a Board for Agriculture, with a president at £2,000. The president took over in the Board's name the staffs and duties of the Veterinary Department, and the land and the tithe commissions, together with the agricultural statistics of the Board of Trade, making a body in all of ninety persons. The Works also passed on to the new Board, in 1903, the Botanic Gardens at Kew. In 1909 the Board of Trade gave up salmon, fresh water and sea fisheries, and " Fisheries " was added to the Board's title. Separable Scottish work was transferred to a separate department created for Scotland, a separate commission was created for forestry, and in 1919 the Board itself, which served only to support a president and had never actually met, was turned into a Ministry of Agriculture and Fisheries. Notwithstanding losses of work and men, the modest staff of ninety in 1889 had grown to 3,500 by 1927.

Education

Formal elementary education depended, till the end of the first third of the nineteenth century, on past and present philanthropy and the patronage of religious bodies. Two of these put on a spurt towards 1801 by forming rival associations. The Church of England founded its National Society for promoting the education of poor children in the principles of the Established Church. Dissenters set up the British and Foreign School Society, which disapproved of all denominational doctrine but the study of the Bible. Both succeeded in fostering numbers of new schools. Government intervention began in 1833 with a grant of £20,000 a year for England and Wales, followed by £10,000 a year for Scotland. The money was divided by the Treasury between the two societies as a bait for voluntary subscriptions. When a new supervising body was required, a Committee of the Privy Council was created by Order in Council in 1839 to supervise the expenditure of the grants. Distrust of Government interference in affairs of the mind was naturally widespread. A motion for rescinding the Order was narrowly defeated in the Commons and easily passed in the Lords, but the Order did not need the Lords' assent, as did legislation, and the provision of money required only the consent of the Commons. A separate Committee of the Council was set up for Scotland; the same president and secretary acted for both till 1885.

The English Committee—the Lords of the Committee of the Privy Council for Education in England and Wales—was made up of four ministers: the Lord President of the Council in the chair, the Lord Privy Seal, the Home Secretary and the Chancellor of the Exchequer. The president appointed as their secretary Dr. Kay, afterwards Sir James Phillips Kay-Shuttleworth, Bart., who had been trained by a physician's practice among the insanitary poor and by four years as assistant to the Poor-Law Commissioners. Not the fleeting ministers but their permanent secretary drove developments ahead during the next ten years, until ill-health forced him to retire with a baronetcy to take up other good works.

The conflicting goals of the Established Church, dissenters, Roman Catholics and unbelievers made evasion and duplicity a necessity of growth. The first proposal of the Committee was to establish colleges to train teachers. Opposition in Parliament was strong enough to scotch this; but the two societies established training colleges of their own, which the committee subsidised, while the secretary personally founded another, in which he took up his residence. From 1846 additional grants were also made to schools which employed teachers

John Palmer

Sir Edwin Chadwick

trained in the colleges. The subsidies to colleges were increased to cover a large proportion of their costs, and the colleges multiplied; by 1886 they numbered forty-three, of which only eight were undenominational; the number had risen to 103 in 1926.

Consent to appoint the first two inspectors of schools was wrung from the Cabinet with difficulty in 1840. Inspectors of factories and poor-law inspectors had existed for some years, but this business of teaching was felt to be more delicate and even more controversial. And rightly so, since the inspectors were teachers of teachers. The formal orders from their inception down to 1903 were to avoid interference by instructions or advice, but to confine themselves to seeing that the conditions attached to State grants were met, and to collecting facts and reporting back. The expectation and practice, as opposed to the written rule, were that they should inspire every practicable improvement. Since the amount of Government grant depended on the inspector's report, his very whisper was potent in the ears of schoolmasters and school managers. And many inspectors were forceful men who did not fear battle even with their Whitehall superiors. Their power was so obvious from the outset that the Church of England secured a concordat under which all the individual appointments that touched Church schools were subject to the approval of an archbishop, the withdrawal of which consent involved dismissal. Appointment as inspectors of Church of England schools was confined to clergy of that denomination, and for equal measure Roman Catholic laymen alone were appointed inspectors for their schools.

Even before the Committee on Education was set up, the Board of Trade was fathering and assisting the æsthetic training of designers for industry; a science division was added to this department in 1853 from the profits of the Great Exhibition, and the whole was renamed the Department of Science and Art. This body, though entitled only to subsidise artistic or scientific training, displayed much courage and ingenuity in stretching or ignoring its terms of reference; apart from technical institutions, elementary day and evening schools financed by the Education Committee drew largely on the Science and Art Department's grants for more advanced or technical courses. Accordingly, the Department of Science and Art was removed from the Board of Trade in 1856 and placed under the president and secretary of the Education Committee, but not under the Committee itself; it remained remote and, below the highest level, self-contained in

L

South Kensington. Of the several institutions which it begot, the Royal School of Mines and the Royal College of Science were merged in a school of London University in 1908; the Royal College of Art, the Victoria and Albert, the Science and the Bethnal Green Museums still maintain a detached life under the Ministry of Education, while the Geological Museum and Survey was transferred in 1919 to the Department of Scientific and Industrial Research.

The transfer of science and art in 1856 was done by Order in Council; the addition in the same year of a vice-president to the Education Committee to provide representation in the Commons required a statute. The vice-president ruled also the Scottish Committee till 1885, when he was replaced by the Secretary for Scotland and a separate permanent secretary was appointed for the Scottish Committee.

The Committee's spending of the parliamentary money aimed at stimulating private benevolence and voluntary effort in particular directions; each slow success was capped by another grant with a further goal. At first, under the Treasury regime, the erection of buildings had been the main objective; the Committee added the training of teachers. To induce managers and teachers to press for reasonably regular attendance, every school which was passed by its inspector as efficient was given from 1853 an extra sum for every child that attended 250 times a year, morning and afternoon counting as two. When it turned out that many children nevertheless left school with little knowledge, payment by results was added. Inspectors examined a sample of regular attendants, and the school received 4s. a head for attendance and up to 8s. a head for successful results. The inspector got £50 extra—1d. a head—if he marked schedules for 12,000 children in a year. The science and art side relied mainly on written examinations and did not employ inspection on a large scale till 1893. But after some forty years it was decided that these examinations were bad for education in elementary schools, and they were dropped.

State expenditure was thus a lever working on the goodwill of others. It increased continually, but the resources of religious bodies and private benevolence were not equally unlimited; the fulcrum for the lever began to be insufficient. Compulsion was applied in 1870 by an Act which allowed the Committee to set up School Boards wherever there were not enough elementary schools. The boards, which were elected locally, were entitled to draw on the rates in addition to receiving Committee grants. The religious atmosphere had changed; denominational schools were expressly debarred from assistance by the rates, a disability which was got over by increasing the State grants; the arrangements for inspection disregarded sects and became purely geographical. Provision of schools was next made obligatory by Whitehall, and school boards were given discretion to make children's attendance compulsory in their areas. Ten years later, in 1880, the Government dared to make compulsion universal up to ten years of age, and this figure was gradually raised.

A new body had now come into the field. The Charity Commission was created in 1853, after enquiries that had lasted a generation, to overhaul the terms and execution of ancient trusts, bequests and endowments, largely educational, which had been thrown out of gear by slackness or the devilries of time. The income at stake was (in 1895) £154,000 a year for elementary but nearly three-quarters of a million for secondary schools. In 1898 the Charity Commissioners began to inspect endowed schools, ostensibly to see how their schemes were working.

The various State entanglements with education below university standard were brought together under a revised Board of Education by an Act of 1899. The Board was still a Committee of the Privy Council, made up of the Lord President, the First Lord of the Treasury, the Chancellor of the Exchequer and all the Secretaries of State, but it was also given a president of its own. The former vice-president was replaced by a parliamentary secretary, who ranked below the permanent secretary of the Board. The Duke of Devonshire, Lord President of the Council, had some difficulty in explaining clearly to Parliament why a Minister for Education was not simply created in place of all this paraphernalia. He could only assure his fellow peers that the alternative had been carefully considered; while he could not now recall the reasons which made a board preferable, they did not matter, since it was perfectly well understood that the Board was a phantom which would never meet. On this the clause was allowed to pass. The Education Committee had not in fact met for some fourteen years, and the Board of Education never met at all.

In the new body the Science and Art Department was completely incorporated with the staff who had dealt with elementary education, though the former Department's physical removal to Whitehall was delayed till 1908. The Board took over also the educational work of the Charity Commissioners and the duties of the Ministry of Agriculture of an educational type.

School boards varied from the energetic and progressive, even beyond their legal powers, to the sceptical and supine. Local authorities were growing in size; technical education was transferred to them in 1899. School boards in the provinces were abolished in 1902, and in London in 1903, in favour of the larger local authorities, which were also given jurisdiction over the managers of voluntary schools in their area. More than 2,500 school boards were replaced by about 300 local educational authorities for elementary education; apart from the schools taken over, these supervised, and in the end had to pay for, more than 14,000 voluntary schools which continued to be run by voluntary managers. A more capable and authoritative administration was thus interposed between the Board of Education and the schools. The system of State grants had to be completely remodelled; it took no further account of success in teaching, but only of numbers and ages, expenditure actually incurred and the poverty or wealth of the local authority; to those that had not, more was to be given. The Board's own administrative and inspecting staff had to be rearranged and reorganised, but its numbers, far from falling, continued slowly to increase.

A Palace revolution was coupled with the Act. (Sir) Robert Morant, after taking a degree in theology, spent seven years in Siam as tutor to the Crown Princes, did more than was in his bond and was thrown out in 1893. In 1895, being in financial straits, he was engaged as his assistant in the newly formed section for special enquiries and research of the Board of Education by its head, the distinguished educationalist, Sir Michael Sadler. This section provided the raw material for legislation. Morant was detached in 1899 to the vice-president's private office, originally to devil for him, but, as it turned out, to lead him, on the impending Bill. The permanent secretary of the Board, Sir George Kekewich, and Sadler favoured the preservation of school boards; the vice-president took the opposite view, and intrigue and rumour agitated officialdom for the next two years. In view of the discords within and without the Board, the leader of the House and Prime Minister, Arthur Balfour, took charge of the complicated and controversial Bill and steered it through all its stages. Its form and contents and final passage into law were regarded as the personal triumph of his Civil Service assistant. Morant, the importation of seven years back, was installed in the place of Kekewich, who, being over sixty, was called on to retire. Sadler soon followed him into retirement. A government Blue Book had to be published to explain away these changes of personnel.

Morant was engaged for the next nine years in the reconstruction of his department and of local educational bodies in accordance with the Act of 1902. He created innumerable foes; in August, 1911, the Government removed him from his post, and in the following November he was appointed as chairman to organise the new National Health Insurance Commission. This unprecedented task accomplished, he passed on to the Ministry of Health as its permanent secretary in 1919 when it absorbed the insurance work.

A " tall and harassed apostle " is how Morant was described at the time when he was foisted like a cuckoo into the Board of Education nest. He could exercise at will an almost mesmeric charm, or, after he reached power, lambaste a lame dog with a tongue of vitriol. He bore not at all with blunt instruments or those that turned in his hand. He had immense driving power, was fertile in expedient, exacting in his choice of men and possessed by a talent, in fact, a genius, for organisation, so that the whole English administration quickened and sharpened after him; but with this gift there went, as with a man inspired, a profound conviction that all opposition derived from the devil. " Beasts," as he called them, beset his every step. That he was over-weeningly ambitious, tortuous and indifferent to common standards of honour, is not in doubt, nor that he committed the unforgivable sin, in the official's decalogue, of disloyalty and intrigue against his own ministers. The best opinion saw in his ambition and chicanery only selfless devotion to an ideal; he was " unprincipled but not corrupt." It is odd that all four great organisers, Cromwell, Pepys, Chadwick and Morant, sooner or later proved unbearable. Morant's Act of 1902 was anything but the last word. Twenty-three new statutes were passed between 1907 and 1921 alone, an average of one in eight months, and many were substantial. Elementary schools were universally forbidden to charge fees in 1918. The momentum continued in further legislation.

The personnel under the Department, whether as Committee or Board, was of three species. Teachers were never its direct employees, but were servants of the body that ran the school. That did not prevent the Committee from instituting, by a brief, light-hearted ukase in 1846, pensions, to be awarded and paid by itself. The pensions were for a long time meant to be supplements to the individual teacher's savings; the basis and figures had to be changed several times before an Act of 1918 put the whole charge on Government, raised the amounts and extended similar pensions to teachers in secondary and technical schools. Contributions to the cost of pensions by the individual were resumed four years later, and in 1928 contributions were also required from local authorities.

The Committee, while refusing to be the employer, nevertheless paid its share of salaries direct to the individual teachers from 1846 to 1862. Thereafter salaries were fixed and paid by the actual employers, and varied widely from place to place. The teachers, however, organised themselves from 1870 onwards in large associations, with which the department had perforce to maintain amicable relations. It could not be indifferent to low salaries, and offered local authorities in 1917 additional money grants, of which the primary aim was to induce an increase of teachers' salaries. After the war was over it obtained by indirect pressure a good deal of uniformity of level. Four model scales, each for a stated type of area or post, were framed by an arbitrator and altered afterwards from time to time by committees of employers and employed, or, when agreement failed, by arbitration awards.

All field work was done by salaried inspectors, whose appointments were made by pure patronage of the president, in his sole discretion after religious loyalties ceased to be regarded in 1870; in practice, the selections were made for him without elaborate machinery from men who had taken first- or second-class honours at a university. Later these were supplemented by assistant inspectors, usually chosen from successful headmasters, and in time they were recruited in part from these assistants. The original inspectorate of two swelled to round about 400 in four grades, apart from whom a numerous corps of medical inspectors was recruited to take care of the body.

The president appointed also the administrative staff at headquarters, assistant secretaries and those who were called principals at a later date, but who were in this Department long entitled examiners. These were the men whose upper ranks shaped policy and whose lower decided its concrete working out; unlike their peers in some offices, they wielded much authority and dictated in the name of " My Lords " indifferently to inspectors, school managers and local authorities.

Being experts in examinations, the Education Department refused to adopt that fashion of recruitment for important grades, whatever the rest of the Civil Service did; it held on to personal selection till 1919, when it was worn down into taking the general line for examiners, and set up a committee with outside members for the selection of inspectors.

A large staff was also needed to record facts and findings, trace precedents and case law, and calculate and pay grants; besides the great mass of routine work involved in keeping details of every teacher's service and calculating and paying the final pension. These writers —boys, assistant clerks, and second division clerks—were provided, as in other departments, by the Civil Service Commission's competitions. Within the office, these clerical colleagues appeared to the administrators to be very paragons of departmental learning, but hopelessly enmeshed in red tape; the inspectors held exactly the same opinion of the examiners.

In addition to the stream of statutes that overlapped like an anteater's scales, the Department itself continually put forth, in the light of experience, additional rules that were woven line upon line into the annual editions of codes, schedules and regulations. Their mass had swollen over nearly a century to 165 printed pages, before a purge was applied and the total reduced to 24 pages in 1926.

Following the realisation from 1914 onwards that the creation of fresh ministerial offices was a constitutional possibility, the notional Committee on Education was abandoned in 1944 and a specific Minister was substituted.

Other Privy Council Offshoots

The Privy Council had meantime become the depository of central control over vaccination and public health in general for the years 1858–71, when this function was transferred to the Local Government Board. When quit of these and other administrative responsibilities it was again called upon to provide a foster-mother for the Midwives Board in 1902; and a good deal later for science. A committee of the Council was constituted for the Department of Scientific and Industrial Research, in its origin a creation of the Royal Society, when it became governmental in 1915. The president further became the political head of the Medical Research Council (first set up as the Medical Research Committee in 1913), when this parted from the

National Health Insurance commissioners on their absorption in 1919 by the Ministry of Health. Yet another committee, made up of the Lord President and three Secretaries of State, with the Ministers of Agriculture and Fisheries, Education, and Housing and Local Government, was created to preside distantly over the Councils created by Royal Charter for Agricultural Research (1931) and for Nature Conservancy (1949). The accretion of a substantial secretariat of scientists to the Lord President quite dwarfed the revered judicial committee of the Council and the ancient but minute office of the clerk, whence, though now drafted elsewhere, orders in Council still issue in spate.

14

WELFARE DEPARTMENTS

THE sheriffs were the King's officers for local business from the Conquest to the Tudors. Besides all else, they were tax-collectors, and their posts were lucrative, as they were not expected to account for the whole sum collected. A sheriffdom cost from £100 to £1,000 by the early twelfth century. The cup of their iniquity ran over, and after a royal inquisition in 1170 most of them were discharged and their posts distributed to officials of the Exchequer and of the Household. Time and again they were called on to account in full, contrary to the provisions of Magna Carta, and about 1240 change of Royal lands, escheats and wards was taken from them and dispersed. But the office still attracted the great; to prevent concentration of such powers in few hands, Edward III agreed in 1340 to a law that no man should be sheriff for more counties than two or for longer than a twelvemonth at a time. Thus continuity was prevented, though many permanent officials took their turns as sheriff. A century later great prices were still said to be paid for a sheriff's office, until the Exchequer once more set aside ancient customs, required sheriffs to account to it in full for their total collections, and abolished their private collection of head pence. In 1456 the posts had again almost ceased to attract men of standing.

The Tudor monarchs created lords lieutenant of counties to take over the sheriffs' military responsibilities; they put Crown taxation in the hands of special officials, and transferred the oversight of local administration to the local men of standing appointed, without pay, to be Justices of the Peace. Whereas sheriffs had been chosen by the Exchequer, justices were appointed by the Lord Chancellor, but their duties were not purely judicial till 1888; they fixed and levied rates on the parish and saw to the maintenance of local services, from roads and bridges to police and gaols.

In consequence of the loss of provision for the indigent after the seizure of the monasteries and the crushing of princely houses, a series

of laws under Elizabeth I made each parish responsible for the relief of
its poor and the provision of work for its unemployed.   The justices
had charge of this activity also; it was so far the heaviest of all local
expenses that the poor rate was regarded as the typical rate for each
parish.   County rates were long rare; when they were standardised,
they were based on the parish poor-law assessments.   The total poor
rate of England and Wales amounted to just over £800,000 a year at
the end of the seventeenth century; it dropped to just over £600,000
by 1750, but in 1785 it had risen to nearly £2,000,000.   Bad harvests
and the Government's fiddling with the currency pushed the cost of
living up during the great French wars.   The J.P.s of Berkshire
accordingly met at Speenhamland near Newbury on 6th May, 1795,
for the purpose of laying down minimum wages for the county, but
they drew up instead a scale of allowances from the rates according to
the price of bread and the size of a family.   This " Act of Speenhamland " was followed, almost as if it were statute law, by half the
counties of England; so strong at that date were local powers.   " To
each according to his need " did not work well.   Wages were kept
down, the work-shy and the wanton prospered, the expenditure rose
to £8,000,000 a year and the smaller ratepayers were well-nigh ruined.
Reform of the Poor Law was considered in almost every session of
Parliament till 1834.

This was in a decade when all the aspirations of the business and
professional world began to be gratified at once.   In 1832 the number
of parliamentary electors was doubled and the constituencies ration-
alised by the Reform Bill; in 1835 mediæval town corporations and
the mode of their electing were remodelled on analogous lines.   A little
earlier, in 1829 under a different Government, the police forces, which
Bow Street magistrates had organised during the past half-century for
London outside the City, had been replaced by Peel by a new force
under the Home Secretary; similar forces under local authorities were
created in 1835 in the boroughs and in 1839 and 1856 for the counties.
Government grants for education began in 1833; in 1834 the national
accounts were improved.

Edwin Chadwick, a disciple and legatee of Jeremy Bentham, was
the principal agent of other changes in the fields of industry, charity,
health and local government.   He was secretary to the Royal Commission on children in factories which produced the first Home Office
inspectors (1833) and vested the control of factory conditions in that

department. The Royal Commission on the anarchic Poor Law employed him as an investigator in 1832; he was advanced next year to be a member of the Commission, wrote most of its report, and was appointed secretary to the executive Poor Law Commission that was set up in 1834 in pursuance of his recommendations. This body of " three bashaws of Somerset House " or " Pinch-paupers," as they were nicknamed, was kept free of politicians and Parliament, the better to do its unpopular work; in practice it was run by Chadwick. He would have preferred a completely centralised State organisation, but was forced to bring into the picture the traditional unit of the parish. Parishes were grouped by the new Poor Law Commission into large " unions "; besides the economies and efficiencies of working on a larger scale, the object was to classify and divide the different sorts of people on the dole. The union areas were drawn up according to the Commission's fancy. On a review in 1882 of the chaos of local authorities, it was found that only eight unions out of more than 600 coincided with a borough, while 143 spread into two, twenty-nine into three and four into four counties. A Board of Guardians, elected in part by local ratepayers and for the rest made up of the J.P.s, was set over each union at its creation and required to apply the fundamental principle that relief for the able-bodied should be more distasteful than work. The detailed work of the Guardians was done by a paid and permanent staff of relieving officers, who were also responsible to the central body, and medical men in local practice were engaged part-time to look after the sick and aged. The principle of local responsibility was thus preserved, but the Guardians were in fact very closely controlled by the central office and its inspectors.

The Liberal Government did well to keep its distance; expenditure on poor relief was promptly reduced by a quarter. It came down from £6,750,000 in 1834 to an average of £4,500,000 in the next five years. But the Commission did a great deal more than cleanse the body politic of some parasites. Chadwick insisted throughout that real destitution was mainly caused by disease and that disease was bred by dirt. Apart from medical attendance on the sick, the Commission employed three physicians on medical surveys of black spots. One of these, Sir James Kay-Shuttleworth, became permanent secretary of the Board of Education; another, Dr. Southwood Smith, famous for having dissected the corpse of Jeremy Bentham during the terrors of a thunderstorm, was taken on as medical officer by the later Board of

Health. These surveys were statistical enquiries, and a similar statistical approach led to the creation, in which Chadwick played a large part, of the General Register Office in 1836. Details of all births, deaths and marriages had henceforth to be furnished to registrars whom the several Boards of Guardians were required to appoint on lines laid down by Chadwick, and to be passed by the registrars to the Registrar-General to be digested. The annual reports of William Farr, F.R.S., Chadwick's compiler of abstracts and statistician from 1838 to 1879, focused attention on wide variations in sickness where local conditions differed.

The Poor Law Commission, or Chadwick's peremptory ways, aroused such irritation that it was remodelled in 1847 and put under a member of Parliament as chairman, but the statistical material and the Commissioners' enquiries and special reports had already established a link between shocking sanitation and much sickness. With the stimulus of an outbreak of cholera, they evoked a Royal Commission, and this resulted in the establishment of the General Board of Health in 1848. Epidemics had occasionally produced temporary bodies of the sort before, of which the last had been a quarantine board, under the appropriate presidency of the deputy-chairman of the Board of Customs, which lasted through the cholera epidemic of 1831. The new Board had a minister at its head—the First Commissioner of Works—who changed four times in its short life; and one paid and one unpaid member. A medical member—Dr. Southwood Smith, of the Factory and Poor Law Commission—was added in 1850. Chadwick transferred forthwith from the Poor Law Commission to be the paid member and dictator of the new Board.

The General Board of Health had a right to control town cemeteries; otherwise it was entitled to intervene in local affairs only on the request of the local authority, or where the death rate exceeded a certain figure over a period of years. In either case it could set up a local health authority and initiate schemes of improvement. The cities were not all inert. Liverpool appointed the first municipal medical officer of health in 1847; the City of London, which escaped the jurisdiction of the General Board, appointed the second in 1848; the latter, Sir John Simon, was engaged by the Board as their chief medical officer in 1855 and continued to do notable service under its successors, the Privy Council and the Local Government Board, till he retired at sixty on a large pension. Chadwick continued to promulgate the economy of stopping disease by removal of filth. Costly carts and cesspools, he said, must be abandoned; the cheapest vehicle was running water, therefore sewerage and water supplies must be developed together.

The General Board succeeded reasonably well; it supervised the creation of local health authorities in 182 different districts and secured the construction by thirty-one of them of waterworks and drainage systems. Two of Chadwick's proposals on the national scale would no longer seem fantastic; he wanted the management both of water supplies and of burials to be taken over in all details by the Civil Service. The latter wish was actually granted by an Act of 1850, but this had to be repealed two years later. Another of his propositions was to supply London with soft water from the Weald; he reckoned that the cost to the community would be covered by their saving on soap, with a further saving on tea as pure gain.

The sands were running out for him. He was an embodiment of the official mind at its worst; stretching to the extreme conclusions reached on evidence that proved incomplete, convinced that only baseness could differ from him, imperious and autocratic. Parliament reasonably demanded his withdrawal as the price of letting the General Board continue, so Chadwick retired on a pension of £1,000 in 1855; a knighthood followed—*longo sed intervallo*—in 1887. Such brilliant Civil Servants need to be damped by the heavy water of a minister. His assistant secretary and successor had brilliance of a different order; he was a future editor of *Punch*, Tom Taylor. A separate president, a member of Parliament, was given to the General Board, and it was permitted to continue in existence, but only from year to year, till 1858, when it was wound up. Its medical duties and staff were transferred to the Privy Council, and its engineering and general duties and staff to the Home Office.

After thirteen years of separate development, the staffs were united again with each other and with the men of the Poor Law Commission in 1871 in a new department—the Local Government Board. A parliamentary president at £2,000 a year, raised to £5,000 in 1910, was at its head; appended to him to make up a Board were the Lord President of the Council, all the Secretaries of State, the Lord Privy Seal, and the Chancellor of the Exchequer, but it was well understood that the Board should never meet and that the president should act alone. The poor-law group not unnaturally took the lead in the considerable secretariat and inspectorate which served under him; the medical men lost the pride of place which they had enjoyed under the Privy Council, and initiated the long debate on pre-eminence for the technologist.

The simplification which had been demanded in the complex of local authorities was carried out in the following year, 1872; in the main, towns were to be run by their elected councils or boards of health, and rural districts by the Poor Law Guardians, with many complications. A further simplification and aggrandisement was effected in 1888, when the system of county councils and county boroughs was set up and the Metropolitan Board of Works, created in 1855, blossomed into the London County Council. Justices of the Peace were relegated to the bench, and their administrative functions were transferred to the elected bodies; and in 1894 a great many surviving *ad hoc* bodies were abolished in favour of urban and rural district councils.

The growth of town and other councils was stimulated not only by the incitements or demands of these Government departments but also by growing Government subsidies. The first liability to be shifted from rates to taxes was half the cost of criminal prosecutions; the whole cost, originally borne by the individual aggrieved, had been placed on the county or borough in the eighteenth century. Local burdens costing £341,000 a year were transferred to taxes in 1846 as a sop to farmers for the abolition of the Corn Laws. Bit by bit the Government took over the local prisons; a quarter, then half the cost of police; and half the cost of medical officers and sanitary inspectors. It agreed in 1874 to pay the amounts which would have been due if Government properties had been subject to rates; a sub-department of the Treasury—the Rates Department—was set up to agree and discharge the annual liability. In 1875 the Public Works Loan Board was set up under independent part-time commissioners to lend money of Treasury provision to local authorities for their capital expenditure. The historians of local government regard the contributions up to this date as proper inducements to develop particular services, but the further grants of the next thirty years as donations to favoured classes. At any rate, grants of nearly £3,000,000 a year were made on the expansion of local authorities in 1888. On top of this came the grants for education. In the present century repeated attempts have been made to construct formulæ which would leave local authorities some motive for economy without stinting the needy ones; the total contribution has risen above £400,000,000 a year.

Although the franchise was greatly enlarged in 1867 and 1884, Government did not start direct payments to the aged, sick or unemployed till the years 1908–11. Humanity was in the air; a new department, the Public Trustee, was set up in 1908 to serve unskilled family estates; a financial department, it was placed under the Lord Chancellor. On the other hand, the large expenditures for the needy were promoted by Treasury ministers, traditionally the high priests of economy. The elaborate machinery for old age pensions took in, as well as the Treasury, the Local Government Board, the Post Office and the Customs, and could not be completed till 1909. Pension Officers were appointed by the Treasury, which used Customs officers in sparsely settled places; pensions were awarded or refused by a committee in each local authority's area after these officers had examined and reported; dubious cases were settled on appeal by the Local Government Board; and the Post Office paid. The Insurance Act, 1911, imposed a stamp tax on the employed and their employers and gave the poorer sick medical attention and a weekly allowance, and the unemployed a dole, but made the latter attend and seek work at the State Labour Exchanges. These had been set up in 1909 to bring vacancies and applicants together. Exchanges and unemployment were under the Board of Trade; the enormous task of creating a taxing and allowance-paying organisation to deal with 12,000,000 individuals was done by the new National Insurance Commission, on which Sir Robert Morant, late of the Board of Education, headed a band of Civil Servants selected from many departments. Medical advance was provided for by a research committee under the Commission.

This exercise in organisation, which had taken twenty-five years in Germany and was put through here in eighteen months, was excellent practice for the labours soon to be required of the Civil Service by the nation in arms. The first structures had a short life. A Ministry of Labour was created in 1917, to which all labour questions, exchanges, insurance, wages, strikes, statistics and the rest were moved from the Board of Trade; conscription for the forces, the new Press Gang, and for industry was added to its functions; the Home Office gave up the factory inspectorate; and after a temporary fission the title of the Ministry became Labour and National Service. The Local

Government Board and the National Health Insurance Commission were fused at the end of the First World War into yet another new body, the Ministry of Health. The payments to various classes of clientele were raised and extended to other classes. The remaining poor relief was taken over by the Government and entitled national assistance; the guardians of the poor were abolished in 1930. After a deal of work with paste and scissors, and the creation and dissolution of fresh departments, the resulting set-up consisted of five departments:

Ministry of Labour and National Service, for problems of employment and unemployment, wages and conscription;

Ministry of Health, for the medical work in England and Wales of three abolished bodies, the Local Government Board, the Insurance Commission (except research, which went to the Privy Council), and the Ministry of Pensions;

Ministry of Housing and Local Government, for the remainder of the Local Government Board work—local administration, burials, coast protection;

Ministry of National Insurance, for regulated payments to widows, the sick, unemployed, parents of children and many of the aged; the collection of charges by stamps; and war pensions, previously dealt with by the Ministry of Pensions; and

Ministry of National Assistance, for payments to other aged persons and additional grants to persons whom its brother ministry left too poor.

In a different field of welfare, Government action was opportunist and accidental. Museums and picture galleries mostly became governmental responsibilities because a collector, to prevent the dispersal of his treasures, offered the white elephant at a bargain price or paid money towards its upkeep. Of the metropolitan State institutions, the first, the British Museum and its Library, owed its birth in 1753 to the offer of Sir Hans Sloane's books and curios for £20,000. The National Gallery was reluctantly founded next, in 1824, under promises of many gifts, in John Angerstein's house by the purchase of his collection. In 1843 it had 183 pictures, of which thirty-eight were Angerstein's, twenty had been bought subsequently, and 130 had been presented or bequeathed. Both these institutions are run by bodies of independent trustees, differently appointed; but as these depend on votes of Parliament for the great bulk of their funds, their officers and

Sir George Rose

servants are in practice Civil Servants. Hence also a Treasury minister is responsible in the House of Commons for informing the inquisitive and placating the critical on questions relating to a trustee museum.

The Great Exhibition of 1851 begot two museums in South Kensington, to be eventually controlled by the Minister of Education—the Museum of Manufactures, which changed its name successively to Museum of Ornamental Art and to Victoria and Albert, and the Science Museum. The British Museum had by this time outgrown its immediate capacity; it was split, and the Natural History Museum migrated in 1851–5 to South Kensington. In that active period the Geological survey created its museum, and another trustee body, the National Portrait Gallery, was founded in 1856.

The Imperial Institute, only in part a museum, was founded to commemorate the Jubilee in 1887, partly from Colonial funds; its administration was divided between the Colonial Office and the Board of Education.

The Wallace Collection was a bequest of 1897. In the same year the Tate Gallery was created by the collection and contributions of Sir Henry Tate. The fairy godfather of the London Museum was Lord Leverhulme, with his gift of Stafford House in 1913. The Imperial War Museum was founded in 1917 and opened in 1920 as a memorial of the First World War. The National Maritime Museum was the creation of Sir James Caird in 1934 to receive his collections.

The Ministry of Education's museums apart, separate boards of trustees have the governance of all these museums and galleries, which thus abstract themselves a little from the infelicity of State affairs.

The Public Record Office is the lumber-room of the State. Some parchments had to be preserved for indefinite periods in quite remote times as records of rights; international diplomacy was bedevilled and acerbated as early as the fourteenth century by the industry and acuteness of Government archivists. Many other records survived because no one was paid to destroy them after their immediate utility was exhausted. With the rise of the first great school of antiquarians, systematic efforts to preserve other administrative records began under the first Elizabeth and culminated in its heyday with the extension of the State Paper Office under Mr. Secretary Williamson. A fresh flush of antiquarians produced from 1800 onwards a series of Record Commissions, with personnel as numerous as they were bored. After the last had dozed off, the Public Record Office was founded in

M

1838 to concentrate the State papers scattered over some seventeen depositories, and Government departments were forbidden for the future to destroy documents without the consent of its head, the Master of the Rolls. The first stone of the central building was not laid till 1851, after a long, vain fight by the Treasury to pile up the papers in the empty Victoria Tower of the new palace of Parliament.

Immense as they are, those departments must rid themselves in part of their dead *paperasserie*. Accordingly, schedules, which must be submitted to Parliament, are drawn up of species of papers which shall be destroyed after so many years, and those which shall survive only so many more, leaving a small proportion—but a huge aggregate—for transfer one day to the Record Office. By foresight and skilled labour the utmost is done on properly regimented lines to keep all that might interest posterity if so much were not preserved.

15

THE PRE-VICTORIANS

Two changes were slowly wrought on the Civil Service during the century and a half before Victoria's accession. The first distinguished the politician from the employee; the second removed the Gothic extravagances which time had made of old offices.

Parliament, until its maturity, was run by the King. The Lords are still presided over by the Lord Chancellor; the Speaker of the Commons, though nominally elected by the House, was selected beforehand by the Crown until the end of the Tudors; he was often one of the permanent Royal servants, and if not already of that service might expect a subsequent appointment. Thus, Speakers between 1450 and 1500 included two Chancellors of the Exchequer, an Under-treasurer, the Duke of York's chamberlain, an Exchequer remembrancer, a Customs official, an attorney of the Duchy of Lancaster and a Justice of Assize. Henry VII's notorious trio, Catesby, Empson and Dudley, were all Speakers of the House of Commons. The customary fee from the Royal purse, which had earlier varied between £50 and £100, became fixed at £100 a session under this King. The Crown service likewise provided the clerk of the Parliaments for the Upper House at an extra £40 a year, and the under-clerk of the Parliaments for the Lower at £5 a year, which both Edward VI and Elizabeth I raised to £10, Mary reverting to the older figure; while one of the Palace sergeants-at-arms was diverted, with his usual wage of 12d. a day, to be doorkeeper.

These officials established their financial independence of the Crown stipend by their own exertions from Elizabethan times onwards. The Speaker extracted fees from all promoters of private Bills; each clerk was paid by them for every stage in a private Bill's progress—for its entry, copying, amendment and final engrossment. The Commons clerk charged the members for entries in his journals, for extracts from these for a copy of a Bill and so on, while the sergeant-at-arms levied toll on both petitioners and members. The two clerks became wealthy men who could afford to employ, or rather sell employment to, under-clerks, and sit back and leave the work to these deputies or assistants; whom in turn, in the end, the Houses accepted as direct servants. The clerk of the Parliaments, for instance, at the end of the eighteenth century, was Sir George Rose. After a spell as a captain's boy in the Navy, he got a permanent Exchequer clerkship at eighteen in 1762; he was made, in addition, Keeper of Records in the Exchequer in 1772 and permanent secretary to the Board of Taxes at £900 in 1777. He resigned the last job to become patronage secretary to the Treasury in 1782, but in view of its insecure tenure would not enter Parliament till he was promised the clerkship of the Parliaments on the next vacancy and had been given a post in the Commons journal office. His finances were further safeguarded by appointment in 1785 for life to be a master of the pleas of the Exchequer. The incumbent dying, Rose became clerk of the parliaments in 1788; he held this post and a seat in the House of Commons till his death in 1818. During those thirty years he was also, when the Tories were in power, variously a secretary to the Treasury, vice-president of the Board of Trade, joint Paymaster-General and Treasurer of the Navy.

As clerk of the Parliaments, Rose, though appointed by the Crown, was agreed to be the servant of the House of Lords. He never attended; a committee of the other House, twenty-two years after his appointment, enquiring if he did so, got the blunt answer, " Certainly not." Rose declared that the duties of his office had been done by deputy since 1483, and pointed out that his immediate predecessor, Ashley Cowper, clerk from 1715 to 1788, had been appointed at fourteen or fifteen and was nearly ninety when he died. Lord Thurlow, the great Lord Chancellor, however, considered the appointment of 1715 to have been an impropriety by the then Lord Chancellor, and the neglect even of supervision a concession to Cowper's ill-health.

Rose's official income from all sources varied from £7,000 to £12,000. The clerkship of the Parliaments alone yielded an average of £3,278 in his first eight years, and this had increased to almost £5,000 in 1817. The source was fees paid by solicitors or persons promoting legislation. The work was wholly done by the clerk-assistant for a salary of £100—but fees of £3,600. Sir George Rose was able to leave the clerkship to his eldest son, Sir George Henry Rose, who thereupon retired from the diplomatic service, sat in the

Commons for Christchurch, like his father, from 1818 to 1844, and continued as clerk of the Parliaments till his death in 1855. The clerk-assistant, a Civil Service commissioner, then at last moved up to the titular post.

That the King's head men should sit in the Great Council of the Realm or House of Lords went without question. The lower House started in the late thirteenth century as an annexe where lesser folk could be conciliated to additional taxation, for which these Commons cautiously sought a return in concessions and changes of law. The machine for calling a Parliament, initiating an election, deciding its result and securing members their fees was the Chancery. Every county was ordered to elect two knights of the shire, and selected towns and cities to elect two burgesses or citizens, to the Commons house and to pay their members 4s. in the case of a shire and 2s. elsewhere for each day of the session and necessary travelling time. Attendance was a duty for which the elected sometimes thought the money too meagre; as late as 1604, an enforced candidate offered £5 to any volunteer who would take his place. The last paid member was Thomas King in 1681. But two centuries before that a seat in the Commons was generally recognised to be to the member's advantage in credit or cash, and more and more candidates, to secure adoption, waived their fees, till they became obsolete.

The Commons hardly grew beyond a taxing and humbly-petitioning body till Henry VIII made it his ally in measures against the Church that without such support might have been frustrated in the upper House with its phalanx of bishops. The Commons were fully the equal of the Lords before the Stuarts were called to the throne. After the Revolution they became the crucial House, though ministers usually sat in the Lords, and big money was spent at times in the eighteenth century to secure a seat. The average value of safe boroughs was reckoned at £7,000.

The King's servants were not a separate caste, and, until the breach between Parliament and Charles II, objection was seldom taken to their seeking the suffrages of a constituency, where indeed they tended to be welcome for their presumed influence with the monarch. Away back in Edward III's reign, petitions were presented in 1348 and 1351 for the exclusion from the Commons of that most odious class, the collectors of revenue. Two hundred years later, the Pilgrimage of Grace assumed that Civil Servants had hitherto been excluded and attributed recent grievances to a change in practice. "The old custom," they said, "was that none of the King's servants should be of the Commons house, yet most of that house were the King's servants," to which another text adds "and their servants." Under Mary, the House itself added to a Bill on the franchise a clause to debar from its membership all officers and servants of the Queen, but this was mere tactics to bring Mary to veto legislation which she wanted and the Commons did not.

Such protests were isolated, and many Royal officers below the peerage level found their way into the Commons. They averaged exactly a quarter of the known membership of the thirty parliaments held or summoned in the seventy years before the accession of Henry VIII, rising to a third or declining to a fifth in particular parliaments. No definite rule was observed; Treasurers and Comptrollers of the Household, Under-treasurers and Chancellors and Chamberlains of the Exchequer, and Chancellors of the Duchy of Lancaster much more often than not were in the Commons, but did not need to be in either House. Three Clerks of the Signet (including the poet, George Ashby), but no Clerk of the Council, found seats. Nor were any of the King's principal secretaries in either House during this period unless they were bishops during their period of office. Of all the Government departments, the Household and Chamber were the best represented, supplying many grooms and ushers as well as men of higher ranks. The Customs ran them close; the great bulk of its elected personnel were customers; a few were surveyors or comptrollers, but searchers, weighers and gaugers also got in. The Exchequer was not far behind; members came from every rank, remembrancers, tellers, auditors, the foreign opposer, and under-clerks. Thomas Bulkly, a messenger there from his teens, who took fourteen years to rise to be a clerk, and as many more to become a sergeant-at-arms at 1s. a day, at last got once into the House. The proportion of Crown servants in the Commons did not greatly change in later reigns; at least a third of the known members of Edward VI's Parliament of 1547 held offices at Court or were closely related to those who did; and Crown servants, with a dozen or so of their servants, numbered 90 to 100 in a Commons house of 460 members in the last parliaments of Elizabeth I. Officials near the top of the hierarchy were by that time accepted as a Government group or informal ministry—"Her Majesty's Privy Council in the Nether House." While planned action was doubtless taken to secure seats for spokesmen and liaison officers, or even at times to pack the House, most Civil Servants seem still to have owed their admission to their own initiative, by using their influence with a locality or a greater man. But neither leading nor lesser officials were expected to speak with one voice at this time, or for a long time to come.

Toleration of officials in the Commons survived the Civil War, but distaste and apprehension became manifest as the schism between King and Commons grew afresh and was increased by the Revolution. The Cavalier or Pensioners' Parliament of Charles II passed a nugatory resolution in its old age, a bare year before its dissolution, against any of its members accepting further office or promise of office while it lasted. After the Revolution, though six Bills for the exclusion of officials that were tabled between 1693 and 1705 failed to pass into law, quite a number of superior revenue officials were debarred from election; the managers of several taxes were interdicted in 1693, commissioners of stamps in 1694 and commissioners of excise in 1699.

One comprehensive measure got through; the Act of Settlement of 1700 made it illegal for anyone who held an office or place of profit under the Crown to be a member of the House of Commons—but not till after the death of Queen Anne. From that date, ministers and Civil Servants would have been restricted to the House of Lords, and the peculiar development of the British constitution would perforce have taken other lines. The embargo was, however, repealed before it came into effect and replaced in 1707 by a less total prohibition. The House of Commons was closed to the incumbent of any office created after 25th October, 1705, or of numerous older posts which were specified, but holders of other offices that existed before the sacred date remained admissible, if the appointment was made before election, or if the member was re-elected. The burden of re-election was lifted from the posts of ministers in 1919. The 1707 law provided, incidentally, a way of escape from the House for members who had changed their minds. A member of Parliament cannot resign; but he loses his seat if he secures an office of profit, of which the Chancellor of the Exchequer has four in his gift for this purpose. They are the old stewardships of the Chiltern Hundreds, of East Hendred, of Northstead and of Hempholme Manor. That none of them carries pay or duty adds to the beauty of strict observance of the law.

Clerks and deputies in the Treasury, Exchequer, Admiralty and nearly a score of other Government departments were added in 1742 to the schedule of old posts which disqualified their holders for membership of the Commons, without allowing re-election, and a dozen further Acts, spread over the next century, nibbled away the freedom of the remaining offices that had existed in 1705. The executive government finally required Civil Servants to resign before seeking election,★ and the distinction then became quite clear between non-political posts and the upper fringe of controlling or merely dignified offices which alone were open to a member of the House of Commons, which convention required to be held usually by a member of one or other House, and which had to be resigned on the fall of a Government. A Civil Servant remained free to sit in the Lords, or a lord to become a Civil Servant.

The jealousy of any buttressing of the power of ministers was strengthened by the presumption that Civil Servants would support their temporary master in the constituencies. It was largely because the number of excisemen would have been swelled and Government supporters in constituencies possibly increased by a mere 110 that Walpole's scheme to replace by excise the customs duties on tea and tobacco had to be withdrawn in 1733 and this reform postponed for fifty years. The embarrassment, if such it was, to parliamentary government was averted by disfranchising Civil Servants from 1782 to 1867.

The elimination of ministers' subordinates from the House of Commons, though so frequently pursued, was not complete or possibly very earnest. 271 members were estimated to hold paid offices or pensions at the accession of George I in 1714, and 257 in 1727; 234 out of 244 supporters of the Government in a close division in 1734 held official posts with total salaries of £200,000. Moreover, a preference in Government contracts or in allotting Government loans could serve as well to conciliate a member as his appointment once and for all to an unimportant post, but this channel of influence was not closed till 1782.

There remained, therefore, till the nineteenth century a considerable number of indeterminate permanent posts, not ministerial, which could be filled by a member of the Commons. Most of these posts had one characteristic: they involved no work, or only such work as

---

★ Order in Council of 29th November, 1884; somewhat relaxed for underlings by Order in Council of 25th July, 1927.

by time-honoured custom could be left to a deputy. They had come into existence in different ways. The enormous incomes at the Exchequer (p. 40) came from leaving fees unchanged when the size of transactions and the volume of business were multiplied many times. In the Customs (p. 98), swollen fees played a part; the reorganisation of methods of checking and account and the ebbing of trade left many posts high and dry. Not infrequently the work, but not its performer, had been abandoned in the course of generations, as with the collector and transmitter of State papers in the Foreign Office, who was paid £500 a year for duties that had passed out of memory. All that was known of the post was that it had " always existed." Generous payment frequently produced sinecures; the incumbent could farm the duties to an efficient substitute at a much lower rate. Thus the Treasury paid its Keeper of Papers £400, while he got the work done for £100. Very lowly persons could do the same; the " necessary woman "—housekeeper and charwoman—at the Home Office gave her rooms and 28 guineas a year to another who did the work.

All the upper posts in the Exchequer, Privy Seal and Signet Offices were sinecures; there were a large number in the Colonies and the Customs; the Excise, nearly as large as the Customs, with a total staff of perhaps 7,500, had only half a dozen; the Post Office only one, the Court Postmaster. The great concentration of sinecures apart from the Exchequer was in the Law Courts. The most curious group was the twenty-four cursitors of Chancery, each appointed by the Lord Chancellor for life, to make out the original writs in cases from specified counties. The cursitors had formed themselves into a corporation in the reign of Elizabeth I; in the late eighteenth and early nineteenth centuries all the work was done by four of the group for about £600 a year each; another four, whose allotted sphere was London and Middlesex, received £1,600 each in idleness, while the remaining sixteen had but £900 to share among them. Nepotism and the sale of subordinate offices were vital elements in the remuneration of the higher judiciary.

Only the most highly paid sinecures in the Civil Service were monopolised by politicians and their families. Civil Servants as well as M.P.s had their cut from the more modest, but M.P.s did not despise even small appointments; Augustus Selwyn held two small posts, worth together about £120 a year, for fifty years; Spencer Perceval, succeeding him, held on to them even when Prime Minister;

and Edmund Burke made mock of one member who was nominally a scullion in the Palace.

The sinecures were used, at least in part, to supplement official emoluments that were deemed inadequate, to make provision for ministers' families, and in substitution for other payments from public funds. The mastership of the Mint provided for the unpaid President of the Board of Trade; appointment as treasurer of the Navy for its unpaid vice-president. After the Treasury was placed in commission, the First Lord was entitled to only £1,600 a year, his share of the £8,000 assigned to the Board of five. This was brought up to £5,000 from the secret service fund until 1782, and from then till 1831 from the Civil List. Even £5,000 a year was regarded as poor, and many a First Lord was in addition Under-Treasurer and Chancellor of the Exchequer, which gave him another £2,500, made up of the two salaries of £100 each, about £700 in fees and an allowance of £1,600 in lieu of old perquisites. Other First Lords—North, Chatham and Liverpool—appointed themselves Wardens of the Cinque Ports—once a key post in the defence of the realm but now purely honorific—which carried an income of £1,100 to £1,500 in the earlier and nearly £3,000 in the later eighteenth century. One way or another, the income of a First Lord of the Treasury was uniformly brought up to £9,000 or £10,000 a year.

Appetites were not insatiable; Chatham and Burke refused to take the greater part of the emoluments of Paymaster of the Forces, and Perceval, while keeping his little Mint perquisite, left undrawn the large emoluments of Chancellor of the Exchequer.

Sir Robert Walpole, First Lord and Chancellor of the Exchequer in 1715 and from 1721 to 1742, was the great family man. He made himself, for life, Customs collector of the port of London, then worth about £2,000 a year, with the reversion of the post to his two elder sons for their lives. His uncle was Auditor of the Exchequer. His eldest son was Clerk of the Pells in the Exchequer till the uncle died and he became Auditor in his turn. The second son was made Clerk of the Pleas of Exchequer, at a paltry £400 a year, then Secretary to the Treasury, later Secretary in Ireland, and finally, when the post was freed by his brother, Clerk of the Pells. The youngest son, Horatio, the letter-writer, was given three Exchequer offices; he was Usher of the Receipts at £2,000, and, in addition, Clerk of Foreign Estreats and Comptroller of the Great Roll, bringing in between them another £500.

A few rangerships and the like were added for small change.   Nevertheless, a pension of £4,000 was granted Sir Robert when he resigned political office.

In other cases appointment to a sinecure was a substitute for a pension.   Three Lord Chancellors—Hardwicke, Northington and Camden—were provided for by appointment as tellers in the Exchequer.   A fourth—Thurlow—was promised, on his appointment to be Lord Chancellor, a pension of £2,800 a year until a teller's post fell vacant.   Pitt, when Prime Minister, diverted the clerkship of the pells from his own enjoyment to replace the pension of £3,200 which had been granted to Barré, late Treasurer of the Navy, by a previous Government.   Again, the perpetual pension of £2,000 conferred by the Commons on the heirs male for ever of the murdered Prime Minister Perceval was saved for the lifetime of the eldest son by his appointment as teller in the Exchequer.

To end their usefulness to the Government was a main motive behind the attack on idle posts by Burke in his " plan for economic reform " of 11th February, 1780.   Indeed, he agreed that the great rich offices of the Exchequer should not be touched.   With the same motive the Commons, two months later, passed the famous resolution that " the influence of the Crown has increased, is increasing and ought to be diminished."   Public savings as well as Crown influence became a burning question.   The Commons appointed a string of hard-working committees after the American War of Independence and the fall of the Government; again during the war against Napoleon, and once more in 1834, to search for overpaid or unnecessary personnel.   The Board of Trade was temporarily abolished in 1782, and some forty offices were marked for lower incomes or for ultimate discontinuance. Change was slow, for the rights of existing holders were respected; the occasions of their deaths alone were taken to stop or cut an emolument, or to transfer a sinecure title to the working deputy, with an advance in his pay if it were very modest.   The change was further assisted by the introduction of systems of retirement pensions for Civil Servants in 1810 and for politicians in 1812.

A good deal of retrenchment was effected, or decided upon as vacancies occurred, between 1782 and 1810.   The emoluments, for instance, of the Auditor of the Exchequer and of the Paymasters of the Forces were limited to £4,000, of the Clerk of the Rolls and the Master of the Mint to £3,000, of the tellers to £2,750.   A fair number of posts had been marked for extinction; some had already fallen in. Nearly 200 posts were to be suppressed in the Customs, of which fifty-five had actually gone in 1810. The fees of clerks in Whitehall offices were pooled in principle from about 1785; after a period during which the individual's income fluctuated with the business of the office, inclusive salaries were fixed, and the fees were eventually paid into the Exchequer.

The Select Committee of 1810 enumerated as still in existence in the British Isles some 240 posts which ought in due course to be abolished or transferred to lower ranks. The list included posts already scheduled for destruction, but was incomplete. The net annual expenditure on these sinecures, after subtracting income tax and the cost of deputies, was put at:

England and Wales	£178,051
Scotland	25,523
Ireland	76,435
	£280,009

The Scottish sinecures were mostly in their Law Courts and Exchequer, with some mediæval survivors like the keepers of the three Seals, and the staff of the Edinburgh Mint, which had been closed for a century. The Irish posts were likewise legal or in the Irish Exchequer.

The Civil Service of Great Britain is estimated to have numbered 16,000 to 18,000 at the beginning of the French war and half as many again at its close. In mere numbers, therefore, sinecure posts may be put at not much over 1 per cent.

There were also ninety posts in Canada and the West Indian islands held by Civil Servants, politicians and others who stayed at home and let the place and the pay at an annual rent to a deputy. The gross salary bill was £19,500, and though the Secretary of the Council of Jamaica drew £2,500, most of the salaries were small. A requirement of residence on new appointments disposed of all but four of these arrangements during the next quarter-century.

A radical change in sentiment on emoluments not directly earned occurred in the nineteenth century, about the period of parliamentary reform. Possibly the tidier mind of business was making itself felt in the Commons. Its Select Committee of 1797 thought that for " smaller persons "—meaning Civil Servants—sinecures held in plurality should be replaced by adequate salaries and a system of pensions. But they considered that the richer sinecures were useful as appendages to peerages that were conferred in reward of individual services, and that they might well be granted also to give decent dignity to retirement after long and meritorious discharge of the duties of high office. The Select Committee of 1834, when a more doctrinaire mood prevailed, pronounced, on the contrary, that " Anything in the nature of a sinecure office . . . is alike indefensible in principle, pernicious as a means of influence and grievous as an undue addition to the general burden of the nation." The report of this committee accordingly called for the abolition of all known sinecures outside the Law Courts that were not definitely ministerial. The Treasury were advised to buy out half a dozen hereditary offices; amongst them were the posts of Chief Usher of the Exchequer, given in perpetuity by Henry II in the twelfth century, long held by a female representative of the Heneage family and worth but £137 a year; of the Remembrancer of First Fruits in the same office, which Charles II had made hereditary; and that of Grand Falconer of England, which dated only from James II. (The Grand Falconer, the Duke of St. Albans, still performed his titular duties, on which he spent half his salary of £965 a year.)

The great majority, however, of Civil Servants in the eighteenth and early nineteenth centuries worked at the employments for which they were paid at moderate rates. Clerks generally started at £45, £50 or £60 and rose to about £90, if not promoted; the grade immediately above ran from about £100 to £160 in the Stamp Office, but in some offices the promotion grade might rise to £225, or even £300. In the Home Office, where each clerk had a separate grading, the lowest had £80; the highest—the chief clerk, corresponding to the present Permanent Under-secretary of State—had £1,000. The average salary of the twelve clerks in 1795 was £285, including receipts, which were numerous, from other Government employment; the chief clerk, for instance, drew an extra £410 as clerk of the Crown in Canada and deputy in the Signet Office. All ranks could expect to continue until they dropped in their tracks, or, exceptionally, to be pensioned off on full salary or something near it.

The whole of Government business was so small and so standardised that all decisions outside the bounds of red tape could be taken by ministers. The Admiralty, for instance, had a total clerical staff of only fifty-five at the end of the war in 1813, and by 1822 had reduced their number to twenty-four. Practically the whole Civil Service could work to rule, and, with individual exceptions, at an easy pace. Office hours were short. The virtuous Stamp Office opened from 7.30 a.m. to 2 p.m., but some offices in the West End only for two or three hours from noon, or later. It was invariably understood, however, that these hours were subject to pressure of business and that all stayed as late as the public interest required. Work in office or field was clearly done conscientiously and thoroughly, but there had to be sufficient staff for the heavy seasons, and often there was leisure and youth enough in the office for skylarking, boisterous games and, in Whitehall, entertainment of friends.

There were no vacations, but holy days were numerous. The Act of 1553, which fixed the number of idle week-days in the year at twenty-eight, was still in force, with the addition to the saints' days and festivals of the Church of the anniversaries of Charles I's execution and Charles II's restoration by a statute of 1660. Guy Fawkes and the Burning of London had been added by other statutes. Each department was a law to itself in allowing further days. The Customs were content with shutting for forty-four week-days a year; the Stamp Office made its total fifty-two; the Excise followed the Customs, outside its headquarter office, which shut for fifty-six. The statutory list was increased, differently in different departments, not only by the inclusion of further saints' days, which one would have thought heretical, if not actually treasonable, but by abstaining from work on other loyal occasions. The Excise thus honoured the accessions of Elizabeth I and George III, the landings in England of William of Orange, George I and George II, and four Royal birthdays.

The pay of many lower grades was raised in the forty years before Queen Victoria's accession, at the very time when ministerial and other high remuneration was reduced. All who were admitted to be permanently employed " on the establishment " were given pensions on retirement after ten years of service, which ranged up to two-thirds of final pay after service of forty years, with further additions for special cases which were gradually eliminated in later times. Discharge between sixty and sixty-five became normal.

The head and under clerks of Whitehall are described by Charles Knight, in his *London* (1843), as " a people apart," who clung together and conversed on technicalities in an esoteric tongue. The subordinate clerks, mostly Cockneys, gradually promoted, were liable to be sent on missions abroad and to become oracles at home. The head clerks, aspiring to be called secretaries, were written down as fetching and carrying machines. They flocked together at night to their chosen suburbs, as to rookeries, within a reasonable walk of the office, but on a bus route in case of rain, and talked incessantly of office trivialities. Head clerks came from all three kingdoms; Scotsmen more than any others became mere office furniture. The type was observed to have changed of late; a new generation had arisen " with more assumption and less character," who affected literary tastes, producing tragedies and dissertations on red tape, the folding of letters and other official matters, like statistics. Mockery apart, they were clearly devoted to and absorbed in their profession: " His heart was at his office, his heart was always there, A-docketing the papers and minuting with care."

16

THE GIANT STRIDE

A N image has been built up in the public mind of a Civil Service that during the first half of the nineteenth century was filled with incompetents by ministers for the sake of votes. Most appointments rested in theory with the minister in charge of each department, or with the patronage secretary of the Treasury for departments which it controlled; but in practice recruits were chosen at different levels. Those for the Admiralty office were selected during 1809–30 by the political but almost permanent secretary Croker, who took the duty conscientiously; while dockyard staff posts were the concern of the Navy Board, and workmen of the local officers or of master-craftsmen. Although Post Office patronage vested solely in the Postmaster-Generals, the permanent secretary seems to have had a free hand in his own office and other permanent officials in theirs; it could never have been convenient to disregard entirely the man responsible for getting work done. The Prime Minister transferred Customs appointments to the commissioners for that service in 1820. Many departments imposed their own tests, conducted, however farcically, by their own officers, in handwriting, arithmetic or other essentials. The Customs had instituted such tests before 1700; they existed by the early nineteenth century in the Treasury, Audit, Admiralty, Emigration, Ordnance, Pay, National Debt, Privy Council, Registry General, Excise, Inland Revenue, Works (for clerk of works) and elsewhere.

Nor was the political motive for courting bad service overwhelmingly strong. Favouritism was needless for pocket boroughs, and a few improper appointments would not catch votes in a large electorate; the oligarchies of moderate size alone could repay nursing. The Treasury patronage secretary practically relinquished his rights as regards most rank-and-file appointments in the provinces to members of Parliament, who cannot have been wholly improvident over employment in their own constituencies. By 1823 the custom of the Treasury on the occurrence of a vacancy in the outposts of Customs, Excise or Stamp

Office was to write to that member of Parliament for the county or borough who generally voted with the Government and invite his recommendation. Members of Parliament came to regard nominations as their right; in 1829 the Duke of Wellington complained, as of an abuse, that the privilege had ceased to depend on any support of Government measures. But by the 1850s many members had become conscious that a power which was so widespread gave each little advantage over his rivals, while it entailed an onerous correspondence and unpleasantness with the many disappointed applicants.

The first restraint on patronage was imposed in 1833 in the recruitment of the attractive Indian Civil Services. The East India Board, or its individual directors, were required by the Charter Act to nominate four times as many candidates as there were vacancies. Three-quarters were then eliminated by competition in academic examination. Macaulay recommended to Parliament this novel way of selecting British nationals to rule India by a eulogy of scholarship as a test of ability, regardless of subject: " If instead of learning Greek we learned the Cherokee, the man who understood the Cherokee best, who made the most correct and melodious verses, who comprehended most accurately the effect of the Cherokee particles, would generally be a superior man to him who was destitute of these accomplishments." Countless generations of mandarins of China would have bowed their approval. The system was adopted for India, only to be dropped in 1837; but sixteen years later, in 1853, nominations were abolished and open competitive examination became the gateway to follow Clive and Hastings.

Sir Charles Trevelyan had spent twelve years (1826–38) in the Bengal Civil Service; he was the Treasury permanent secretary—assistant secretary as the title then was—from 1840 to 1859, when he returned to India to be Governor of Madras and later, Finance Minister. He was a brilliant, unbalanced man who was not impressed with the quality of Whitehall staffs. (Sir) Stafford Northcote, afterwards first Earl of Iddesleigh, had been private secretary to Gladstone at the Board of Trade and the Mint in his youth; then a legal assistant in the Board of Trade, and latterly a secretary of the Great Exhibition. Gladstone, as Chancellor of the Exchequer, appointed these two to enquire into the organisation of the permanent Civil Service.

The report which they made on 23rd November, 1853, was scathing. It premised that the growth of business, the other preoccupations of

N

ministers, and the rapidity with which they changed, made it impossible for the government to be carried on without " the Permanent Civil Service of the Country," " to advise, assist and to some extent influence those who are from time to time set over them." Recruits to these important services normally entered in the bottom grade, were employed for many years on copying and routine, and advanced several steps during a long life by seniority alone, but were not trained for and could seldom hope to be promoted to the very highest posts. In some departments they were even ineligible for these. Admission to the service was " eagerly sought, but it is only for the unambitious and the indolent or incapable that it is chiefly desired." With " numerous honourable exceptions," most entrants had little thought of rising to public eminence. On the contrary, the certainty of pension " furnished strong inducements to the parents and friends of sickly youths to endeavour to obtain for them " Government employment, while at higher ages " the dregs of all other professions are attracted to the public service as to a secure asylum." As these officers were unlikely to reach, so they remained unfit for, the highest posts in their department, which were therefore filled in the public interest by appointments from outside. But the outsiders chosen were, according to the report, often poor creatures, no better than the rejected, and so the result was to increase the despondency in the lower ranks.

This was a dark picture; but it was a figment. Having tacitly excluded two-thirds of the service, the report stated that it covered 16,000 persons,* whose grades and whereabouts were left to be guessed. This vagueness left the way open for a bright, epigrammatic report, of which the sweeping strictures have no relevance to offices that are certainly included, such as St. Martin's le Grand and its provincial surveyors and postmasters, the staffs of the Customs and the Excise and the Stamp Office. The report becomes intelligible, though still false, if the authors are presumed to have had in mind only the offices round Whitehall and their very few hundred clerks. Some of these should have been discharged during their probation, but the attractions of the Government service seem also to have brought in, to keep ledgers, copy letters, and fetch and put away files, men who on the whole were too good for the task. After Trevelyan's time lower and lower levels of recruitment were explored, but still the cry went on of wasted capacity.

---

* The census of 1851 registered 53,000 Civil Servants; many people thought 16,000 a gross exaggeration; all depends on definition.

Since dull chores made up nine-tenths of the work that had to be done, and posts requiring great qualities were very few, budding statesmen were likely to be spoiled by a lifetime of routine. A second line of recruitment near the top was necessary, as it always had been. The authorities might have been as reckless as was alleged over entries of rank and file, but they were unlikely to be indifferent to the quality of these special appointments of their key personnel. None of the alleged " numerous " instances of appointments of " men of very slender capacity and perhaps of questionable character " could be identified. The heads of departments of the time seem to have been more than competent. All departments did not need paragons. No Foreign Secretary would have tolerated advice from his highest official for half a century yet. But in the Colonial Office, where, on the contrary, the shaping of policy devolved on the permanent head from an early date, three successive under-secretaries, each appointed from outside after relevant Government experience, fully justified their choice. Sir James Stephen, colloquially " Mr. Over-Secretary Stephen," " literally ruled the colonial empire " from 1836 to 1847; Herman Merivale, who followed him from 1848 to 1859 and left to be Permanent Secretary at the India Office, was a man of great distinction and energy; his successor, Sir Frederic Rogers, Lord Blatchford, likewise " governed " the colonies till 1871. Indeed, political ministers in the Colonial Office, though three-quarters of the papers were formally submitted to them, contributed nothing but their initials till Joseph Chamberlain's appointment in 1893. Even the top Treasury staff under Trevelyan himself was very capable.

The allegations of the report were refuted with almost a single voice by statesmen and leading Civil Servants.

The two reformers propounded a mixed board of educational experts and officials with a Privy Councillor at their head to investigate the age, health, moral fitness and bodily activity of all candidates, and subject those who were not found to be flawed to one of two competitive written examinations " for intelligence as well as attainments." One examination for the more exacting posts should be of University standard and taken between eighteen and twenty-five years of age; the other should be based on an ordinary commercial education and be taken at seventeen to twenty-one at local centres dispersed throughout the country. Specialist competitions were also contemplated. To provide a good field, all vacancies and impending vacancies were to be pooled. A beneficial effect on University education was confidently foretold; schoolmasters warmly welcomed the promised market for their wares.

While admitting that "a very large majority" of Civil Servants would object strongly to promotion by merit, detailed proposals were made to temper seniority by regard for it. Provided that members of the staff of other departments were first considered, direct appointments from outside to the highest posts were, however, to continue.

The Government in power fell; the succeeding Palmerston ministry shared a fairly general scepticism, but went far enough to impede unsuitable recruits. An Order in Council on 21st May, 1855, set up a commission of three for the admission of persons to the Civil Service of the Crown. Selection by the department concerned continued to be the first step, but before it could take effect the nominee had to obtain from the Civil Service Commission its certificate of satisfaction with his age, health, character and ability—which last implied examinations. An exception was made for men of mature age and special attainments if the head of the department certified the necessity for such an appointment.

The first three commissioners were:

Sir Edward Ryan, F.R.S., a former Chief Justice of Bengal, a member of the Judicial Committee of the Privy Council, a railway commissioner and assistant Comptroller-General of the Exchequer; Sir John George Shaw Lefevre, F.R.S., clerk of the Parliaments; and Edward Romilly, Chairman of the Board of Audit.

Romilly withdrew after six months on grounds of health and his other occupations. Lefevre resigned in 1862 and was succeeded by an ex-Governor-General of Canada. The number of commissioners remained at two until 1875.

The commissioners threw their net much wider than the Northcote–Trevelyan exploration called for. Their mild survey took in during the first eighteen months the staffs of the Houses both of Lords and of Commons, of Chelsea Hospital, the Ecclesiastical Commissioners, police courts and offices, Irish Constabulary, and Northern Lighthouses, as well as Consuls, diplomatic attachés and Ceylon writers; from their third year they conducted the examinations for the Indian Civil Service and for Army commissions.

In the main, merely qualifying examinations were held for home posts; for the few that purported to be competitive, the nominating departments either put in a number of candidates which did not much exceed the vacancies, or, if they put up three candidates for one post, two of them were men of straw. The commissioners on their part felt their functions to be "so novel and peculiar" that they trod very gingerly. They took over the conduct of the previous internal examinations by departments, but were careful not to raise the standard, except in the solitary case of one "competitive" examination for two Treasury vacancies, for which there were four candidates. In framing new examinations for posts that had not hitherto been subject to qualifying tests, the commissioners embodied the most trifling and probably unconscious divergencies in the proposals of different departments, although the staffs affected were identical and despite their own preference for uniformity.

With the commissioners to take the burden, nominating departments made no effort to weed out the unsuitable. Out of 3,004 candidates dealt with by the Commission in its first eighteen months, ninety-nine were passed on the bare word of the sponsor; sixty were outside the prescribed age limits; twelve were physically unfit and ten were rejected on grounds of character; only 1,587 received certificates. Of the balance, 880 were wholly rejected, but 219 were more kindly declared unsuccessful. The wholly rejected to the end of 1859 numbered 1,972; of these 95 per cent had been rejected for spelling or arithmetic. Among less elementary blunderers, one candidate conceived that Marlborough fought the Spanish Armada and thoroughly destroyed it; another that the Roman Wall in England was built to keep the Tartars out; a poor geographer thought that the Alps were in Hungary and Germany in the Caspian Sea. The commissioners emphasised that the posts were in the main humble—tidewaiters, letter-carriers, or junior clerks—and that the failures reflected more on the sponsoring departments than on the educational system.

The Commission's best efforts on entries could not have altered the upper staff of the Civil Service in five years, but on that body, amongst others, the mischances of the Crimean War were unjustly blamed. A Select Committee of 1860 declared that the Commission's Order in Council had been largely evaded and that its competitions were "shams" and "a fertile source of abuse." It again recommended two general examinations, of University and commercial education standard respectively, for clerks, with suitable educational tests for outdoor staff, but with the proviso that at least three qualified candidates should be nominated for each vacancy.

The Civil Service Commission was strengthened in 1862 by the grant of a salary as First Commissioner to Sir Edward Ryan, on which he resigned his other appointments. The three-to-one ratio was observed, and some small advance was made in offices towards classifying work by engaging supplementary clerks or hiring writers, on piecework, from law stationers to do their copying. Some offices had brought in copying presses, which continued in service till the 1914–18 war; otherwise all duplicates had to be written by hand.

The idea of untrammelled competition by scholastic ability for Government triumphed at last in an Order in Council which was put through on 4th June, 1870, by that tempestuous Chancellor of the Exchequer, the Robert Lowe of the epitaph:

> " Here lie the bones of Robert Lowe;
> Where he's gone to we don't know.
> If to the realms of peace and love,
> Farewell to happiness above."

Open competitive examination on behalf of the Civil Service Commissioners was instituted for all office appointments, except those definitely excepted in a gazetted list. The exceptions included the multitude of humble, menial or temporary employments, posts that required professional or specialised qualifications and a small number filled by Order in Council, under the Royal sign manual or under the Great Seal. Treasury approval was made necessary for any addition to or removal from the list, and Treasury powers over personnel generally were asserted. Clerical posts were still divided between only two examinations, of which the stiffer was for the group called successively Scheme I, Higher Division, Class I and Administrative Class, and the less advanced for that called Scheme II, Lower or Second Division.

The improvement of the upper group was the principal target of Northcote and Trevelyan; how far was it secured? The Board of Education, the experts in schools, stood out against the new ways and continued to recruit their administrative class with much success by mere nomination. The Treasury, after a decent interval, by-passed the Class I examination for years at a time by alleging that they had no vacancies; after the lists were closed, they selected their upper staff from those who had been tried out for a year or two in other departments. Anthony Trollope, a practical man who organised the Post Office in the provinces, could find no benefit in the competitions. Sir C. Rivers Wilson, the first entrant to the Treasury by examination, concluded at the end of his long life that the new system had not supplied better men than the best of the old, but that it had raised the average and reduced the number of "Q.H.B.'s," the Queen's Hard Bargains, the absolute failures. And a reduction in hypothetical Q.H.B.'s was as much as heads of other departments would concede to the system. A craft or profession of coaching candidates through Government examinations was their immediate product; apparently it vitiated the tests, for every subsequent enquiry tried to defeat the coaches.

Only twenty recruits had been admitted by the Class I examination, 1870 vintage, when another Chancellor of the Exchequer—the Northcote who had acted with Trevelyan—set up a committee in 1874 of six heads of departments, with one M.P. member and another—the brilliant Lyon Playfair—as chairman, to consider recruitment and grading afresh. This committee introduced a new grade at the bottom—boy clerks, who were to obtain promotion by examination or be discharged at nineteen; it improved pay; and it recommended that promotion to posts above the first grade of Scheme I entrants, whose numbers were to be kept small, should be made by merit throughout the service and irrespective of department. Nothing came of the last recommendation.

Up to this date, action had been taken in the main by the Treasury. The restoration of the franchise to Civil Servants generally in 1867, the growing strength of their unions and associations (which began in the Post Office about that date) and of other pressure groups, and magnified numbers caused future controversy to be remitted to Royal Commissions. These had in practice to concern themselves principally with improving the pay and prospects of those already in the service. Levelling up and uniformity went together, and uniformity strengthened the associations further. The first of the Royal Commissions was appointed in 1886 under the chairmanship of Sir Matthew White Ridley, in response to laments by the lower division, and sat for four years. It recommended general increases of pay for the various office classes, and standardisation throughout the departments of holidays and sick leave and of an attendance, including meal times, of seven hours daily; six and a half hours had been common. All departments were asked to recruit their messengers in part, as the War Office already did wholly, from time-expired soldiers. About half did so in the course of a quarter of a century.

The upper division had indeed been limited; it was only employed in the small Whitehall departments, the Admiralty, War Office, Inland Revenue and Customs and Excise, which last presently dropped it. The lower division was not competent in all places to deal with the work upon which it was employed. The Admiralty started four separate examinations of intermediate standard for four of their book-keeping sub-departments; these examinations were amalgamated by the Civil Service Commissioners in 1896, and the new intermediate class of clerk was very gradually extended to other offices—the Ordnance factories in 1903, then the Audit office, the Estate Duty office in 1907, the Bankruptcy department of the Board of Trade in 1911. Another new general class of assistant clerks or abstractors was created by Order in Council in 1898 to save from discharge boy clerks or copyists who could not pass the lower division examination for promotion. Boy clerks, however, were being ousted by machines. After the Inland Revenue tried the experiment of typists in the seventies, the Treasury sought steadily to force girls and women, as typists and shorthand typists, on all departments. They had succeeded with about half by 1911. A mischievous tale attributes to the Sea Lords the refusal of the Admiralty : " My Lords cannot conceal their preference for boys." The Post Office and Inland Revenue, being large users, ran open competitions for the new type. All other departments reverted gladly to personal selection. The Secretary to the Treasury, Sir George Murray, explained blandly to the next Royal Commission that this, his only bit of personal patronage, was used to benefit the orphans of dead officials, provided they were competent, but he did not expect to convince; nor did he.

The crop of new departments in the years 1908–11 required large staffs. The Office of the Public Trustee was created in 1908 for the management of testators' estates and family trusts. Its permanent head, having been appointed by the Lord Chancellor, was supplied with funds and left to engage and employ at his sole discretion his staff of some 240, who were regarded as his servants. Personal staffs of this sort, once so common, were still the rule in many Government units— the offices of the solicitors of all departments, of consuls and vice-consuls abroad and of surveyors and inspectors of taxes at home. The clerks of the last, however, succeeded in this year (1908) in getting transferred to direct Government employment.

The Road Board and the Development Commission, created in 1909, were mainly filled by selection of Civil Servants from other departments. The Labour Exchanges of the Board of Trade, which began to operate in September 1909, and the National Health Insurance Commission offices of July 1911, required recruitment from outside on a large scale. Committees of officials of the responsible department advertised for and sifted applications; a second series of committees of the department and the Civil Service Commission interviewed the survivors and selected from them names, still numerous, for appointment by the minister. Choice here, too, had gone back to personal impressions.

The second Royal Commission was appointed under the chairmanship of Lord MacDonnell in 1912 to give a sympathetic hearing to the many hungry claimants. Its task was reduced by the contemporary appointment of a Select Committee on the pay of post-office employees, and it decided to omit the industrial staffs of dockyards, arsenals and manufacturing departments. Even so, it reckoned that it had to deal with about 60,000 persons. Every member found it expedient to make in the fourth and main report one or more minority findings on his or her particular interest. It fused boy clerks with assistant clerks, and second division with intermediate clerks, in a junior and a senior clerical class with improvements in pay, and made the departmental first divisions a common administrative group with uniform pay. It recommended that transfers and promotions between departments should be free and frequent, with adequate machinery to ensure fairness. A hard-headed minority of three held that this nomadic habit would suit the individual better than the business of the State and drew attention, not unnaturally in view of the many millions of words delivered to the Commission, to the " lamentable amount of time " spent by Civil Servants, some in composing, and others in answering, memorials on grievances.

All patronage and personal selection that still survived were to cease; and open competition, or at least competition amongst nominees, was to be applied even to the most specialised work in a museum. While not denying the success of the steps recently taken to obtain Labour Exchange and insurance personnel, the Commission hoped that they would not be repeated. It abolished indirect employment by supporting the transfer of personal employees to the more generous service of the State. Ex-soldiers were given a leg up; practically all messenger jobs were to become unpensionable and to be reserved for them in future.

Women were a particularly thorny topic. Their employment was confined to certain large blocks of work which they monopolised. The suffragette organisations demanded their employment everywhere at the same pay as men. The entry and early promotion of women to make up for lost time were asked for strictly on their merits, if these sufficed; but if they did not, enough merit should be imputed to secure the result. The theory that women should be paid the same as men in all posts with similar names could not be so quietly compromised; party interest seemed to require the plunder of the public purse. Those out of power have ever since then clamoured for acquiescence, while those in power postponed it till easier days. " Petticoats up " has always been the cry; equality by " Trousers down " attracts no votes. Neither did it pay to recall that normal women were somewhat less useful in those spheres, though to rate them at a half, as in one department's estimate, seems low. So the constant drips wore away not too stony hearts, and in 1955 the compliment of the same pay was given, subject to a lowering of the rates drawn by a few men, which would have been too grotesque for their female counterparts, and to a modest differential where male duties were patently more onerous. The increase was spread over seven years to lessen immediate consequences.

Action on the MacDonnell proposals was delayed by the First World War. The Civil Service, already increased by a half since 1900, was doubled in number during its course. Old departments bulged and spread; new departments were founded. The Ministry of Munitions alone soared from nothing to a staff of 25,000, who were dispersed over more than 100 buildings in London. The expansion was met by collecting temporary staff by mere nomination or selection, much as in the old days, but on a grander scale. It was organised and officered by ample transfers and promotions of Civil Servants, whose unsatisfying remuneration had yet attracted abilities far beyond their previous duties; and by bringing in large numbers of heads of successful businesses. Some of these even displaced ministers. Whether employed at high or low levels, they naturally clung to those direct and personal methods which had already served them well, and this influx of different experience, with the urgency of the times and the general flux of personnel, was the death of many elaborations of Civil Service routine.

Four developments may be traced to these contacts with the world of business and their renewal in the Second World War. First, machines began to dominate the office as well as the factory. The Treasury found it necessary in the end to form a special section within itself to foster and guide resort to mechanical applicances throughout the Civil Service. It is doubtful, indeed, whether the output of top copies by a typist, allowing for the labours of controls and checks, exceeds that of the ancient writer by hand; the gain is in the simultaneous production of copies. The carbon and the card-punching and sorting machine are the linchpins of modern administration.

Secondly, after two centuries of turning the entourages of great officials into impersonal hierarchies, the private office came back into its own. " Five private secretaries? " said Sir Eric Geddes when he became First Lord of the Admiralty : " I will have fifteen." Leading ministers had their " circuses," but personal assistants were in time accorded to officials far down the scale; to every man, a maiden or two.

Thirdly, oral discussion and conference replaced more formal communications between departments on controversial or complex questions. Central administration reverted, as under the Restoration Privy Council, to a denser cloud of committees. Sceptics declared that no question was decided after the Second World War unless it was large enough to warrant a conference, where it was not decided.

And fourthly, the sanctity of written examinations became suspect; more and more, interviews—competitive, of course—and even more elaborate methods, were demanded as correctives, until the Civil Service Commissioners recently dispensed with examinations altogether for London clerkships.

Since Government activities did not shrink to the old level after the First World War, one of the first tasks was to transfer the sweets of office from those taken on during its course to men whose careers had been interrupted by the war. Special arrangements were made for their selection for permanent employment in the upper grades. In the routine classes the numbers and the need were great, and the minimum standard of attainments was put low. The result was a large new class of unestablished ex-service clerks, of whom the best were above the examination average and were rapidly promoted; but the ruck was only explicable as a mass political appointment.

The internal governance of the Civil Service was radically altered during and after this war. The change seems to have sprung originally from the abandonment of the gold sovereign. The purely paper money which ensued and the wages paid in it did not long keep their value; an arbitration court had to be set up to raise nominal wages; and a special division of this was assigned to the Civil Service. The ultimate control of Civil Service remuneration, for all grades up to a prescribed level, was thus transferred to a standing body which was outside Government control.

The Government also endeavoured to bring private employers and employed closer together by recommending the formation of councils in which the two sides of an industry or factory would thresh out its problems. The Civil Service proved a kindlier field for the new experiment than that for which it was originally meant. Here the employers were themselves employees, and no nice calculations of profit and loss had to be made. A single Whitley Council for all Government staffs other than industrial was set up in 1919 for the discussion of general questions up to a level at which the employers' side might cease to be disinterested. The two sides, each some twenty-seven strong, were composed respectively of high officials from the larger departments and secretaries of or delegates from the various staff organisations. Similar bodies of departmental membership and scope were set up in each department. The staff organisations remained free to pursue their sectional interests, with ultimate reference to the Industrial Court. The great industrial Trade Unions refused to take part on behalf of their members; separate bodies with precautions against trespass on what the Unions regarded as their peculiar field were set up for industrial staffs. Impressive hierarchies were developed for handling these conclaves and arbitrations; whole sub-departments were created in the Treasury and each of the larger departments whose sole business was management of personnel, conduct of negotiations and application of the ever-growing body of agreed rules.

These exhaustive arrangements for increasing the cost of the Civil Service in the manner most agreeable to its members did not avert a further Royal Commission which was appointed in 1929 under Lord Tomlin and sat for two years considering their grievances. This Commission advanced still further the growing uniformity between different departments; it laid down new scales, compromised over the pay and employment of women and abolished employments which were called temporary, but which holders could seldom be persuaded to quit, by transfers after a certain period to the permanent and pensionable list.

In another eight years another war brought on another period of expansion, rapid promotion and renewed depreciation of money. Twelve new departments were created in the years 1939–45. After the end of the war, the Government decided to take over permanently large spheres which had hitherto been left in private control—railways, mines, electricity, gas, central banking, and so on. Their employees, however, instead of being absorbed into direct Government service, were left in the charge of corporations which were formed for the purpose. Universal health benefits and Cripps's devaluation of the pound followed. Within the Civil Service, large personnel departments, Whitley councils and arbitration courts could not keep pace with the changing conditions and rising demands, with which a fourth Royal Commission is now struggling.

Government servants are still (end of 1954) more than a million in number. The workers by hand in dockyards, arsenals and other manufactories number some 430,000; these are distinguished as industrials. Of the rest, nearly a quarter of a million are employed in a single great department, the Post Office; the fighting departments and their two supply departments account for 134,000; 257,000 odd are left for all civil departments other than the Post Office. This great force is split up among a hundred separate departments, which differ greatly in size. The entry, promotion, allotment of duties and retirement, at last, of its members are governed by elaborate rules. Obviously an organisation so wide and so diversified must operate on the whole within rule and precedent.

Mere change of scale has shifted even the higher responsibilities from ministry to Civil Service. The Northcote–Trevelyan report, 100 years ago, appears to be the first recognition that ministers' servants might influence policy. The statement was belated for some departments, premature for others, but " the formation of policy " has now been included for a generation in the defined duties of the administrative class, which is some 3,000 strong. The transient political head of each department is none the less held responsible for all that is done or left undone therein, although his power of changing even his immediate subordinates is limited and his knowledge of necessity tenuous. His control is assured by inviolable practice and the irresistible force of professional etiquette. Even if parliamentary debate and question and his own bright notions of reforming the world did not elicit a stream of reports, his department consider it his duty more than his right to decide on all that may have public repercussions or large implications, or on any question which his pledges or prejudices might affect. The innocent, but wily, politician cannot escape anything short of complete responsibility, even if it has to be thrust upon him. There have been ministers in the long ago who compromised by deciding in pencil and using a rubber if the event went agley; dabs of gum foiled such retreats. But evasion by a minister who has been troubled on too light a matter is accepted: "I do not," one wrote many years ago at the foot of an exactly balanced submission, "comprehend the conclusion of your memorandum, but I agree with it."

Owner-drivers became owners with chauffeurs, as it were, as the car of State grew more complex. These ministerial owners decide destination, pace, the colour of the car or what else they will, but depend on their chauffeurs to deal with technical detail and with choices of roadway.

17

LITERARY LIGHTS

THE old King's Service needed all the arts and employed recognised exponents of each in their several spheres. It was the patron of architects and nurse of medallists. The King's musicians enlivened his Court, and though painters and sculptors were commonly employed on commission, a Master of the King's Pictures was taken on the salaried strength soon after the Restoration. The claims of literature were honoured about the same time by the distinction and modest emoluments of Poets Laureate and later by a succession of Civil List pensions.

All in all, the art of the written word has had little connection with the craft of administration and with clerks. The universal efflorescence of the Tudor age touched officialdom as it touched everybody else. Masters of the pen were drawn in during the Commonwealth and again after the Revolution for much the same reasons as lie behind public relations officers in our day. The Board of Trade was afterwards reputed 'a nest of singing birds', and there were similar concentrations in later times in the Colonial Office, Consular and Diplomatic services and Post Office.

The list below does not pretend to completeness or entire consistency. Later writers on their own departments, of the type of the author of the Dialogue on the Exchequer, have been disregarded. Gower and Gibbon have been included; but others whose connection with the Civil Service was as fleeting have been omitted. Specialist writers like Sir Isaac Newton and, on a lower level, J. D. Hume of the Customs, Sir Edward Ryan of the Civil Service Commission and Sir John Simon of the Local Government Board, have been considered not to qualify. Ministers, from Bacon to Canning and Disraeli, would be out of place, but Croker as a hybrid has been admitted.

The list stops with entries into the service before the Boer War, in view of the growth in the itch for writing; in the Treasury alone, in the next two decades, at least six of an upper staff of twenty produced books of some note—economic, historical, linguistic, mathematical, even poetry. The list is arranged in rough chronological order. The epithet appended to each writer is an identifying rather than a descriptive label. The dates are those during which public office was held.

Ely, Richard of, Dialogus — Treasurer, *c.* 1156–96
Bury, Richard of, bibliographer — Privy Seal, Treasurer, *c.* 1327–40
Chaucer, Geoffrey, poet — Customs, Works, Woods, 1374–1400
Gower, John, poet — Customs, 1378–?
Hoccleve, Thomas, poet — Privy Seal, *c.* 1387–1450
Lyndwood, Bishop William, canonist — Privy Seal, *c.* 1417–46
Ashby, George, poet — Signet, 1438–60
Hawes, Stephen, poet — Chamber, *c.* 1500–30
Bourchier, Sir John, Lord Berners, translator — Exchequer, 1516

Elyot, Sir Thomas, novelist — Privy Council, Diplomatic, 1523–35
Thynne, Francis, editor of Chaucer — Clerk of Kitchen, *c.* 1530
Wyatt, Sir Thomas, poet — Jewel House, Diplomatic, 1524–?, 1537–40

Ascham, Roger, educationalist — Diplomatic, Latin secretary, 1550–?68
Spenser, Edmund, poet — Irish Offices, 1580–94
Greville, Sir Fulke, Lord Brooke — Secretariat, Exchequer, 1583–1628
Donne, John, poet — Chancery, 1596–1601
Sackville, Thomas, Earl of Dorset, poet — Treasurer, 1599–1606
Carew, Thomas, poet — Household, ?1613–39
Wotton, Sir Henry — Diplomatic, 1604–24
Alexander, William, Earl of Stirling, poet — Taxes, Requests, Secretary for Scotland, 1608–40
Ashmole, Elias, antiquarian — Excise, 1644–?, 1660–3
Milton, John, poet — Latin secretary, 1649–60
Marvell, Andrew, poet — Foreign and Latin secretary, Diplomatic, 1653–65

Evelyn, John, F.R.S., diarist — Sick and wounded seamen, Trade, 1653–72

Waller, Edmund, poet — Trade, 1655–60
Denham, Sir John, poet — Works, 1660–9
Pepys, Samuel, F.R.S., diarist and historian — Navy Board, Admiralty, 1660–79, 1684–9
Howard, Sir Robert, dramatist — Treasury and Exchequer, 1671–98
Locke, John, F.R.S., philosopher — Trade, 1672–3, 1696–1700
Burchett, Josiah, historian — Admiralty, 1680–1742
Dryden, John, F.R.S., poet laureate — Customs, 1683–8
Prior, Matthew, poet — Diplomatic, Trade, Customs, 1689–1714

Congreve, William, dramatist — Wine and coach licensing, 1695–1714
Defoe, Daniel, journalist — Glass duty, 1695–9

Vanbrugh, Sir John, dramatist	Works, 1702–26
Addison, Joseph, poet	Excise, Secretariat, Records, 1704–18
Steele, Sir Richard, essayist	Gazette, Stamp Office, 1707–13
Mottley, John, dramatist, historian	Excise, 1708–20
Rowe, Nicholas, dramatist	Secretariat, Customs, 1709–?17
Gay, John, poet, dramatist	Lottery commission, 1722–31
Fountaine, Sir Andrew, antiquarian	Mint, 1727–54
Weston, Edward, moralist	Secretariat, 1730–64
Popple, William, dramatist	Trade, colonial governor, 1730–64
Harris, Joseph, scientist, economist	Mint, 1737–64
Walpole, Horace, letter-writer	Exchequer etc., 1738–97
Cumberland, Richard, dramatist	Board of Trade, Ireland, Board of Trade, 1748–84
Wood, Robert, explorer	Secretariat, 1756–70
Paine, Thomas, pamphleteer	Customs, 1761–5, 1768–74
Bruce, James, explorer	Consular, 1763–5
Hume, David, historian, philosopher	Foreign Office, 1763–8
Burgess, Sir James Blair, poet	Bankruptcy, Foreign Office, 1779–1825
Gibbon, Edward, historian	Trade, 1779–82
Byng, John, 5th Viscount Torrington, diarist	Stamps, 1782–1813
Chalmers, George, antiquarian, biographer, economist	Trade, 1786–1825
Burns, Robert, poet	Excise, 1788–96
Lamb, Charles, essayist	India House, 1792–1825
Young, Arthur, novelist, economist	Agriculture, 1793–1820
Marsden, William, F.R.S., orientalist	Admiralty, 1795–1807
Moore, Thomas, poet	Colonial service, 1803–19?
Barrow, Sir John, explorer	Admiralty, 1804–45
Hallam, Henry, historian	Stamps, 1806–26
Hunt, James Henry Leigh, poet, essayist	War Office, 1806–8
Morier, James Justinian, novelist	Diplomatic, 1807–17
Croker, John Wilson, F.R.S., journalist	Admiralty, 1809–30
Hook, Theodore Edward, humorist	Colonial service, 1813–18
Stephen, Sir James, journalist	Colonial Office, 1813–47
Smith, John Thomas, humorist	British Museum, 1816–33
Peacock, Thomas Love, novelist	India House, 1819–56
Cole, Sir Henry, " Felix Summerly ", publicist	Record Office, Treasury, Education, 1823–73
Taylor, Sir Henry, poet	Colonial Office, 1824–72
Merivale, John Harman, poet	Bankruptcy, 1831–44
Lever, Charles James, novelist	Health, 1831–3
Procter, Bryan Waller (Barry Cornwall), poet	Lunacy, 1832–61
Praed, Winthrop Mackworth, poet	Control, 1834–5
Chadwick, Sir Edwin, journalist	Poor Law, Health, 1834–54
Trollope, Anthony, novelist	Post Office, 1834–67

O

Spedding, James, Baconian — Colonial Office, Civil Service Commission, 1835–58

Head, Sir Edmund Walker, F.R.S., poet, translator — Colonial governorships, Civil Service Commission, 1836–68

Palgrave, Sir Francis, historian — Record Office, 1838–61

McCullough, James Ramsay, economist — Stationery Office, 1838–64

Scudamore, Frank Ives, humorist — Post Office, 1841–75

Rosetti, William Michael, biographer — Inland Revenue, 1845–94

Hawes, Sir Benjamin, political writer — Colonial and War Offices, 1846–62

Patmore, Coventry Kearney Deighton, poet — British Museum, 1846–65

Doyle, Sir Francis Hastings Charles, poet — Customs, 1846–88

Yates, Edmund, humorist — Post Office, 1847–72

Merivale, Herman, varied prose — Colonial and India Offices, 1847–74

Lytton, Edward Robert Bulwer, poet — Diplomatic, 1849–91

Taylor, Tom, dramatist, editor of *Punch* — Health, Local Government Board, 1850–72

James, George Payne Rainsford, novelist — Consular, 1850–60

Arnold, Matthew, poet, critic — Education inspectorate, 1851–86

Murray, Grenville, journalist — Diplomatic, 1851–69

Clough, Arthur Hugh, poet — Education, 1853–61

Forster, John, biographer — Lunacy, 1855–72

Dobson, Henry Austin, poet, biographer — Trade, 1856–1901

Monkhouse, William Cosmo, poet, critic — Trade, 1856–1901

Garnett, Richard, poet, critic — British Museum, 1851–99

Walpole, Sir Spencer, historian — War Office, Fisheries, Post Office, 1857–99

Blunt, Wilfrid Scawen, poet — Diplomatic, 1858–69

Rogers, Sir Frederic, Lord Blatchford, journalist — Colonial Office, 1860–71

Helps, Sir Arthur, essayist, biographer — Privy Council, 1860–75

Forman, Henry Buxton, editor — Post Office, 1860–1907

Burton, Sir Richard Francis, travel — Consular, 1861–90

O'Shaughnessy, Arthur, poet — British Museum, 1861–81

Courthope, William John, critic, translator — Education, Civil Service Commission, 1869–1907

Lee, Hamilton Eugene, poet, novelist — Diplomatic, 1869–73

Shorter, Clement King, journalist — Exchequer and Audit, 1877–90

Jacobs, William Wymark, short story writer — Post Office Savings Bank, 1883–99

Hewlitt, Maurice Henry, novelist — Land Revenue Records, 1896–1900

BIBLIOGRAPHY

General :

ANSON, Sir WILLIAM R. *The Law and Custom of the Constitution*, 4th Edition (Oxford, 1935).

COHEN, E. W. *The Growth of the British Civil Service, 1780–1939* (Allen & Unwin, 1941).

DALE, H. E. *The Higher Civil Service of Great Britain* (Oxford, 1941).

DAVIS, H. W. C. *England under the Normans and Angevins* (Methuen, 1912).

ELTON, S. R. *The Tudor Revolution in Government* (Cambridge, 1953).

GRIFFITH, WYN. *The British Civil Service, 1854–1954* (H.M. Stationery Office, 1954).

HALSBURY, LORD. *Laws of England* (Butterworth, 1931–1942).

HARVEY, JOHN. *The Gothic World, 1100–1600* (Batsford, 1950).

History of Parliament, *Biographies and Register of Members of the Commons House, 1439–1509* (H.M. Stationery Office, 1936, 1938).

HOLDSWORTH, W. S. *A History of English Law*, 3rd Edition (Methuen, 1922).

KNIGHT, CHARLES (Ed.) *London* (Knight, 1843).

MACKIE, J. D. *The Earlier Tudors* (Oxford, 1952).

NEALE, J. E. *Elizabeth I and Her Parliaments, 1559–81* (Cape, 1953).

„   „   *The Elizabethan House of Commons* (Cape, 1949).

POOLE, A. L. *From Domesday Book to Magna Carta, 1087–1216* (Oxford, 1951).

PORRITT, E. and A. G. *The Unreformed House of Commons* (Cambridge, 1903).

POWICKE, Sir MAURICE. *The Thirteenth Century, 1216–1307* (Oxford, 1953).

ROWSE, A. L. *The England of Elizabeth* (Macmillan, 1950).

STENTON, F. M. *Anglo-Saxon England* (Oxford, 1943).

TASWELL-LANGMEAD, THOMAS. *English Constitutional History.* Ed. Theodore F. T. Plunknett (Sweet & Maxwell, 1946).

Reports of House of Commons Committee on Salaries, fees, gratuities, perquisites and emoluments . . . . in the several public offices, 1787.

Reports of House of Commons Committee on Finance, 1797–8; 36 reports reprinted by Order, 1803.

Reports of House of Commons Committee on Sinecure Offices, 20.6.1810; 18.6.1811, and 23.4.1812.

Reports of House of Commons Committee on Sinecure Offices, 25.7.1834.

Reports of House of Commons Committee on Official Salaries, 25.7.1850.

Report of Northcote Committee, 1853 (reprinted in *Journal of Institute of Public Administration*, XXXII, Spring 1954).

Report of Playfair Committee, 1874.

Reports of Royal Commissions on the Civil Service:
   (Ridley) 1890.
   (MacDonnell) 1914.
   (Tomlin) 1931.

Specific Departments :

LYTE, Sir H. C. MAXWELL.   *The Great Seal of England* (H.M. Stationery Office, 1926).

SCACCARIO, DIALOGUS DE, including CONSTITUTIO DOMUS REGIS.   Ed. Charles Johnson (Nelson, 1950).

ROUND, I. HORACE.   *The King's Sergeants and Officers of State* (Nisbet, 1911).

MADOX, THOMAS.   *The History and Antiquities of the Exchequer . . . to Edward II* (1711).

BONNER, Sir GEORGE ALBERT.   *The Office of the King's Remembrancer in England* (Butterworth, 1930).

CRAIG, Sir JOHN.   *The Mint* (Cambridge, 1953).

EVANS, Miss F. G.   *The Principal Secretary of State, 1558–1680* (Manchester University Publications, 1924).

TROUP, Sir EDWARD.   *The Home Office* (Putnam, 1925).

NEWSAM, Sir FRANK.   *The Home Office* (Allen & Unwin, 1954).

TILLEY, Sir JOHN, and GASELEE, STEPHEN.   *The Foreign Office* (Putnam, 1933).

HERTSLET, Sir EDWARD.   *Recollections of the Old Foreign Office* (Murray, 1901).

FIDDES, Sir GEORGE V.   *The Dominions and Colonial Offices* (Putnam, 1926).

SETON, Sir MALCOLM.   *The India Office* (Putnam, 1925).

HEATH, Sir THOMAS LITTLE.   *The Treasury* (Putnam, 1927).

DOWELL, STEPHEN.   *History of Taxes in England* (Longmans, Green, 1884).

POWER, EILEEN, and POSTAN, M. M.   *Studies in English Trade in the Fifteenth Century* (Routledge, 1933).

MURRAY, Sir OSWYN.   *The Admiralty* (uncompleted); in " Mariner's Mirror ' (Cambridge, 1937–9).

LEWIS, MICHAEL.   *England's Sea Officers* (Allen & Unwin, 1939).

JOHNS, A. W.   *The Principal Officers of the Navy.*   " Mariner's Mirror," XIV, Jan., 1928 (Cambridge, 1928).

TOOLEY, RONALD VERE.   *Maps and Map-makers*, 2nd Edition (Batsford, 1952).

SMITH, Sir HUBERT LLEWELLYN.   *The Board of Trade* (Putnam, 1928).

FLOUDE, Sir FRANCIS L. C.   *The Ministry of Agriculture and Fisheries* (Putnam, 1927).

SELBY-BIGGE, Sir LEWIS AMHERST.   *The Board of Education*, 2nd Edition (Putnam, 1934).

NEWSHOLME, Sir ARTHUR.   *The Ministry of Health* (Putnam, 1925).

REDLICH, JOSEF, and HIRST, FRANCIS W.   *Local Government in England* (Macmillan, 1903).

SIMON, Sir JOHN.   *English Sanitary Institutions* (Cassell, 1890).

GORDON, HAMPDEN.   *The War Office* (Putnam, 1935).

ROBINSON, HOWARD.   *Britain's Post Office* (Oxford, 1953).

CRUTCHLEY, E. T.   *GPO* (Cambridge, 1938).

YATES, EDMUND H.   *Edmund Yates, his Recollections and Experiences* (R. Bentley & Sons, 1884).

JOYCE, HERBERT. *The History of the Post Office* (R. Bentley, 1853).

Individuals :

Dictionary of National Biography.
   And also for the following individuals :
BAINES, F. E. *Forty years at the Post Office.* F. E. Baines (R. Bentley & Son, 1895).
BARROW, Sir JOHN. *An Autobiographical Memoir.* Sir John Barrow (Murray, 1847).
CHADWICK, Sir EDWIN. *The Life and Times of Sir Edwin Chadwick.* Samuel E. Finer (Methuen, 1952).
COLE, Sir HENRY. *Fifty Years of Public Work.* Sir Henry Cole (Bell, 1884).
CROKER, JOHN WILSON. *John Wilson Croker.* Myron F. Brightfield (University of California, 1940).
HUBERT de BURGH. *Hubert de Burgh.* Clarence Ellis (Phoenix House, 1952).
HAWKINS, Sir JOHN. *Hawkins of Plymouth.* James A. Williamson (Black, 1949).
HILL, Sir ROWLAND. *Life of Sir Rowland Hill.* George Birkbeck Hill (De La Rue, 1880).
KYNNERSLEY, E. M. SNEYD. *H.M.I. Some Passages in the Life of one of H.M. Inspectors of Schools* (Macmillan, 1908).
MORANT, Sir ROBERT :
      1. *Diaries* (1912–24). Beatrice Webb (ed. Margaret L. Cole) (Longmans, 1952).
      2. *Journal of Institute of Public Administration*, Vol. XXVIII, Summer, 1950. D. N. Chester.
      3. *Journal of Institute of Public Administration*, Vol. XXVIII, Winter, 1950. Violet Markham.
      4. *Sir Robert Morant, A Great Public Servant.* Bernard Allen (Macmillan, 1934).
PEPYS, SAMUEL :
      Samuel Pepys : The Man in the Making.
      Samuel Pepys : The Years of Peril.
      Samuel Pepys : The Saviour of the Navy.
         Arthur Bryant (Cambridge, 1934, 1935, 1938).
ROSE, Sir GEORGE. *The English Nation : a History of England in the Lives of Englishmen* (A. Fullarton & Co., 1863–8).
SADLER, MICHAEL ERNEST. *Michael Ernest Sadler, 1861–1943.* Michael T. H. Sadleir (Constable, 1949).
SHUTTLEWORTH, KAY-, Sir J. P. K. *Four Periods of Public Education.* Kay Shuttleworth. (Longmans, Green, 1862).
      The Life and Work of Sir James Kay-Shuttleworth. Frank Smith (Murray, 1923).
TROLLOPE, ANTHONY. *An Autobiography.* Anthony Trollope (1883) (Williams & Norgate, 1946).
WALPOLE, HORACE. *Horace Walpole, 1717–1797.* Lewis Melville (Hutchinson, 1930).

WALPOLE, ROBERT. *Twelve English Statesmen*. John Morley (Macmillan, 1889).

WILSON, Sir C. RIVERS. *Chapters from my Official Life*. Sir C. Rivers Wilson (Edward Arnold, 1916).

INDEX OF SUBJECTS

ADMINISTRATIVE class, 188, 190, 191, 195
Admiral, Lord High, 8, 108–11, 119–20
Admiralty, 111, 117, 120–2, 136, 144, 147
Agricultural Research, 158
Agriculture, Ministry of, 75, 148–9, 154
Air Ministry, 76, 129
Almoner, King's, 28
Arbitration Court, 194
Art education, 146, 151–2
Assessment, triple, 105
Assistance, public, 166
Assistant clerks, 190, 191
Attendance books, 56, 87
Audit Commissioners, 38
Auditor of Exchequer, 38–40, 78
Auditor of Land Revenues, 30
Auditor of Prests, 38
Augmentations, Court of, 35–6

Bank of England, 4, 39, 115
Bankruptcy Department, 147
Bates' case, 92
Benevolent funds, 99
Bills, Customs, of entry, 99
Board and lodging, 8, 9, 15, 20, 59
Boy clerks, 189, 190, 191
Budget, 33, 37, 88
Burma Office, 77
Butler, chief and deputy, 7, 8, 37, 92

Candle perquisites, 9
Celibacy, 53
Cemeteries, 162, 163
Chamberlain, Lord Great, 6–9
Chamberlains of Exchequer, 24, 28, 32, 38
Chancellor, Lord, 8–10, 13, 14–15, 28, 53, 54
Chancellor of Exchequer, 28, 32, 37, 46, 79, 86
Chancery, 15–16, 19, 50, 171
Charity Commission, 153, 154
Chelsea pensioners, 86
Chemist, Government, 107

Chequer Board, 26–7
Cinque Ports, Warden of, 176
Civil List, 11, 71, 84, 86
Civil Service Commission, 2, 185–9
Civil Service defined, 2–5
Colonial appointments, 178
Colonial Office, 76, 144, 185
Colonies, 76, 143–6
Commissariat, Treasury, 126, 127
Competence, tests of, 87, 96, 134, 182, 186–90, 193
Comptroller of Household, 11, 12
Constable, Lord High, 7, 8, 28
Control, Board of, 76
Copyhold Commissioners, 149
Copying press, 188
Cramming, 189
Crimean war, 187
Crown Agents, 35, 36, 85
Crown Lands, 35, 36, 48
Currency, control, 86, 89, 143, 146; bullion value demanded, 29; value of, 10, 193–4; devaluation, 34, 195; devaluation proposed, 81
Cursitors of Chancery, 175
Customs, 91–9, 107, 162, 165

Deputies, 9, 15, 22–3, 28, 38, 44, 45, 94, 110, 116, 170, 175; forbidden, 32; ended, 177
Development Commission, 191
Diplomatic and Consular services, 4–5, 54–5, 62–3, 74
Dockyards, 112
Dominions Office, 76

Earl Marshal, 7, 8
Ecclesiastical Commission, 2, 3, 37
Ecclesiastical connections, 10, 15, 17–18, 24, 53, 54
Education, 149–57, 167, 186
Escheators, 31
Establishments, 87, 140, 194
Estreats, clerk of, 30, 40
Examination system, 182, 183, 193
Exchequer, 24–41, 78, 159

Exchequer and Audit, 41, 88
Exchequer Bills, 89
Excise, 99–102, 107, 174
Ex-service men, 100, 192, 193

Factory inspectorate, 160, 165
Falconer, Grand, 179
Farming duties out, 93, 95, 96, 99, 100, 104, 114, 132, 133, 134, 135
Fees, 14, 20, 27, 70, 83, 117, 126, 169, 178
Fictitious Boards, 48, 79, 86, 145, 149, 153, 163
First fruits, 34–5, 36–7
Fisheries, 149
Foreign Office, 72–4
Foreign Opposer, 30, 40
Forestry, 149
Franchise, 174, 189
Franking of letters, 132

Gazette, London, 67
General Register Office, 162
Geological Survey and Museum, 124, 152, 167
Gifts at new year, 83, 84, 85; of lands, 13, 29; on conclusion of treaties, 71
Government Actuary, 86
Government Chemist, 107
Great Officers of State, 8
Great Seal, 16, 17, 29
Green Cloth, Board of, 56
Grievances, 191
Groom of State, 11

Hamper or Hanaper, clerk of, 15
Health, 157, 161, 162–3, 166
Heralds, College of, 3
Hereditary tenures, 9, 24, 29, 32, 42, 44, 179
Holidays, 180, 189
Home Office, 71, 74–5, 76, 126, 127, 145, 149, 160, 163
Honours, 54, 113
Hours, 180, 189
Household, Royal, 6–12, 159
Housing, Ministry of, 166

Immunity, privilege of, 43
Income tax, 105–7
Indian Civil Service, 183, 186
India Office, East India Commission, 3, 76, 183
Indirect and personal employment, 15, 21, 44, 51, 61–2, 69, 71, 190–1, 192

Industrial Civil Servants, 4, 195
Inland revenue, 107, 190
Inspectorate, 75, 106, 151, 156
Insurance Commissions and Ministry, 155, 165, 166, 191
Intermediate class, 190, 191

Judiciary, 3, 4, 5, 27, 110, 175
Justices of the Peace, 56, 159–60, 161, 164
Justiciar, 11

Knights, 7, 25

Labour and National Service, 129, 148, 165, 166, 191
Lancaster, Duchy of, 32, 34, 35
Land Commission, 106, 149
Land tax, 82, 105–6
Literary activities, 197–200
Local authorities, 75, 160, 164
Local Government Board, 75, 162, 165, 166
London County Council, 84, 164
Lords Lieutenant, 159

MacDonnell Commission, 191
Machines, 193
Marshal of Exchequer, 30, 32
Medical Research Council, 157, 165
Melter of Exchequer, 29
Messengers, 29, 70, 72, 190, 192
Midwives, 157
Mines, 75, 148, 195
Mines, School of, 152
Mint, 36, 42–6
Monasteries, 50, 52, 55–6
Moneyers, Company of, 44
Money Order Office, 137
Monopolies, 146
Munitions, Ministry of, 129, 195
Museums, 146, 152, 166–7

National Debt Office, 86
Nature Conservancy, 158
Navy Board, 112–19, 122
Nichills clerk, 30, 41
Northcote–Trevelyan Report. *See* Trevelyan Report.
Nova Scotia, founding of, 144
Numbers employed, 3, 14, 30, 31, 62, 66, 72, 84–5, 86, 89, 119, 140, 146, 178, 180, 184, 191, 192, 195

Officialese, 13, 180
Ordnance Board, 123–8

Ordnance Survey, 124
Overseas Trade, 146

Paper Office, State, 68, 71, 167
Parliament, 15–16, 169–171
Parliament, Civil Servants in, 5, 171–5
Parliaments, clerk of, 16, 170
Part time, private employments, 45–6, 47
Patent Office, 147
Patronage, 83, 101, 182–3, 191
Pay, 7–9, 14, 15, 20, 22, 29, 38, 39–41, 46–7, 59, 67, 69–72, 79, 81, 84–5, 95, 97–8, 101–102, 103, 111, 113, 122, 127, 137, 144, 145, 169–70, 176, 179
Pay Office, 38, 126–7
Pells, clerk of, 30, 39, 40
Penny post, 138
Pensions, Civil Service and political, 36, 38, 64, 121, 122, 135, 139, 177; old age, 139, 165; systematic, 87, 177, 180; teachers', 156
Pensions, Ministry of, 129, 166
Permanency of tenure, 33, 36, 38, 64, 72, 82, 84, 194
Perquisites, 73, 116, 136, 137. *See also* Board and lodging, Fees, Gifts, Ecclesiastical connections.
Piece rates, 44
Pipe, clerk of the, 30, 39, 40
Plantations Office, 76
Playfair Committee, 189
Pluralism, 55, 71, 72, 80, 85, 179
Police, 4, 75, 160
Policy, Civil Servants' position— Foreign Office, 73–4; Home Office, 75; Colonial Office, 76; Treasury, 89; Education Department, 150; Poor Law Commissioners, 161; modern, 195–6
Poor Law Commission, 160–3
Post Office, 130–41, 165, 191
Prisons, 164
Privy Council, 21–2, 45, 56–7, 86, 142– 158, 163, 172
Privy Seal, 17–19, 21, 22–3, 116
Promotion, principles of, 18–19, 20, 32–3, 72, 85, 86, 96, 103, 184, 186
Public Record Office, 167–8
Public Relations, 197
Public Trustee, 165, 190
Public Works Loan Board, 164
Purchase of Offices, 11, 17, 25, 64, 65, 67, 68, 70, 125, 159, 170, 175

Queen Anne's Bounty, 37
Queen's Hard Bargains, 189

Railways, 147, 195
Rates Department, 164
Rates, local, 160, 164–5
Recruitment, 32, 43–4, 55, 65, 70, 82, 85, 94, 111, 112, 118, 134, 151, 156–7, 165, 185, 190, 191, 192, 193
Red tape, abolished, 88; exemplified, 68, 117, 144; referred to, 73, 181. *See also* Routines.
Relieving officers, 161
Remembrancers, Queen's and Lord Treasurer's, 30, 40, 41; of First Fruits, 179
Requests, Court of, 56
Retrenchment, 36, 38, 45, 47, 87, 102, 114, 115, 137, 177–8
Revenue, 25, 49, 104, 105, 138
Ridley Commission, 189
Road Board, 191
Rolls, Master of, 15
Roman numerals, 27
Routines—Chancery and Seal Offices, 19, 22; Exchequer, 28, 31, 37, 39; Secretaries of State Offices, 73–4; and Council, 144; Treasury, 78, 79; in obtaining patents, 146–7
Royal Engineers, 124

Sanitation, 161, 163
Savings banks, 139
School boards, 152, 154
Science and art, 151, 152, 153
Scientific and industrial research, 124, 152, 157
Scotland, 75, 76, 149, 150, 152, 178
Seals of Chancellor of Exchequer, 37– 41; Augmentations, 35; Wards, 35
Seamen's Registry, 147
Second division clerks, 188, 190, 191
Secretaries, King's, 17, 54; of State, 59–76; at War, 125; French, 55; Latin, 69–70
Secret service, 63, 132
Settlement, Act of, 173
Sheriffs, 25, 28, 33, 41, 56, 159
Ship money, 27
Shipping, control of, 147
Signet, 19–23, 59
Simplification of statutes, etc., 97, 157
Sinecures, 45, 98, 118, 145, 175–9 and *passim*
Six clerks, sixty clerks, 15, 53

Smuggling, 94, 98
Speaker, 34, 81, 86, 169
Speenhamland, Act of, 160
Spigurnel, 16, 95
Stamps Office, 102–3, 107, 180
Standardisation, 189, 194
Stationery Office, 71, 88
Statistical approaches, 146, 147, 162
Steward, Lord High, 6–9

Tallies, 26, 38, 41
Tally cutter, 30, 38
Tax Commissioners, various, 82
Teachers' training, 150
Telegraphs and Telephones, 139–40
Tellers of Exchequer, 29, 38, 39, 40
Tithe Commission, 149
Tobacco, 92, 101
Tomlin Commission, 194
Trade, Board of, 45, 75–6, 98, 99, 125, 143–8, 149, 151, 165, 177, 197
Transfers of staff, 30, 191, 192
Transport, Ministry of, 124
Treasurer, Lord High, 6, 24, 27, 28, 37, 78, 80
Treasurer, Under-, 41; of Household, 12
Treasury, 38, 79–90, 188, 189, 193
Treasury control, 87
Trevelyan Report, 183–8, 195

Trinity House, 3, 5
Typists, 73, 190

Unions and associations, 156, 189, 194
University of London, 152
Usher of Exchequer, 29, 32, 179

Vaccination, 157
Veterinary Department, 149
Victualling Board, 116, 119, 122

Wardrobe, 13, 17, 31, 34
Wards, Court of, 35, 37
War Office, 76, 125–9
Wars, effect of, 33, 127, 129, 192, 195
Water supply, 163
Weigher of Exchequer, 29
Weights and Measures, 147
Whips, Government, 79
Whitehall Palace, 37, 52, 89
Winchester, 24–5
Women, 8, 190, 192
Woods and Forests, 47–8, 147
Works Department, 46–8, 88
Writer of Tallies, 26, 30, 38
Writing office, 11, 13, 15, 29; Master of, 25, 28

Yeomen of the Guard, 124–5

INDEX OF PERSONS

(excluding Chapter XVII)

ACWORTH, Jacob, 118
Aelfwine, 13, 14
Allen, Ralph, 134–5, 137
Arlington, Sir Henry Bennet, Lord, 69, 133
Ashby, George, 172
Aust, George, 72

Bainbridge, Cardinal Christopher, 54
Baines, Frederick Ebenezer, 139
Baker, Sir John, 36
Banstead, John of, 17
Barlow, Thomas, 115
Barrow, Sir John, 121
Batten, Adm. Sir William, 115, 118
Beckington, Thomas, 18, 54
Bele, Richard, 18–19
Benson, William, 47
Bentinck, Lord William Cavendish, 40
Berkeley of Stratton, Lord, 115
Bertie, Charles, 80
Bishop, Col. Henry, 132
Blake, Edmund, 46
Blakeney, John, 18
Blaythwayte, William, 70, 125, 144
Blyke, Theophilus, 126
Body, William, 57
Bolman, Robert, 19
Bowes, Thomas, 122
Bowles, Phineas, 118
Bray, Sir Reginald, 32
Bridgeman, William, 68
Brisbane, John, 117
Brown, John, 33
Buch, Peter, 113
Bulkly, Thomas, 172
Burchett, Josiah, 121
Burgh, Hubert de, 14
Burke, Edmund, 39, 176, 177
Burns, Robert, 101

Calvert, George, 1st Lord Baltimore, 63, 64
Camden, Marquess, 40
Carkesse, C., 97
Carteret, Sir George, 115

Cecil, Sir Robert, Marquess of Salisbury, 61–3, 78
Cecil, William, Lord Burleigh, 60–3, 65, 78
Chadwick, Sir Edward, 160–3
Chalmers, George, 145
Chamberlain, Thomas, 18
Chaucer, Geoffrey, 46, 93
Chinnery, —, 39
Clark, Sir William, 125
Cliff, John, 21
Coke, Sir John, 65
Cole, Sir Henry, 139
Conway, Henry, 20
Cooke, John, 69–70
Cornhill, Henry and Reginald of, 108
Coventry, Sir Henry, 69
Coventry, Sir William, 69
Cowper, Ashley, 170
Croker, John Wilson, 122, 182
Cromwell, Sir Thomas, Earl of Essex, 36, 51, 52–8

Danby, Earl of, 81
Davy, Sir Humphry, 148
Denham, Sir John, 47
de Questers, 131
Derby, Thomas, 20, 57
Dockwra, William, 133
Downing, Sir George, 80, 116
Dudley, Edmund, 34

Edmonds, Thomas, 62
Empson, Richard, 55

Falkland, Viscount, 65
Farr, William, 162
Faunt, Nicholas, 62, 89
Fenn, Hugh, 33
Finlayson family, 86
Fitzalan, Henry, 12th Earl of Arundel, 142
Fowler, Richard, 32
Fraser, William, 72
Freeling, Sir Francis, 134, 137
Freeling, Sir George, 134

Frizzell, William, 131
Furnell, William of, 93, 108

Gardiner, Dr. Stephen, 51, 55
Godolphin, Sidney, Lord, 2, 69, 83
Godsalve, Sir John, 20
Gonson, Benjamin, 115
Gonson, William, 114
Gostwick, John, 51, 57
Gower, Edward, 46
Gray, John de, 10, 11
Guildford, Earl of, 98
Guildford, Sir Richard, 122
Gunthorpe, John, 19
Guy, Henry, 80, 81

Hamilton, Sir George Alexander, 84
Hammond, Edmond, 1st Lord, 72, 73
Harley, Thomas, 82
Harrington, Lord, 130
Hatcliff, William, 54
Hawes, Sir Benjamin, 128
Hawkins, Sir John, 114–15
Hayter, Thomas, 117
Heath, Sir Thomas Little, 89
Hedges, Sir Charles, 67
Herbert, Mr. Secondary, 61, 64
Herbert, Sir William, 142
Herfast, 13
Heron, Sir John, 1–2
Hill, Sir Rowland, and family, 138–9
Hoccleve, Thomas, 18
Honnyng, William, 21
Howard, Sir Robert, 80
Hume, James Deacon, 97

Jenkins, Sir Leoline, 69
Jennings, Robert, 40
Johnson, Edward, 133
Jones, Inigo, 47
Juxon, William, Archbishop, 53, 80

Kay-Shuttleworth, Sir James, 150, 161
Kekewich, Sir George, 154, 155
Kent, William, 90

Lake, Sir Thomas, 62
Laud, William, Archbishop, 53
Lefevre, Sir John George Shaw, 186
Lematon, John, 46
Lever, Charles, 74
Leyburn, William of, 108
Lingen, Sir Ralph, 1st Lord, 84
Liverpool, Earl of, 98
Locke, John, 81, 144

Locke, Matthew, 125
Louth, John, 123
Lowndes, William, 81–2
Lyndwood, William, 17

Maberley, William Leader, 137, 139
Macaulay, Lord, 183
Mahon, Lord, 41
Manchester, Duke of, 98
Manly, John, 132
Marny, Henry Lord, 18
Marsden, William, 122
Marvell, Andrew, 66
Mason, Sir John, 130
Merbury, Nicholas, 123
Merivale, Herman, 185
Middlesex, Earl of, 95
Mildmay, Sir Walter, 36
Milton, John, 66
Moleyns, Adam, 21
Montagu, Charles, Earl of Halifax, 83
Montagu, Edward, Earl of Sandwich, 115–16
Morant, Sir Robert, 154–5, 156
Morland, Sir Samuel, 132
Morrice, Sir William, 69
Morton, John, 34
Morton, Sir Albert, 64
Mowatt, Sir Francis, 84
Muddiman, Henry, 67
Munck, Levinius, 63
Murray, Sir George, 190

Nanfan, Sir Richard, 49
Naunton, Robert, 63
Newton, Sir Isaac, 42, 81, 102
Nicholas, Sir Edward, 65, 67, 125
Nigel, Bishop of Ely, 24
Northcote, Sir Stafford, 1st Earl of Iddesleigh, 183, 189

Oisel, Hugh, 93
O'Neile, Daniel, 132

Pace, Richard, 51, 54, 55
Paget, William, Lord, 20, 60, 142
Palmer, John, 134, 135
Palmerston, Henry Temple, Lord, 72, 73
Paulet, Sir William, Marquess of Winchester, 36, 51
Peckham, Sir Edmund, 36
Pelham, Henry, 83
Penn, Sir William, 115
Pepys, Samuel, 2, 68, 81, 115–18, 119

Perceval, Spencer, 175, 176, 177
Petre, Sir William, and family, 57, 60, 62, 142
Petts family, 113–14, 115, 116
Phillips, Thomas, 62
Poer, Roger le, and family, 24
Pollard, Richard, 57
Popple family, 144
Potshead, Henry, 58
Potts, Henry, 134
Pratt, Thomas, 85–6
Prideaux, Edmond, 131

Questers, de, 131

Randolph, John, 130
Ray, Major General William, 124
Richard, Bishop of London, 24–5
Rivaulx, Peter des, 31
Roberts, E. W., 40
Robinson, John, Bishop of Bristol, 53
Rochester, Sir Robert, 142
Rogers, Sir Frederic, 1st Lord Blatchford, 185
Romilly, Edward, 186
Rose, Sir George, 39, 170
Rose, Sir George Henry, 39–40
Ruthall, Dr. Thomas, 55
Ryan, Sir Edward, 186, 188

Sadleir, Ralph, 57, 60
Sadler, Sir Michael, 154
Sampson, Richard, Bishop, 54
Sanderson, Thomas, 1st Lord, 73
Saxton, Christopher, 124
Scudamore, Frank Ives, 139
Selwyn, Augustus, 175
Sepping, Sir Robert, 119
Shrewsbury, Lord, 79
Sigillo, Robert de, 9
Simon, Sir John, 162
Sinclair, Sir John, 148
Slingsby, Capt. Robert, 115
Smith, Dr. Southwood, 161, 162
Smyth, Sir Thomas, 95
Somerset, John, 46
Soulemont, Thomas, 57
Spearman, Sir Alexander, 84
Spencer, Robert, Earl of Sunderland, 69
Spert, Sir Thomas, 113
Stanhope, John, 130
Stapeldon, Walter de, 31

Stephen, Sir James, 185
Stevens, Sir Philip, 121
Stonehewer, Richard, 72
Stoughton, Thomas and John, 94–5

Taverner, Richard, 57
Taylor, Tom, 163
Tekell, John, 40
Thirlby, Bishop Thomas, 142
Throgmorton, John, 32
Thurloe, John, 66, 132
Thynne, Henry, 70
Todd, Anthony, 134–7
Tomson, Lawrence, 62
Tressor, Sir John, 69
Trevelyan, Sir Charles, 84, 87, 183
Trollope, Anthony, 189
Tucker, —, 121
Tuke, Sir Brian, 130
Tuke, Sir Henry, 2

Vane, Sir Henry, 65
Vannes, Pietro, 51

Walker, Sir Edward, 125
Walpole, Sir Robert, and family, 176
Walsingham, Sir Francis, 61, 62, 95
Walter, Hubert, 1
Warwick, Sir Philip, 80
Weckerlin, John Randolph, 66
Welby, Sir Reginald, 1st Lord, 84
Wickham, William of, 17
Wildman, John, 132, 133
Williamson, Sir Joseph, 67–8, 167
Willis, Simon, 63
Wilson, Sir C. Rivers, 189
Windebank, Sir Francis, 65
Windebank, Thomas, 63
Winwood, Sir Ralph, 64
Witherings, Thomas, 131–2
Wolsey, Cardinal Thomas, 49–52
Wood, John, 123
Worsley, Benjamin, 144
Wren, Sir Christopher, 47
Wriothesley, Sir Thomas, Earl of Southampton, 2, 20, 51–2, 57
Wrotham, William of, 93, 108
Wynne, Dr. Owen, 70

Yaxley, Francis, 21
Yetsweirt, Nicholas, 21
Young, Arthur, 148